WALLACE WADE

WALLACE WADE

Championship Years at Alabama and Duke

Lewis Bowling

Library of Congress Cataloging-in-Publication Data

Bowling, Lewis.

Wallace Wade : championship years at Alabama and Duke / by Lewis Bowling.

p.   cm.

Includes bibliographical references and index.

ISBN-13: 978-1-59460-231-3 (alk. paper)

ISBN-10: 1-59460-231-X

1. Wade, Wallace, 1892-1986. 2. Football coaches--United States--Biography. 3. University of Alabama--Football--History. 4. Alabama Crimson Tide (Football team)--History. 5. Duke University--Football--History. I. Title.

GV939.W2B68 2006

796.332092--dc22

[B]   2006028235

CAROLINA ACADEMIC PRESS

700 Kent Street
Durham, North Carolina 27701
Telephone (919) 489-7486
Fax (919) 493-5668
www.cap-press.com

Printed in the United States of America

To Beth Harward. You are the best.

CONTENTS

PREFACE

The great majority of the references I have used are documents, newspapers, magazines, game programs, scrapbooks, and various archival material from the early 1900s to 1950. Player comments from Coach Wade's teams at Alabama came mostly from old newspaper clippings, for, as far as I have been able to research, none of Coach Wade's former players at Alabama survive from his Tuscaloosa years of 1923 to 1931. Many of Coach Wade's former Duke players are still going strong, and I have had personal contact with over forty of them through letters, email, or on the phone.

This book is meant to be more oriented to the general public than to academicians, so footnotes are not used. That being said, I made every attempt to accurately attribute my sources: all sources of information that I read as background material, quoted from, or drew upon for content are listed in the reference section.

ACKNOWLEDGMENTS

I owe a sincere thank you to many people for helping me to write this biography of Wallace Wade. Keith Sipe, Kasia Krzysztoforska, Linda Sipe, and L. Taylor Arnold of Carolina Academic Press were most helpful in editing and publishing this book.

Al Buehler, Duke University professor emeritus, is a legend on the Duke campus himself. Coach Buehler is enshrined in the National Track Hall of Fame, the NC Sports Hall of Fame, and the Duke Sports Hall of Fame. He has served as an Olympic track coach also. These honors came to him from his many years as head track and cross-country coach at Duke University. Coach Buehler also has been an athletic administrator and director of the physical education department at Duke.

Coach Buehler simply knows everybody at Duke, or so it seems, and his help and guidance has been absolutely indispensable to me. Having known Wallace Wade after Wade had retired, Coach Buehler was a great person to go to for information about Coach Wade. Once a week for close to a year, I would sit down with him and talk about Coach Wade. Coach Buehler's office in Cameron Indoor Stadium was formerly occupied by another man I have enjoyed getting to know from writing this book ... Wallace Wade. My association with Coach Buehler was simply invaluable in preparing this book.

Beth Harward is one of the most loyal Duke fans I know. She absolutely loves Duke basketball, although hopefully this book might just remind her that there was a time when football was by far the most popular sport on the Duke campus. A longtime teacher in Granville County, NC, Beth was the one I turned to for help in the actual writing of the manuscript more than anyone else, and she always came through for me, just as she always has. Without her typing, editing, support, and encouragement, this book could not have been done. Thank you Beth.

Betty Hilliard of Duke University is one of the nicest ladies one could ever meet, and a fast and accurate typist. Helen Fuller typed much of this book also, and delivered when I had a tight deadline. Thanks Betty and Helen.

The Duke University Archives supplied the majority of information on Coach Wade. Tim Pyatt, Tom Harkins, Jill Katte, and Kimberly Sims were all very helpful, and this book could not have been done without their archival information and their kindness in assisting me.

Many former players for Coach Wade either wrote me or shared their experiences with me in conversations. Bob Barnett, the captain of the great 1941 team that played in the 1942 Rose Bowl, was the one who I turned to most. Mr. Barnett was very gracious with his time over several rather long phone conversations, and was just a wealth of knowledge. Other players who shared their thoughts of Coach Wade were Werner Brown, E.P. Bethune Jr., John Carey, Billy Cox, W.D. McRoy, Richard Lenox, Paul Stephanz, James Wolfe Jr., Jasper Davis, C.A. Adams, Jim Groome, Ralph Felty, Leonard Darnell, George Clark, Bernard Jack, Walter Lenox, James Gibson Jr., Blaine Earon, Leonard Smith, Winston {and Anne, his wife} Siegfried, Robert Deyton, Charles Looper, Walter Smith, William Mozingo, Larry Karl, Hunter Hadley Jr., Clyde Bryant, Robert Smith, John Mueller, Don Bafford, Robert Bickel, George McAfee, Charles Smith, and Paul Conway. Student managers who helped were Howard Ris and Robert Price.

The Duke Sports Information Department was very helpful in supplying much written information on Coach Wade, and also many fine photographs.

Most of my information on Coach Wade's career at Alabama came from the Paul W. Bryant Museum at the University of Alabama. Brad Green met my every request in my visits to the museum and through many emails. Taylor Watson also assisted me, and it was a pleasure meeting Clem Gryska. Tom Land and Donnelly Lancaster of the W.S. Hoole Special Collections Library at the University of Alabama were also very helpful. Kirk McNair of Bama Magazine and Fred Sington Jr., son of the great All-American Fred Sington, who played and coached for Wade, were supportive also.

Fred Culp and Nell Breeden assisted me greatly on my visit to Trenton, Tennessee, where Coach Wade grew up. Mrs. Breeden once cared for a sister of Wade's, Lucille, and Mr. Culp is a great historian of Trenton and Gibson County. It was also a pleasure to talk to Louise Faulkner and Evelyn Wade Harwood. Mrs. Harwood is now 105 years old, and is related to Coach Wade. She grew up in Trenton and still lives there.

Mrs. Anita Caldwell met Herschel Caldwell while both were students at the University of Alabama, and she came to know Coach Wade well as her husband served as an assistant to Wade at Duke. Mrs. Caldwell still attends Duke football games at the age of 98, and I enjoyed listening to her still vivid memories of her days at Alabama and Duke. Herschel Caldwell Jr. was also very helpful and supportive. Lee Caldwell supplied me with several good pictures.

Two of Coach Wade's granddaughters, Nancy Wade and Diane Withrow, were very supportive to me and supplied me with information on Coach Wade away from the football field. What courage Bob Withrow, Diane's husband, showed as a young man upon meeting Coach Wade for the first time, when asked what he planned to do for a living by his grandfather-in-law, replied, "I want to be a football coach, sir." And Bob did, becoming a very successful high school football coach.

I either talked or corresponded with all of the following: Patrick Miller, Bill Turpin, Bobby King, Allen Barra, author of *The Last Coach*, Warren St. John, author of *Rammer Jammer Yellow Hammer*, James Harward, Dorothy Harward, Clyde Bolton, Will Fitzgerald, Ken Stephens of the College Football Hall of Fame, Larry Leathers and Chris Skinker of Vanderbilt, Senator Jesse Helms, John Carroll, Peter Mackie and David Thompson of Brown University, Scott Nave, son of Doyle Nave, who threw the touchdown pass in the 1939 Rose Bowl for USC to beat Duke, Jay Wilkinson, son of the legendary Buzz Wilkinson, Pam Matheson and Mary Dinkins of the Duke Varsity Club, Add Penfield, Bob Harris, Johnny Moore, Southern Conference Commissioner John Iamarino, Mike McGee, Mike Flynn of Appalachian State University, Barry Kritzberg of Morgan Park Academy, Matt Eviston of Elon University, Mady Salvani of the sports information department at Army, Bob Kinney, Andrew Doyle, Tobin Lim, Dr. Galen Wagner, Ron Brister, Bob Moyer, Robert Durden, and Christian Hoffman of VMI.

WALLACE WADE

INTRODUCTION

February 15/1930

Mr. Wallace Wade
The University of Alabama
Tuscaloosa, Ala.

Dear Mr. Wade:

I am writing you this letter in the strictest confidence, knowing from what I have seen of you that you will treat it in that way. And I am also presuming on your willingness to be of help to us here in a matter that I feel sure you are deeply interested in, that of securing as big and good a head coach for football as is possibly available. I say "presume" upon your willingness, for from what I have seen of you in my brief association with you in the three meetings of the Southern Conference I have formed a high opinion of you both as man and as leader of youth in sports.

As you probably know we have now completed here an unusually fine outlay for college sports, one in keeping with the great university development we are rapidly making. It is our earnest desire to build the very best possible physical *plant* and to provide for the coaching of our teams the best leaders we can secure. We are determined to integrate the sports of youth with the whole program of the university. In the last analysis it is on the men in charge of sports that we must rely. I know you have a broad and sane and experienced opinion on all that pertains to this part of college education. I am therefore as Dean of the University and as Chairman of the Faculty Committee on Athletics asking if you will be good enough to write me frankly as to who in your opinion is the best man we could probably secure as head coach of football. If you feel that an interview with you would be a better means for a discussion of the whole question please say so, and I will see that it is provided.

We should like if possible to have the man come to us even this spring, but since it is now rather late for that we shall probably have to engage him to come early next fall, in time for football drill prior to the opening of college late in September. We have already begun spring practice and it will proceed under the men here. Of course the man we bring in will have entire direction of the team and we will bring in the assistants he will want.

We are very desirous of getting this vitally important question settled as promptly as possible and I shall be grateful to you for a prompt reply. If you should prefer an interview, feel free to wire me. You will readily understand that we wish to avoid publicity now, for we do not want to go through the deluge of applications and suggestions that will come as soon as it is known that the head coach position is vacant.

With the best of good wishes, I am

Very truly yours,

Dr. W. H. Wannamaker
Office of the Dean
Duke University Durham, N.C.

Feb 18, 1930

Dr. W. H. Wannamaker
Duke University
Durham, N.C.

Dear Sir:

I fully appreciate the compliment which you pay me in your kind letter of Feb 15th. I am very glad to do anything that I can to assist you. I, also, am greatly impressed with the idea that your fine institution has a future probably second to none in this country.

I have taken twenty-four hours in which to think about your situation. I doubt very much if you are going to be able to get the kind of man that you want in time to take charge of your team for the 1930 season. Most likely such a man would have obligations for next season that he would be unwilling to ask to be relieved of at this late date. If you cannot get the right man now, would it not be better to continue with your present staff another year, than to try an unsatisfactory man, with the prospect of having to make another early change. It has been my observation that frequent changes in coaching organizations are very demoralizing.

There are four men whom I would be willing to suggest as having the possibilities of filling your requirement: Henry Crisp has been line coach here for seven years, and varsity basketball coach the same length of time. Lewis Hardage has been backfield coach at Vanderbilt eight years. Roy Morrison has been head coach at Southern Methodist University of Dallas about eight years. Clark Shaughnessy has been head coach at Loyola University of New Orleans for three years. He was head coach of Tulane for several years before that. I believe that anyone of these men would make you a good man. I doubt if any one of them would be available before the season of 1931.

If you decide to wait until the season of 1931 I should be glad to talk with you about this position for myself. If you care to discuss the matter further I expect to be in Atlanta March 2–4th for the conference basketball tournament.

I should be glad to have you call on me if you feel that I can be of any further assistance to you.

Very truly yours,

Wallace Wade

The exchange of these two letters started negotiations that led to Wallace Wade's resignation as coach at Alabama. He would become Duke's coach in 1931. Wade had established the Crimson Tide as a national power, and he would go on to do the same at Duke. In fact, in the ten seasons from 1932 to 1941, Duke would have the best record in the nation by winning 80 games against only 16 losses, with two Rose Bowl appearances.

By 1930, Coach Wade's opinion was a much sought out commodity. He had won the first two national championships in Alabama history, with three Southern Conference titles. Looking back years later, Bear Bryant would give credit to Wade for establishing the great football tradition of Alabama: "There's no question that Coach Wade started the tradition of good football around here. His great teams got the ball rolling." Dr. Wannamaker of Duke certainly knew of Wade's amazing record as a coach at Alabama, but more than that, he had gotten to know Wade as a man and leader. As a leader in athletics at Duke, Wannamaker had attended the meetings of the Southern Conference along with

Wade, who represented Alabama as head football coach and athletic director. A person could not help but be impressed upon meeting Wade. Almost six feet tall, weighing around 180 pounds with handsome features, Wade always dressed sharply. His piercing eyes struck terror into his players and according to Clem Gryska, longtime Alabama assistant coach under Bryant who knew Wade, when Wade walked into a room, he drew everyone's attention; "Coach Wade just had a regal bearing, always well dressed, and he carried himself with authority. Even Coach Bryant was a little intimidated around Coach Wade, for whom he had great respect." So along with others, Dr. Wannamaker wanted the advice of this impressive man, knowing that Wade was a man of integrity and would keep Duke's search for a coach confidential. Little did he know that Wade himself was ready for a change.

Why did Wade leave Alabama, after eight years of championship football in Tuscaloosa? There were many reasons, among them, having the opportunity to have total control of football, a chance to build another program, and to work at a private university again, such as Duke was. Wade had been an assistant at Vanderbilt previous to accepting the head coaching job at Alabama. Another reason, no doubt, was money. Duke, flush with the money of tobacco magnate James B. Duke, offered Wade what was an extraordinary salary in 1930, $12,500 a year, plus a percentage of gate receipts. The contract was conservatively estimated to come to at least $100,000 over the five years it covered.

By March of 1930 Wade had agreed to become Duke's coach, but he insisted on honoring the remaining year of his contract at Alabama. The football season of 1930 became foremost in Coach Wade's focus, and the results that followed further stamped Wallace Wade's legacy on the Alabama football tradition.

November 27, 1930

Birmingham, Alabama
Legion Field
Alabama vs. Georgia

The game has just ended. The concrete girders of Legion Field vibrate. Chants of Wade! Wade! Wade! reverberate in a thunderous roar, escaping through and over the top of this historic stadium and to the steel mills of Birmingham and the downtown district. Alabama beats Georgia 13 to 0. A fourth Southern Conference title under Wade, the first four conference championships for the Crimson Tide in its history

1930 Alabama football team. Courtesy of Duke Sports Information Department.

January 1, 1931

Rose Bowl
Pasadena, California

Fred Sington, Frank Howard, Johnny Cain, and the rest of Alabama's team simply steamroll Washington State, 24 to 0. The first three of what are now twelve national championships belong to Alabama. Amazingly, opponents only scored 13 points against Alabama the entire season, which ended 10 and 0. Alabama scores 271 points. With 61 wins against only 13 losses, the three national championships, and four Southern Conference championships, Wallace Wade now moves to Duke. But the foundation has been built for the Crimson Tide to be one of the dominant teams of the 20th century.

Coach Wade not only built the first great teams in Tuscaloosa, but also played a large role in two other great coaches coming to the Capstone. Largely upon the recommendation of Wade, President George Denny hires an assistant coach from Georgia to take over, Frank Thomas. In fact, Wade made the first contact with Thomas regarding the opening. Thomas would go on to have great success also. Bear Bryant, the greatest coach in Alabama's history, and perhaps in college football, would become coach in 1958, but he became a fan of Wade's Alabama teams as a young man growing up in Arkansas. Bryant even left an all-star game in Dallas at halftime on the day Wade's team beat Washington State in the Rose Bowl so he could get back to his hotel to listen to the game on the radio. The Bear was a guest of an Arkansas coach, who was trying to bring Bryant to campus to play for the Razorbacks. But Bear Bryant's heart was in Alabama.

Mighty teams were to follow in Durham with the Blue Devils. Thad Stem, a Duke student during the 1930s while Wade was there, wrote the following poem. It sums up what the coaching and leadership of Wade meant to a university that was on the precipice of greatness as a football power and an academic institution of higher learning.

> "In all the days of future years,
> his name and fame will shine,
> our brilliant, Iron Colonel,
> of our old Blue Devil line."
>
> "And men will tell their children,
> although other memories fade,
> how they played for the
> Mighty Dukes of Durham,
> And 'old man' Wallace Wade."

CHAPTER ONE

THE EARLY YEARS

A little boy named Wallace was born in the small town of Trenton, in a farming community of West Tennessee on June 15, 1892. Born on a farm, raised on a farm, Wallace would eventually retire as a cattle farmer. In between these years, Wallace Wade attained recognition and respect nationwide as one of the premier college football coaches ever.

A little less than five months after Wade was born, on November 11, 1892, the University of Alabama would play its first football game. Four years earlier, in 1888, Duke University, then called Trinity College, defeated the University of North Carolina 16 to 0 in its first football game. The little farm boy of West Tennessee would lead these two teams to national prominence, first starting at Alabama in 1923 and retiring from Duke in 1950. During these years, Wade's teams accumulated three national championships, ten Southern Conference championships, five Rose Bowl appearances, and the second-most shutouts ever registered by a college football coach. Along the way, he did more than any coach in the history of the game to put southern college football on the map.

Trenton, located in Gibson County, Tennessee, is 92 miles from Memphis and 45 miles east of the Mississippi River. Chickasaw Indians once claimed this area of the Volunteer state as prime hunting ground. In 1818, Andrew Jackson and Governor Isaac Shelby of Kentucky, acting on behalf of the United States government, bought much of this land from the Chickasaw. Davy Crockett once lived in Gibson County, and a bronze bust of this great frontiersman is now in the yard of the county courthouse. A replica of his cabin is in Rutherford, just a few miles from Trenton. Wallace grew up hearing about this great man of West Tennessee, who reportedly killed forty-seven bears in one month, who could outshoot anyone around with his famous rifle Betsy, who fought Indians, and became a hero of the Alamo. Crockett's motto was: "Be sure you're right, then go ahead." This type of focus and belief in oneself would characterize much of Wade's life.

Gibson County furnished a large number of troops in the Civil War, and a significant battle occurred in Trenton. After the Battle of Shiloh and the fall of Memphis, the Mobile and Ohio Railroad through the area was used to sup-

Gibson County Courthouse in Trenton, Tennessee. Courtesy of the author.

ply the Union Army as General U.S. Grant made plans to move south toward Vicksburg, Mississippi. Union troops were placed at points along the railroad to protect the supply route from Confederates, and one of the largest of these forces was stationed at Trenton. Brigadier General Nathan Bedford Forrest was ordered to attack this Union supply line. Choosing to attack at Trenton, Forrest and his Confederate troops arrived on December 20, 1862. Union troops were barricaded on the depot platform behind cotton bales and hogsheads of tobacco. Colonel Jacob Fry was in command of these men, and he also placed twenty-five sharp shooters on a building across the street from the depot, the top of which was protected by a three-foot high wall. Six more men were placed in another building, with good sight lines from windows.

The battle commenced as General Forrest dashed down Lexington Street with his troops. About one hundred yards from the depot, the Union sharpshooters opened fire on the Confederates, and the men behind the barricades soon followed suit. Forced to withdraw some 200 yards from the depot, Forrest dismounted his men and sent some to nearby houses and buildings to afford some cover and to be better able to fight back. He then ordered a cannon in the Confederate arsenal to be placed on a piece of elevated land south of the depot. After a number of these cannon shots, white flags were soon waving from the Union held depot.

Meeting General Forrest, Colonel Fry asked about the terms of surrender, to which came the short and to the point reply, "Unconditional." Fry then remarked that his sword had been in his family for forty years. "Keep it," Forrest said, "but I hope, sir, when next worn, it will be in a better cause than in an attempt to subjugate your countrymen."

This surrender of the Union troops in Trenton resulted in over 400 prisoners of war, the capture of 1,000 horses and mules, and 400,000 rounds of small arms ammunition, among other items. Also taken was a fine imported sword of Damascus steel. General Forrest had the blade sharpened on both sides to a fine point and carried it throughout the rest of the war. Being ambidextrous, he wielded the sword very much to the advantage of the Confederate cause.

* * *

Thus into this land of the Indians, Davy Crockett, and Civil War battles Wallace was born in 1892. His parents were Robert Bruce Wade and Sallie Ann Mitchell, who had married in 1879. Robert, who went by R.B., was a farmer, mostly concentrating on a crop this section of Tennessee was known for: strawberries. A slight, rather austere man, R.B. worked hard and provided well for his family. Lucille, the youngest daughter, recalled in her later years that she could never remember her father hugging her, although she knew she was loved dearly. Showing much emotion just was not R.B. Wade. Sallie was a very loving mother, who tended to stay home and look after the kids, cook, sew, and be the one who expressed the motherly love that young children cling to. R.B. and Sallie lived in a nice house on a farm with several hundred acres not far from downtown Trenton.

The first Wade child was Davis, born in 1880. Eight more were to follow: Lycurgus in 1882, Carolyn in 1884, Mark in 1887, Bruce in 1889, Wallace three years later, Rebecca in 1894, Isham in 1897, and Lucille in 1903. Mark and Isham would go on to own one of the largest apple orchards in the United States, located in Wenatchee, Washington. Davis became a very successful commission merchant in Texas. Lucille, as a young woman, won many prizes riding horses.

Bruce was perhaps the most talented and brilliant of all the offspring; he entered Vanderbilt University in 1909, earning his bachelor's degree in 1913 and masters in 1914. The 1914 Commodore yearbook had this to say about Bruce's years there:

> Through his whole college course, Wade stood high in his classes and was extremely popular. For three years he was a member of the Reserve eleven and was elected captain in the fall of 1912. He was a star

R.B. and Sallie, the parents of Wallace Wade, are seated. Standing from left to right are Lucille, Isham, Rebecca, Wallace, Carolyn, Mark, and Davis. 1929 Trenton, Tennessee. Courtesy of Nell Breeden.

on the varsity five and was also a member of the varsity track team for two years. He closed his brilliant career as undergraduate by being elected Bachelor of Ugliness, the highest honor conferred by the student body of Vanderbilt.

Bruce then entered Johns Hopkins University in October of 1914, receiving his Doctor of Philosophy degree in 1917 with the major subjects of geology and paleontology. Bruce went on to become one of America's greatest geologists; possibly his greatest contribution was his discovery of the world famous Coon Creek fossil site in McNairy County, Tennessee. The preservation and variety of fossils from Coon Creek filled an important gap in the fossil record, including significant populations of gastropods, bivalves, cephalopods, crabs, lobsters, and shark teeth. Bruce also found in Harding County, Tennessee, the first insect in amber reported in North America. A publisher of many professional papers, Wade also served as Tennessee State Geologist and as an oil exploration geologist in Mexico. It would seem that Wallace's remark later in life that "Bruce had most of the smarts in the family" was close to the truth.

* * *

Working on the farm, attending school, and playing sports took up most of young Wallace's formative years in Trenton. Agriculture was the field through which most people in the area made a living. Evidence of this was reported in the local newspaper, the *Trenton Herald Democrat*, in the early 1900s. An annual tradition in Trenton was a town festival on the first Monday in August, called First Monday. This day was a celebration of bountiful harvests. The paper reported, "Many hundreds of Gibson countians released from the handles of the plows came to town just to knock about amongst the boys and swap yarns." Local merchants advertised farm implements such as middle busters, spike tooth harrows, cultivators, stalk cutters, corn planters, wagon gears, and fertilizer distributors. Carloads of mules were listed in the local paper almost weekly. In the Trenton paper in 1906, an advertisement was taken out for "Curing a Kicking Cow," which consisted of tying a rope in front of the udder and in back of the hip joints, which would "render a cow almost helpless from the standpoint of kicking." Along with strawberries, farmers grew cotton, corn, potatoes, asparagus, onions, cucumbers, cantaloupes, and pepper, among other staples. R.B. served for a time as the vice-president of the Trenton Fruit and Vegetable Growers Association. At the annual Gibson County Fair, a brochure in 1910 promoted farm life thusly,

> The farmer who owns a farm is the particular person who is fixed. Banks may fail and factories close, workmen strike and mines suspend. Times may be panicky and even crops may be short, but the farmer who owns his acres will get along. He will live in comfort and quiet, with plenty to eat, drink, and wear. He is the most independent man on earth.

A local poet added his praise of this hard working life:

> Twas on the farm where I was born,
> Where the birds their nests would build,
> By the light of the moon down on the farm,
> We would hear the notes of the whippoorwill.

From a young age, hard work seemed to be just fine with Wallace, who helped pick buckets of strawberries, milk cows, clear land for planting, or do whatever else his father and mother needed done. Wallace had great respect for both his parents, and he learned at an early age that when his father told him

R.B. Wade at the Wade home in Trenton. Courtesy of Nell Breeden.

to do something, it was best done promptly and well. No doubt, the stern discipline for which Wallace came to be known as a coach was inculcated in him,
to a large degree, by his father. Wallace actually enjoyed physical labor and activity; Hays Bennett, who grew up in Trenton and was a buddy of Wallace, recalled in 1932 that "Wallace and I used to work side-by-side on his father's
farm, and he enjoyed work more than anyone I have ever known."

This tenacity carried over to Wallace's football playing days at Peabody High
School in Trenton and later at Brown. Bennett played with Wallace at Peabody
and said, "He was the fightingest football player I ever saw." Their coach was
Everett (Tuck) Faucett. Faucett also spoke about the spirit young Wade displayed, saying "Wallace was the scrappiest player on the team. He wasn't big,
but he was a regular bulldog for tackling and holding on. That hard work on
the farm put him in good shape for football. He just never seemed to get tired
and would battle you all day long." Wallace himself reflected on this fighting
spirit in recalling his playing days at Brown University. When he got there, he
was having a hard time getting his coach to give him a starting position, so
Wade determined to show his coach that he was tougher than this teammate.
Wade said,

> I just decided that every single day when I went up against this chap
> in practice that I would just simply beat the hell out of him. I could

scrap with most anybody, so after a while my coach decided that I warranted a starting position, I think mostly because of my spirit and willingness to mix it up, more so than my talent, such as it was.

* * *

Football was not even played around Trenton until 1904. The local newspaper announced the game on October 20 of that year, pitting the Fitzgerald School team of Trenton against the Cobb and Nichols School of Dresden. The football game was the first "ever played in this section, and will be played on the Adams lot, just west of the fair grounds." (Trenton Herald Democrat) Mark, one of Wallace's older brothers, participated in this game. Wallace was just twelve at this time, but eventually, Wallace would follow Mark to three schools to play this new game of football: Fitzgerald School, a prep school in Chicago, and then Brown. In later years, Wallace said, "Mark was a more talented player than me, I just really kind of tagged along behind him."

The first attempts at establishing football in the area met stiff resistance. The *Trenton Herald Democrat* editorialized in 1905 that

> it is proper for boys and young men to engage in active outdoor sports and games, but these may be carried too far. Indeed, they have been carried too far in the foot ball game as at presently played. Some schools seem to be paying more attention to their foot ball teams and match games than to the mental and moral training of the young. A halt should be called at once in foot ball as the game is now played. It is simply brutal and is on a plane with prize fighting. The great number killed in this game, and the very much larger number who have been permanently injured is alarming. The game encourages brutality and coarseness. It has long since passed the point of a boyish sport or manly exercise.
>
> Surely few parents would care to send their boys off to school to be brought home with broken backs, mashed noses, or sent home a corpse. Much interest is being aroused on this subject, and it is to be hoped that the present day foot ball will soon be a thing of the past.

Across the country, especially in 1905, there were vehement calls for change in football. The game had evolved since the first intercollegiate game between Princeton and Rutgers in 1869 and became a popular sport by 1905, especially on eastern college campuses. But many problems existed; rough play and poor sportsmanship were rampant. There was even a rule called "three slugs and you're out," which allowed players to hit an opposing player three times before being ejected. It was not uncommon for players to do their slugging before the ball was even snapped. Once a player left a game, he could not return, thus injured players would usually stay in the contest until they literally collapsed. A play called the "flying wedge," was invented by a Harvard team advisor by the name of Lorin Deland. Deland admired and studied the great military leader, Napoleon, who believed in a concentration of maximum force at a given point on the battlefield. Deland devised the flying wedge with Napoleon's tactics in mind. Basically a group of teammates would converge together to form a wall of running human bodies to protect the ball carrier. *The New York Times* at first praised this new play, or formation, by saying, "What a grand play! A half-ton of bone and muscle coming into collision with a player weighing 160 or 170 pounds." But it did not take long for injuries resulting from this mass formation play to start raising eyebrows.

Equipment to protect players was poor. Helmets were not even required; in fact, some players grew their hair excessively long to offer some protection from the violent collisions. Even deaths occurred on a regular basis. The *Newark Evening News* reported, "It is mere good fortune when out of a game some promising young man does not become crippled or disfigured for life." Charles Eliot, who served as president of Harvard from 1875 to 1909, became the leading spokesman against football brutality. Eliot believed that there was something "exquisitely inappropriate in the extravagant expenditure on athletic sports," and that football was not only unsafe to players, but also begat violence in those who watched it. He said,

> The sensibilities both of the players and of habitual spectators are blunted by such sights. To become brutal and brutalizing is the natural tendency of all sports, which involve violent personal collision between the players, and the game of football is a *non-exception* to this rule.

Injuries became so prevalent in 1893 that President Grover Cleveland cancelled the Army-Navy game. In 1897, Richard Gammon of Georgia was killed as a result of rough play in a game against Virginia in Atlanta. Some colleges abolished football during the 1890s, two of them being Duke and Alabama, the two schools Wade would lead to acclaim in the 1920s and 1930s.

Other problems existed in football. Many, such as Eliot, claimed that athletics sometimes took away time better spent on academics, that football in particular contributed to a moral decay in America's youth. "Ringers," non-students who were hired or recruited to play for teams, were a problem. In fact, it was not uncommon for a player to play for one team one week and switch to another the very next week. Many critics of football also claimed that the game provided an atmosphere that promoted gambling and drinking among students.

By 1904 (when the first football game was played in the Trenton area) and 1905 (a year in which concerns for the game seemed to reach a crescendo), football was in a survival crisis. Proponents of the game defended its virtues. President Theodore Roosevelt spoke vigorously in defense of "manly" sports:

> Since I left college, I have worked hard in a good many ways and sports has always been a mere accessory to my other business, yet I managed to ride across the country a good deal, to play polo, and to shoot, and the like. I was knocked senseless at polo once, and it was a couple of hours until I came to. I broke an arm once riding to the hounds, and I broke my nose another time, and out on the roundup I once broke a rib and at another time, the point of my shoulder.

His injuries incurred while participating in vigorous exercise, or what he termed the "strenuous life," were recalled with pride and considered a part of the game. Other football advocates chimed in. Henry Van Dyke, a professor at Princeton, wrote,

> The University is no place for men who will not or cannot study. Neither is it a place for men to neglect their bodies, ruin their health, and become physical weaklings and incapables ... no American university can prosper or do its work without athletics. The question is not whether we will have them, but how shall we best conduct them.

Charles Young, an astronomy professor at Princeton, wrote that sports provided "a safety valve for the superabundant physical effervescence of young men." A university president noted that he favored college sports such as football, but he warned,

> They [sports] are ever liable to run to excess and to tempt numbers from the regular and systematic prosecution of their studies. The enthusiasm of some students is expended on their muscular feats rather than on intellectual exercises, and the hero of the class is one who stands high, not in literature, or science, or philosophy, but in mere physical agility.

By 1905, even Roosevelt was concerned for the survival of the game. He invited representatives of what were then considered the "Big Three" of college football, Harvard, Princeton, and Yale, to the White House for a conference. Walter Camp of Yale, the "father of American football," was one of the participants. Using the "bully pulpit" of the presidency, Roosevelt urged the college representatives to work together and observe rules of fair play for the good of the game. This meeting did much to lead to the formation of the Inter Collegiate Athletic Association, or ICAA, which a few years later would change its name to the National Collegiate Athletic Association, or NCAA.

The intervention of Roosevelt helped to put the issue of football in the national spotlight, and reform started to change the game. Rules were changed, such as the creation of a neutral zone at the line of scrimmage, increasing the number of officials, and the assessment of larger penalties for infractions. The safety and quality of play slowly increased over the years.

* * *

Wallace no doubt tagged along with Mark to watch his older brother play the intriguing game of football. Considered too young and slight of frame to take part in 1904, when the first attempts at football in Trenton took place, Wade looked up to Mark, who was a member of that first Peabody High team. Tough, strong men appealed to Wade, who had plenty of this type to admire during his adolescent years of the very early 1900s. His father and brother were certainly in this mold, and Wade enjoyed attending the Carl Hagenbeck and Great Wallace Shows circus when it made its annual stop in Gibson County. The strong man performers especially caught the eye of Wade, who all his life stressed the importance of physical fitness, or what was called physical culture in these boyhood years. Of course, Davy Crockett was a local legend, and the "strenuous life" espoused by Roosevelt rang loudly in the ears of the young Wade. Thousands of young boys of this era grew up hearing about the exploits of President Roosevelt, who had used exercise and sports to transform himself from a sickly youth into a robust man.

* * *

Wallace Wade first played organized football at Peabody High School in Trenton. The year was 1909. A scrappy young lad with plenty of intestinal fortitude, Wade's first coach was Everett (Tuck) Faucett. Coach Faucett was the first to admit he did not really know that much about football, but he was a good and respected man of the community who had a good rapport with young boys. So here, in the midst of whooping farm boys and the small town of Trenton, Wade learned the beginnings of the sport that was to carry him to fame across the nation.

Coach Faucett recalled,

> I didn't know but three plays, but we made up others as we went along. The center buck, off-tackle, and end run were our standard plays and when we got tired of one we'd use a combination of all three. We just

had a sort of nondescript team, with little or nothing in the shape of uniforms and headgear. We'd go across the hill in the afternoons and play the Fitzgerald team. They'd take us for a ride most of the time, but occasionally we would slip one over on them. I remember one time we stopped a game when we heard the fire alarm, and the whole team commandeered a farmer's wagon and rode to the blaze.

Coach Faucett eventually gave up coaching and played some professional baseball before participating in World War I.

* * *

As football grew in popularity around Trenton, so too, did the town. The Forked Deer Roller Mills was one of the most important manufacturing industries, along with the Trenton Cotton Mill. This cotton mill employed one hundred and sixty people in 1901, and two thousand bales of raw ginned cotton were converted into cloth and battings per year. The production of the mill in woven goods was more than 250,000 yards per year.

An attraction that remains today in Trenton is the world's largest collection of night light teapots. These little teapots were used for more than a century as a mode of brewing and serving floral or herb teas to babies during the night hours. The ornamental, yet functional, teapots offered the advantages of both providing medication that gave comfort to a restless baby as well as offering light at a time before electricity was available.

Today, downtown Trenton is dominated by a beautiful courthouse that was dedicated in 1901. More than likely, Wade and his family attended the dedication of this grand structure, which became the center of the town's activities.

In 1910, Wade started attending the Fitzgerald and Clark School in Trenton. Here, under coach W. A. Bridges, instruction in football improved over what it had been at Peabody High School. Wade played tackle and guard and made up for his lack of great size with his feistiness and his determination to always be prepared and do his very best.

The captain of the 1910 team was Guy Joyner, and in a 1938 interview he said,

> Wallace played guard and tackle. Had a lot of fire and fight and after he went to Brown he really got to be a good player. But in high school, well, he was average. Wallace lived outside Trenton in the country. Used to come to school riding a horse. Always had his pockets filled with apples, and the boys were glad to see him. Played baseball in the spring and a pretty good man at that, too. Weighed about 150 pounds, would play wherever we needed him most. He was easygoing, very quiet but rather aggressive. Hasn't changed a lick either.

**Fitzgerald and Clark School, Trenton, Tennessee, 1911 baseball team.
Wallace Wade is in the back row, far right. Courtesy of Will Fitzgerald.**

The 1910 and 1911 Fitzgerald and Clark teams, on which Wade played, only lost a total of two games. Coach Bridges was well-respected and had an ability to get the best out of his players. A big victory in 1911 was over Middle Tennessee State Normal, then a two-year college, on Thanksgiving Day.

Interestingly, Wade and William Fitzgerald, one of the founders of the Fitzgerald and Clark School, followed an amazingly similar path through their careers. Fitzgerald graduated from Vanderbilt, where Wade would one day coach, and Fitzgerald accepted teaching positions at Alabama and Duke, while Wade coached at both schools.

* * *

At the conclusion of the 1912 school year at Fitzgerald, Wade had no doubt that he wanted to continue his education and athletic pursuits. There also was little doubt about where he wanted to do this. Mark had just graduated from a prep school in Chicago called Morgan Park Academy, where he played under one of the great football coaches, Amos Alonzo Stagg. Stagg coached the University of Chicago and the Morgan Park prep teams at the same time, with help from his college and former players. During the 1909 season, Mark

UNIVERSITY SCHOOL DORMITORIES, TRENTON, TENN.

Above: Fitzgerald and Clark School, 1910 football team. Wallace Wade is at left guard. Courtesy of Fred Culp.
Below: Fitzgerald and Clark School (at one time called University School).

played guard on a team that won six out of seven games, outscoring its opponents 346 to 8, with the only loss to Culver, Indiana, 8 to 2. This Morgan Park team was declared Illinois state champion. The 1910 team was 5-0-1, and Mark served as captain of the 1911 team.

Even though Mark had graduated by the fall of 1912 when Wallace arrived, Wallace knew that this military boarding school was just what he wanted. Rigid discipline, high academic standards, and a love of sports were right in line with his interests.

By the time Wade arrived, Coach Stagg had put John Anderson, one of his former Chicago players, in the position of head coach, but Stagg still attended practices occasionally. Coach Stagg even sometimes scrimmaged his Chicago team against the Morgan Park team and allowed Morgan Park to play some games at Marshall Field, home of the university. The knowledge that he would have an opportunity to be tutored by either Coach Stagg or his players, coupled with the fact that Mark had achieved such success there, played a significant role in Wallace's decision to go to Morgan Park.

"All modern football stems from Stagg," said Knute Rockne, the great Notre Dame coach, and being in the proximity of Stagg had a lasting influence on Wade. Many others referred to Coach Stagg as the "Grand Old Man of College Football." Coach Stagg coached from 1890 to 1948, which included the years 1891 to 1932 at Chicago. He won 314 games during his lifetime at the college level and was credited with starting many innovations in football, such as diagrammed playbooks, various backfield shifts, men in motion, and the fake kick. Coach Stagg always stressed good sportsmanship, something that Wade, too, became known for. Thorough preparation, clean living, the value of physical conditioning, and the importance of sports to a well-rounded education were other traits that Wallace picked up from Coach Stagg.

As he had already attended Peabody High School and the Fitzgerald and Clark School in Trenton, Wallace only needed one year at Morgan Park to graduate, which he did in 1913. The 1912 football team won three out of five games, and Wallace also played on the baseball team.

Upon graduating from Morgan Park, Wallace Wade once again decided to follow Mark, this time to Brown University in Rhode Island. There Wallace would continue to learn the skills that later in his life landed him in the College Football Hall of Fame.

CHAPTER TWO

A BROWN BEAR

Joe Paterno and John Heisman played football at Brown University. Fritz Pollard attained All-America status at Brown and later became the first black head coach in pro football. Wallace Wade played at Brown, and Weeb Ewbank coached there.

Brown football has a rich tradition that dates back to 1878 when Amherst was the opponent in its first game ever. Amherst won this first contest handily. The Brown student paper, the *Brunonian*, summed it up this way: "We went, we saw, we (were) conquered." Football continued to improve, though in 1890 the *Brunonian* conceded that "signs indicate that at last we are to have a worthy football eleven, but capable men would not train for football because Brown's situation in the heart of the city makes too accessible the attendant gaiety and dissipation." In 1893, Brown had its first really good season, going 6 and 3. This team featured a player who would become a great coach at Brown and for whom Wallace Wade would play: Edward North Robinson. The team also had a player called "Big." Big Smith stood 6'6" and weighed 205 pounds. In this era he was considered a giant. In a game later in his career against Yale, Smith was described as scoring a touchdown in this way: "Yale men were bowled over by the rambling giant as fast as they arose in his path." Brown tied mighty Yale 6 to 6 in this 1895 game, and it was considered one of the great "victories" in the university's history. Yale was one of the giants of early college football; from 1876 to 1895, Yale won 179 games against only five losses with ten ties, a dominance that is hard to match in the history of the game.

In 1887 John Heisman arrived on the picturesque Brown campus. As he recalled in a later article for Colliers magazine,

One blissful September afternoon in 1887, I set forth for Providence and Brown University. I was seventeen and football mad. Eventually I arrived on the campus of Brown on the beautiful hill overlooking the city of Providence. Was I impressed with the ivy-clad halls? Did the enchantment, which clothes the college vistas for wide-eyed freshmen grip me? Ah, no. I gave but a fleeting glance to the buildings, for there at my feet on the campus a game of football was in progress.

Heisman later achieved coaching stardom, serving tenures at Auburn, Clemson, and Georgia Tech, among other schools. His overall record was 184-68-16. The Heisman Trophy was named in his honor in 1936.

A football team manager for the 1896 team went on to become the richest man in the world, John D. Rockefeller, Jr. Even then, "Johnny Rock," as he was affectionately known on campus, knew how to "pinch pennies" as he worked diligently and turned a profit for the football association during his term as manager.

In 1898 Edward Robinson was chosen to coach Brown, and he stayed until 1901. Robinson, known as "Robbie," returned in 1904 to coach through the 1907 season. In 1910, Robinson was hired again, and this time he coached through the 1925 season. The 1910 season was historic in that Brown beat Yale for the first time. Led by its All-American quarterback, William Sprackling, Brown shut out Yale 21 to 0. Sprackling yielded a performance in this game that is still remembered and written about. He kicked three field goals, completed five of six passes for 180 yards and a touchdown, carried the ball for 36 yards, and gained 150 yards in punt returns and 90 on kickoff returns. Of Brown's total yardage, 608, Sprackling had 456. When news of the game reached Providence, cries of "Freshmen, get wood!" could be heard across campus, signaling the start of a gigantic bonfire in celebration of the great victory.

* * *

In 1912 Mark Wade arrived to play for Coach Robinson. A letter written in 1975 referred to his time at Brown:

> Wade Orchards, Inc.
> Wenatchee, Washington

Brown Football Association
Providence, Rhode Island

Gentlemen,

In 1912 I graduated from Morgan Park Military Academy in Chicago as president of the class and captain of the football team. During the three years I was at Morgan Park I was coached under the instruction of the famous coach, Alonzo Stagg.

The Brown Club of Chicago, under the leadership of Elmer Stevens, secured for me a scholarship. I arrived in Providence in September

1912, ten days after the football team had started practice. When I arrived at Andrews Field Coach Robinson gave me the devil for not showing up at the start of practice. He gave me a suit and I wound up as left tackle on the varsity team.

The first real tough team we went up against was Pennsylvania University, coached by Andy Smith. I was scheduled to play left tackle in that game. I had figured the time from the university to Andrews Field and left in time to catch the streetcar and get there. To my surprise all the streetcars were full. I waited, then finally just caught a hold of one and hung on the railing to get to the field.

When the game was over, we defeated Pennsylvania 30 to 7. In the meantime I had broken ribs, a broken thumb, and a broken nose. I remember getting as far as the dressing room and then I passed out. I woke up at the home of Dr. Monroe, the father of one of my fraternity brothers. I asked what kind of shape I was in. Dr. Monroe said, "Outside of a few broken bones, you are all right."

The next Saturday we played Harvard. I had a splint on my hand to protect my broken finger, a nose guard to protect my broken nose, and I was strapped up to protect my broken ribs. We took a defeat from Harvard.

Thanksgiving Day, 1912, we played the Carlisle Indians and Coach Robinson told us that if we could defeat them with Pop Warner as coach, we could still stand reasonably in the ratings. Make no mistake, Jim Thorpe of Carlisle was the best player I ever played against.

The team of 1916, which I was not on, played in the Rose Bowl. My brother, Wallace Wade, was on that team. His class was 1917. Wallace didn't make All-American as a player, but is in the Hall of Fame as a coach. He is five years younger than I am.

The only reason I didn't come back to Brown is that in 1913 I came to Wenatchee to buy 100 carloads of apples. I expected to sell them and return to Brown. The only way to get 100 carloads was to buy direct from the farmers and that required staying after the first of the term — too late for football.

I bought the apples from a company in Wenatchee called Boston *Okanogan* Orchards. They had 1,500 acres planted in fruit trees. The rest of the homestead was developed into reservoirs for irrigation and stock ponds. Eventually, in 1943 I bought the entire holdings of Boston *Okanogan* Orchards and incorporated the holdings under Jim Wade Orchards, Inc. The fruit here has an international reputation for quality.

By the way, I saw Coach Stagg's last game, played in Tacoma, Washington, the night before Pearl Harbor. I was at the banquet and talked with Coach Stagg, who, in my judgment, was the best coach in American history and a great builder of men.

> Sincerely,
> James M. Wade

The Carlisle game referred to in the letter was Thorpe's last game as a college player. Brown increased the seating capacity of its home stadium, Andrews Field, to 10,000 in anticipation of a large crowd. Thorpe scored three touchdowns against Mark Wade and his Brown teammates. A memorable play in this game was an encounter between Thorpe and George Crowther of Brown, who weighed all of 130 pounds. The *New York Tribune* reported that on a long run Thorpe

> got by everyone but Crowther. Crowther barely got him by his sweater, just above the belt. Crowther hung on desperately, and for ten yards more the big Indian tore along, with Crowther pulled clean off the ground. At last, Crowther pulled himself up to the redskin, twined his legs into Thorpe's massive underpinnings and made him stumble.... Thorpe went down on the eight-yard line.

* * *

This is part of the tradition of Brown football into which Wallace Wade entered upon arriving on campus in the fall of 1913. Mark, as he wrote about in his letter, ended up not coming back because he was getting started in the apple business, which ended with him owning one of the largest apple orchards in the country.

Wallace would make the varsity team in 1914. Edward Robinson was still the coach. "Robbie" remains the coach with the most wins in Brown football history, recording 140 victories against 82 losses and 12 ties. In an interview in his later years, Wade said,

> Coach Robinson taught me a lot about football. He was a good coach who stressed fundamentals like blocking and tackling, and he was a good organizer. Many things I learned under Coach Robinson I used

later in my coaching career. I must have thought a lot of him because my brother Mark had already played for him at Brown, and he persuaded me to go there.

The most significant game in 1914 was on November 14, when Brown held mighty Harvard to a scoreless tie. Harvard had beaten Brown thirteen times straight since their first game. To give an idea of how good Harvard, coached by Percy Haughton, was, they won 71 games against only seven losses and five ties during the years of 1908 to 1916. So the tie in 1914 was sufficient for the *New York Tribune* to make the headline, "Haughty Harvard Humbled." At a chapel meeting shortly after the game, President Faunce of Brown brought the game ball in a paper bag. At an appropriate time, he removed the ball and the students rose to their feet and cheered wildly. Brown finished a very respectable 5-2-2.

The year 1915 brought to campus what many consider to be Brown's greatest football player ever. Fritz Pollard was called "one of the greatest runners these eyes have ever seen," by the authority Walter Camp. Camp was so impressed with Pollard that he put him on his All-American team in 1916, the first black player to be so honored. As noted earlier, Pollard also became the first black man to be a head coach in pro football.

Also impressed with his teammate was Wade, who as a guard opened many of the holes in the defense for Pollard. Wade said, "Pollard was a great runner. He ran with considerable drive and force, and he changed directions very well." Wade was particularly fond of Pollard's cross-step dodge, in which Pollard would fake to the inside or outside, and then cross one foot over the other, all the while moving forward. It was a good move "because when he crossed, that gave him a lot of force and with that kick he'd knock that tackle off," Wade said. After becoming a coach, Wade always stressed to his players the importance of constantly moving forward. He didn't like for his players to move sideways or backward, even if it was to elude oncoming tacklers. "Fritz was one of the best runners that I've known in all my football experience," Wade said, "including Grange and all those fellows. I've studied Grange. Seen Grange play. Fritz could go up with any of them."

In 1915, Pollard was one of only two black students on campus. When Wade's father, R.B., found out that Pollard was on the team, he traveled to Providence and threatened to take Wallace out of school if Pollard remained. R.B. Wade had always lived in a very segregated society in the South. Wallace stood up to his father, explaining to his dad that Fritz was a good person and a good teammate. Coach Robinson also talked to R.B., and the result was that Wallace stayed in school and he and Fritz became the best of friends. In an interview later in life, Wallace said,

I was proud to have Fritz as a teammate and friend. He was a good chap. We would eat together at the training table. I remember one day I saw Fritz walking on campus with his head down and looking kind of droopy and sad. He told me that he had just been told that his term bill was due, and he didn't have enough money to pay it. Well, us boys got together and decided to all use Fritz's clothes pressing service he had started. I also contributed a dollar to his fund. It was all I could do. I didn't have much money either.

Wallace befriended Pollard, as did other of his teammates, and almost everyone came to accept him. This was not easy to do at a time in U.S. history where separation of the races was accepted in many states. Wade showed courage and intelligence in this act of independence at Brown, and he would be very instrumental in integrating college football in the south at a later time. Wade genuinely liked Fritz, and Fritz appreciated it. After becoming coach at Alabama, Fritz contacted Wade when Wade's team was in California for a Rose Bowl, and the two met to catch up on old times. There was another reason for Wade and his teammates to get along with Pollard: they knew Fritz was the best player on the team and dramatically increased their chances of winning.

* * *

Perhaps the biggest victory of the 1915 season for Brown was the 3 to 0 victory over Yale in November. The only points were a dropkick field goal by team captain Harold "Buzz" Andrews, who had never even attempted a field goal in a game. Postcards were printed after the game with only Andrews' right foot in a football shoe showing, with the inscription: 1915 Brown 3 Yale 0 The Toe That Did It. Brown beat Carlisle in the last regular season game 39 to 3, to finish 5-3-1. The overall record was hardly spectacular, but the good finish and the victories over highly regarded programs like Yale and Carlisle gave Brown national publicity.

November of 1915 brought great news to the Brown campus. The Rose Bowl had selected Brown's football team to play Washington State in California. Michigan and Syracuse had also been considered, but the committee chose Brown as the "eastern" football representative. Celebrations broke out over campus as faculty, students, alumni, and fans of Brown football realized what the national exposure could do for their program.

The Brown-Washington State match-up would only be the second Rose Bowl game. Michigan had defeated Stanford 49 to 0 in the first game back in 1902. It was such a mismatch that the Stanford coach pleaded with Fielding Yost, the Michigan coach, to stop the game before it officially ended. Yost and

Wade as a player at Brown.

his powerful Michigan teams of this era simply did not believe in mercy, as evidenced by the fact that from 1901 to 1905 his teams scored 2,821 points to their opponents 42. During that time Michigan was 55-1-1. Earlier in 1902, before the Rose Bowl, Yost and his team had beaten Michigan State 119 to 0 and Iowa 107 to 0. Yost's response to the Stanford coach, when asked to stop the slaughter, was typical of his way of playing, "No sirree, let's get on with it!"

Playing for Michigan was a man who would have a huge impact on Wallace Wade. Dan McGugin, a left guard, later became head coach at Vanderbilt and hired Wade as an assistant. McGugin and his teammates obviously did their job, out gaining Stanford 503 yards to 57, with All-American halfback Willie Heston getting 170 yards on 18 carries.

This one-sided match-up helped to convince the Rose Bowl organizers that perhaps playing a football game as part of this New Year's Day Festival wasn't such a grand idea. From 1903 to 1915 other events took the place of football. There were chariot races, rodeo events, automobile races, and ostrich races. In 1913 a race between an elephant and a camel was even staged (the elephant won). But by 1916, football was reinstituted.

* * *

The team left Providence for their cross-country train journey on December 22. The president of Brown excused all students from morning classes to give the team a rousing sendoff. Practically every student joined in a snake dance down to Union Station Depot to the party of twenty-six, of whom

**1915 Brown team. Wade is in the front row, third from left.
Fritz Pollard is far right in the back row.**

twenty-one were players. At the station there were cheers and songs, and "Buzz" Andrews, the team captain, promised the gathering that the team would bring home "a good long slice of Washington bacon."

Wade was by now called "Wally" around campus. He had been reluctant for Brown to make the trip because he had a job during the Christmas holidays and needed it badly to pay his college expenses. Years later he said, "I did a bunch of odd jobs, whatever I could do. I had to pay my school and living expenses. I ran a laundry service, ran errands, shoveled snow. I grew up working hard on my father's farm, these little jobs at Brown were easy compared to that." Wade's anxiety was eased when the *Providence Journal* newspaper hired him to write about the trip.

If anything, Wade's teammates might have been a little overconfident as they began their journey west. Eastern football was then considered to be the best in the nation. But they should have known better. Washington State came into the Rose Bowl undefeated, outscoring its opponents 190 to 10. But Wade recalled, "I believe we had one of the most confident teams ever to play in Pasadena. We took the whole jaunt as a lark, because west coast football was considered to be far inferior to our eastern brand."

Preparations for the journey had been gone over in detail. A large supply of Rhode Island drinking water was taken aboard. Extra insurance was taken out for everyone making the trip. A modern all-steel Pullman train was to be used.

The players enjoyed the sights as they made their way across the country. According to his report written for the *Providence Journal*, studying was practiced by most. "Morning and afternoon, the boys spent considerable time plugging away on their books, not one member of the squad having forgotten he is a student first and a football player second," Wade wrote. There was also ample time for a little recreation, and many a game of Red Dog card playing took place.

A band greeted the train upon arrival in Chicago. Brown had made arrangements for practice at Northwestern's field. A number of Brown alumni provided private cars to carry the team the twelve miles to the Northwestern campus, but upon arrival, the team realized they had left their equipment, including uniforms, on the train. Graciously, Northwestern officials opened their equipment room to Brown's players and let them borrow what they needed.

After the practice, the team was feted at a banquet at the University Club in Chicago. Continuing its journey after the rejuvenating Chicago stop, the team headed into Kansas, which was covered with snow. During a brief stop in Emporia, some of the players got into a little snowball fighting on the depot platform, which caught some innocent spectators in the crossfire. They took it good naturedly, though, as they had been warned that the "rah-rahs" from Brown were about to disembark.

At a stop in Oklahoma, Wade's country boy instincts took over, and he took several of his teammates off the train to show them his skills at hunting rabbits. They barely made it back to the train before departure time. Also in Oklahoma, the issue of race arose. Ray Ward, a Brown player, wrote,

> We had just sat down to a table in the dining car when Fritz sat at our table. The headwaiter came up to Fritz and informed him that he could not sit down with a white man in the state of Oklahoma. This nearly started a riot, but things were finally worked out so that Pollard sat alone at a table and then it was okay if we sat down with him. Evidently, it was okay if white men sat down with colored men, but no good for a colored man to sit with a white man.

Arriving in Albuquerque, New Mexico, on Christmas Day, the team exchanged small gifts they had bought in Chicago. A brief workout was held on the University of New Mexico field but had to be cut short because of their unfamiliarity with the high altitude. Later in the day, alumni arranged a dinner for the team at the Alvarado Hotel and a dance at the Albuquerque Country Club. A report on the dance stated that "the fellows made a fine impression, especially with the handsome Spanish-American senoritas."

By midnight the team was back on the train and headed to Pasadena, arriving at 5 a.m. on December 27. They went straight to their quarters, the

Hotel Raymond, which was owned by Walter Raymond, a Harvard graduate. Raymond made sure that his fellow northeasterners felt at home, even greeting them upon their arrival decked out in an actual Harvard football uniform that he had gotten the university to ship him.

Shortly after arrival, it started raining, and it kept raining off and on right through the day of the game. Nevertheless, Brown practiced daily at the Horace Mann School, named after the famous educator and philosopher who was an 1819 Brown graduate. In the final practice before the game, Wade reported that the starting team "tore the scrubs to tatters."

It certainly was not all work and no play. Several parties, dinners, and sightseeing tours were given for the team. Fritz Pollard recalled that they were "entertained very lavishly and were taken to outstanding places in Pasadena and also to all the movie studios and met several of the movie stars of that era." Pollard also remembered that the hotel had a side elevator, which "the fellows used to go out, stay over their time and sneak up to their rooms so that the coaches waiting on the main floor to catch them didn't know they were out." It is worth noting here that Wade, as a coach, simply would not have tolerated this type of behavior. A couple of days before the game, the team visited an ostrich farm, where some ate too many unripened oranges and contracted diarrhea.

Meanwhile, Washington State had arrived more than a week earlier than Brown. Washington State was coached by William "Lone Star" Dietz, a Sioux who was one of the most colorful coaches around. He dressed in a most flamboyant manner; even to games he would wear a silk hat, striped trousers, and yellow gloves, and he would carry a stylish walking stick.

The Bears of Brown were the definite favorites, due more to the regard for eastern football than a comparison of the two teams. But by game time, none of that mattered as the two teams started play in a hard rain, which soon made the field a quagmire. The crowd was estimated at 7,000. The tournament committee lost money, as it had guaranteed $5,000 to the two teams.

Using mostly line plunges out of its double-wing formation, the Bears of Brown drove to Washington State's four-yard line in the first half before being stopped. Pollard ran gallantly, but ended up with only forty-seven yards on thirteen carries for the game. Brown was not to score the entire afternoon.

Early in the game, two of Brown's ends, Josh Weeks and John Butner, were injured. Coach Dietz directed his rushing attack against this weakened part of the Brown defense in the second half, with outstanding results. Washington State accumulated 202 yards on the ground in the second half to only 17 for Brown. The final whistle signaled a 14 to 0 Washington State victory. Wallace Wade would return to the Rose Bowl *ten* years later with a determination to make amends, and in the process he became the first person to play and coach in a Rose Bowl game.

Why did Brown lose this game? It lost because on that day it was simply outplayed. Overconfidence hurt the players, and the slippery field negated the elusive running ability of their main weapon, Fritz Pollard. Another reason was offered by the *Pasadena Star*: "The Brown men were of a rounder, filled-out type, typical of Eastern colleges, while the Washington men were of the square shouldered, rangy type, which the ranges and mountains of the West produce."

For the trip home, each player was given $21 for meal money, so that he could buy his own meals, since many had expressed displeasure about the food on the way to Pasadena. Jimmy Murphy got home with $17 left over, as he took advantage of several free lunch counters. It is a very good bet that Wade saved much of his meal money too, as he needed it, and also, at least in his later years (according to some who knew him), he was thrifty. It should be noted, though, that he left Duke University a $100,000 endowment fund after his death.

Even in defeat, the Rose Bowl game of 1916 gained much national attention for Brown. With WWI raging and President Woodrow Wilson doing his best to maintain American neutrality, the news of this east-west confrontation must have provided a much needed diversion. Besides the increased recognition, the extra weeks of practice the team gained from having to prepare for the bowl helped to get it ready for the 1916 season. This season would end up as one of Brown's best.

* * *

Fritz Pollard, Wally Wade, Ray Ward, and Josh Weeks were among the returnees for 1916. Hopes were high. After opening with easy wins over Rhode Island, Trinity, Amherst, Williams, Rutgers, and Vermont, Brown traveled to Yale, and it, too, was defeated (by a score of 21 to 6). A caustic remark by a Brown player during the game characterized the team's growing belief and confidence in itself. Cupid Black, Yale's captain, said to Brown's Furber Marshall, "You think you are pretty good, don't you, young fellow," and Marshall replied, "No, but I do shine in these practice games." Pollard showed why he would end the season as an All-American, gaining 307 of the 437 total yards for Brown, despite derisive chants of "Bye, bye, blackbird" from Yale fans.

Next came Harvard, who had in its last two games shut out Virginia and Princeton by a combined score of 54 to 0. Percy Haughton, the Harvard coach, had gone to the extreme of blackening the face of one of his players in practice who was running the plays that Pollard would be using in the game. Over

32,000 fans filled Harvard's stadium as Brown defeated the Crimson for the first time; 1916 also marked the first time that any team had defeated both Yale and Harvard in the same year.

Wade's team was 8 and 0 going into its last game against Colgate. To the surprise of most, Colgate won 28 to 0. Hopes for a national championship were ripped to pieces.

During his last three years at Brown, the team won 18 games, lost seven, and tied three. Wade made a couple of All-Eastern teams in 1916. He had made many friends, gained valuable football knowledge from Coach Robinson, and graduated in 1917. Wade had a strong premonition that WWI would dictate the next stage of his life.

CHAPTER THREE

FITZGERALD AND CLARK

After graduating from Brown, Wade was drafted into the service for World War I. He achieved the rank of captain, but never went overseas for duty. From August of 1917, when he was drafted, to September of 1919, Wade was stationed at Camp Sevier, South Carolina, Camp Shelby, Mississippi, and Camp Gordon, Georgia.

Upon discharge from the army in 1919, Wade applied for and got the position of football coach at Fitzgerald and Clark School, now in Tullahoma, Tennessee. Wade knew the founder of the school, William Fitzgerald, from when he had attended the school in 1910–11 when it was located in Trenton, Tennessee, where he grew up. Wade remembered Mr. Fitzgerald very fondly in a letter to Will Fitzgerald, Mr. Fitzgerald's grandson:

"I first became acquainted with Mr. Fitzgerald in the early 1900s when he founded the Fitzgerald School at Trenton, Tennessee, where I grew up on a nearby farm. At this time "Mr. Fritz" was a handsome, athletic looking young man. He had played on the Vanderbilt University football team and was an excellent tennis player. At that time I was attending the Trenton public schools and often saw him pass by in a very fast walk with several young people hurrying after him in order to hear his words of wisdom and interesting comments. He coached his first football team that I ever saw. I later attended and played football at the Fitzgerald and Clark School, before it was moved to Tullahoma, Tennessee."

"Mr. Fitzgerald was an outstanding teacher and leader of young people. His favorite subjects were English and Latin. He strongly emphasized the grammatical aspects and the mental disciplinary influences of these subjects. It is unfortunate that the young people of today do not have the benefit of the training in the fundamentals of education that Mr. Fitzgerald emphasized. Mr. Fitzgerald's last teaching assignment was in remedial English at Duke University."

"Although a great teacher of languages, I feel that Mr. Fitzgerald's greatest asset was his inspirational leadership. Many young people such as I, a poor farm boy, were inspired by his influence to seek and make the effort for higher education and greater achievement. I definitely owe a great deal to him."

Wallace Wade during WWI. Courtesy of Nancy Wade.

"In my opinion he was at his best in the daily thirty-minute assemblies. At these a short devotional service was conducted and then he would give an extemporaneous discussion on values and conduct of life, such as morality, integrity, honesty, loyalty, fair play, ambition, determination, etiquette, speaking and writing the English language, and many other worthwhile thoughts. Even though I am now past 85, I still remember many of his sayings, such as, "Don't say I want to thank you, but say I thank you."

William Fitzgerald's influence on Wade while Wade was a student and coach at Fitzgerald and Clark cannot be overemphasized. In later interviews, Wade mentions the teachings and leadership of Mr. Fitzgerald, and of course, followed him to Tullahoma after the school had moved from Trenton. Interestingly, Mr. Fitzgerald later followed Wade, first to Alabama where he taught, and then to Duke. The two men had a lifelong admiration for each other.

William Fitzgerald and William Clark, the two headmasters, moved the school to Tullahoma in 1911, yielding to the solicitations of leading business men in Tullahoma, about 75 miles from Nashville. Because of World War I, Fitzgerald and Clark became a military school in 1918.

Needing a job after WWI, Wade, now 27, would take the job as football coach. It was logical since Wade played at Fitzgerald and Clark when it was in Trenton; William Fitzgerald was still at the school, now in Tullahoma; and Wade had played on the famous Brown Rose Bowl team.

Fitzgerald and Clark School, Tullahoma, Tennessee.

Wade showed his savviness early in the 1919 season. His team had a game with the Sewanee prep school, then a part of the University of the South. Arriving in Sewanee on a Friday before Saturday's game, the Sewanee coach invited Wade's team to attend a party his team had prepared for the visitors. Wade, even then a no-nonsense type, said no but thanked the coach. But after the Sewanee coach said the party had been planned all week, Wade relented.

Before the party, however, Wade told his players to eat absolutely nothing while at the party. After the party was over, Wade dropped by to see an old friend, Earl Abell, who was head coach of Sewanee University and had been a player for Colgate whom Wade had played against while at Brown. Wade had stepped into another room momentarily when the Sewanee prep school coach walked into Abell's house. Abell innocently asked the coach how the party went. The prep coach, not realizing Wade was within earshot, replied "That darned coach wouldn't let his boys eat anything after we had all that rich food prepared for them."

Wade won 16 games at Fitzgerald and Clark in his two years there, 1919 and 1920, while losing only three. In 1920 his team would go undefeated and win the Tennessee state prep championship. The 1920 team simply dominated its competition, beating such teams as Montgomery Bell Academy, Tennessee Military Institute, Sewanee Military Academy, St. Andrews, and Branham and

Fitzgerald and Clark School, Tullahoma, Tennessee, 1921, baseball team. Wade is in the back row, second from left. Courtesy of Will Fitzgerald.

Hughes. In the final game of 1920, the game that won the state championship, Fitzgerald and Clark beat Bryson College of Fayetteville 21 to 13 before a crowd of over 3,000. After the game, the *Nashville Banner* reported on Wade's team: "The season has come and gone, records have been made according to games won and lost, and the annual task of setting up a state championship team is at hand. View the situation in its natural, clear light, and the only eleven worthy of wearing the laurels of the victor is none other than Fitzgerald and Clark Military Academy of Tullahoma, Tennessee. It has done the phenomenal thing of picking the state's first order teams and scoring 339 points against them in opposition to 30. It has outclassed every team of the season by so many taps that no symbol of doubt remained at the conclusion of the final quarter of any of these games. Perhaps no factor in the success of the team has been more prominent than that of its coach, Wallace Wade."

The 1920 team was loaded with future college players, most prominent of them Lynn Bomar, who became an All-American at Vanderbilt, and played for Wade there in 1921 and 1922, where Wade was an assistant to Dan McGugin. Pos Elam and Jack Wakefield also went to Vanderbilt and played football for the Commodores. Billy Bone played at Tennessee, Lautzenhauser played at Chattanooga, and Dick Bear played at Washington and Lee. Captain Dale Smoot was planning on following Wade to Vanderbilt in 1921, but he contracted pneumonia and died in late 1920, the year he led the Tullahoma team to the state crown.

Football Team 1920-1921.
(State Champions)
From Left to Right—Wade (Coach), Sullivan, Holland, Coles, Bone, Lockhart, Day, Danner, Lautzenheiser, Beard, Wakefield, Bulman, Smoot (Captain), Gray, S. Franklin.

Fitzgerald and Clark School, Tullahoma, Tennessee, 1920 football team. Courtesy of Will Fitzgerald.

Jack Wakefield was perhaps the most gifted of the players on the 1920 team. Jack was Hek Wakefield's brother, who was a great player at Vanderbilt. Lynn Bomar always maintained that Jack was the best backfield player he had seen. The great sportswriter Fred Russell described Jack Wakefield: "Standing 6'1", weighing 197, he was thick, fast, had arms like a gorilla, enormous hands, could pass 50 yards with either hand and kick well with either foot. He was the most punishing football competitor I ever saw that one freshman year."

After Wakefield's freshman season at Vanderbilt, he got into academic trouble, dropped out, and tragically committed suicide shortly after.

Lynn Bomar remembered Wade at Fitzgerald and Clark. "The games were a hell of a lot easier than his practices," he said. "He was a great coach, but he was a stickler for fundamentals and we learned to regard all Saturdays as rest days."

Wade's first year salary at Tullahoma was $1,800 a year, for coaching football, basketball, and baseball, plus he did some math tutoring.

One of the most famous coaches in all of college football, Dan McGugin of Vanderbilt, got word of Wade, this young coach who was making a name for himself down in Tullahoma. McGugin wanted him on his staff, and in 1921 Wade headed for Nashville to become part of one of the nation's best football programs.

CHAPTER FOUR

UNDEFEATED SEASONS
AT VANDERBILT

After compiling such an outstanding record at Fitzgerald and Clark, college teams started to notice the young 29-year-old Wallace Wade and his coaching potential. One who had was Dan McGugin of Vanderbilt who coached the Commodores for 30 years, 1904 to 1934, with the exception of 1918 for WWI. For most of the early 1900s, McGugin had the best team in the south, winning ten Southern Conference championships. His overall record was 197 victories against 55 defeats with 19 ties. Not only did McGugin's teams at Vanderbilt win most of the time, rarely did opposing teams score. In fact, McGugin has the distinction of being the coach who recorded the most shutouts in NCAA history. Of the 291 games he coached, his teams shut out their opponents 137 times; 47% of the times Vandy played under his tenure, they registered shutouts. Speaking of shutouts, Wallace Wade had the second most shutouts in the history of the game with 118. But based on percentage, Wade coached teams at Alabama and Duke shut out opponents an amazing 51% of the time. That's right; 118 times out of 230 total games the opposition scored no points.

McGugin hired young Wade as a coach and a director of athletics, and with these two defensive minded coaches together, scoring against Vanderbilt was almost impossible. In the 17 games Vanderbilt played while Wade coached under McGugin, only four teams scored, and those four totaled only 37 points over the two seasons.

Defense was not all that Wade learned from the Vanderbilt head coach; McGugin knew how to inspire men to perform to the best of their ability. Grantland Rice, the famed sportswriter, wrote this about McGugin: "I have known a long parade of football coaches through my career, but I have never met one who combined more of the qualities needed to make a great coach than Dan McGugin carried." Fred Russell, another sportswriter who knew McGugin well, wrote that he was a clever strategist, a quick thinker, and was a keen judge of men. One of McGugin's greatest faculties was the ability to adapt himself to the material at hand. If ever a coach gave his life to the college he served, Dan McGugin gave his to Vanderbilt. His name will never die.

A speech Coach McGugin gave in 1930, toward the end of a long career, probably best sums up his own philosophy as a leader. He said that

the lure of the football field to the coach consists not in newspaper publicity, which is either very often too great in praise or too severe in criticism, nor in the applause or recriminations of the multitudes, but in the opportunity it gives to go straight to the hearts of young men and to bring forth in them the qualities which they admire. The greatest single factor in the winning of games is this thing called team spirit. A lad needs to learn a goal is something to be struggled for, that no matter what his disappointments may be, he must gather himself together and push on ahead. He may even find himself tackled until his teeth rattle. He may make mistakes, he may lose his temper, he may be thrown for almost disgraceful losses, but he knows that he must get up and push forward and struggle and fight and endure in order to advance toward the goal, and that he must be all these things according to the rules."

McGugin closed his speech quoting a poem that he truly believed in:

Dear Lord, in the battle which goes on through life,
I ask but a field that is fair;
The chance that is equal with all in the strife.
The chance but to do and to dare;
And if I should win, I win by the code,
With my faith and my courage held high;
And if I should fail, may I stand by the road,
And cheer as the winners go by.

Wallace Wade would carry these traits into his coaching career, as he, too, emphasized teaching his players to win the right way and that playing football was serious business that helped to prepare one for later life. There is no doubt that the two years Wade spent under McGugin had a huge, lasting impact on the coaching career that was to come at Alabama and Duke.

* * *

As of 2006, Vanderbilt football has not had a winning season since 1982, when they went 8 and 4 under George MacIntyre. Vanderbilt is a university of elite standards, with academic requirements second to few. It plays in the powerful Southeastern Conference and has to go to battle with the likes of Alabama, Georgia, Tennessee, Florida, LSU, and Auburn. As Art Guepe, Vandy head man from 1953 to 1962, said, "There is no way you can be Harvard Monday through Friday and try to be Alabama on Saturday." But when Dan McGugin presided in Nashville, opposing teams feared the mighty Commodores.

The years 1904, '05, '06, '07, '10, '11, '12, '21, '22, and '23 all saw the Southern Conference championship brought to the Vanderbilt campus. McGugin's teams pioneered intersectional football for the south, playing against Michigan, the Carlisle Indians, Ohio State, Navy, Harvard, Yale, and Minnesota. Vanderbilt usually lost these games, but by close scores. From 1869, when the first college game was played, through the early 1900s, the southern brand of football was without doubt inferior to northern and midwestern teams. But Vanderbilt chipped away at this wall of separation, and Alabama, under Wade, would tear down that wall for eternity.

Wade was brought to Vanderbilt not only to be an assistant football coach, but also the head coach of basketball and baseball. He had just produced championship teams in all three sports at Fitzgerald and Clark, and that, combined with his highly regarded playing career at Brown, made him a welcome addition on campus in 1921.

After going 8 and 8 in his first year at the helm of basketball, Wade coached the team to 16 wins with eight losses in 1923. The 1923 Vanderbilt yearbook, the *Commodore*, stated,

> Winning sixteen out of twenty-four games is a good record; it is a remarkable record when you consider that four of those eight defeats were to powerful teams of the North, where basketball has reached its highest development, and one other was to Wabash, the crème de crème of college teams, national champions, who came South during the holidays and left a train of tombstones behind them. The development of the Commodores has been spectacular; it is a lasting crown of glory to Coach Wade, who took his bumps last year without a murmur.

The Commodore goes on to describe some of the players on the 1923 team:

> Bomar, footballer de luxe, with all his size, trips over the basketball floor with fairy lightness and has been a powerful cog in the passing part of the machine. Captain "Doc" Kuhn shines best at doing the helicopter act and picking off tall passes out of the atmosphere. "Pep" Bell flashes here and there like a diminutive water bug.

Lynn Bomar, who played at the Fitzgerald and Clark School where Wade coached, was a consensus All-American in football in 1923 as well and became the first player for Wade that made it to the College Football Hall of Fame, although many were to follow. Notable victories in 1923 were wins over Chicago, Mississippi A and M, and Tennessee. The 16 wins were the most victories in school history up to that time.

The 1922 baseball team won 14 games against seven losses. Wins against Ohio State, Michigan, and Auburn were highlights of the season. In 1923 the team won 14 with five losses, with two wins over Auburn and a win over Notre Dame.

* * *

Opening the 1921 football season with easy wins over Middle Tennessee and Mercer, Kentucky then scored 14 points against the vaunted Vanderbilt defense, but the Commodores scored 21. On October 21 McGugin, Wade, and Lewis Hardage, a former great player at Vanderbilt, made up the coaching staff as the team went to Dallas to play Texas, which had won 12 games in a row dating back to the 1920 season. Before the game, McGugin lit a fire under his boys, telling them,

> You are about to be put to an ordeal which will show the stuff that's in you. What a glorious chance you have. Every one of you is going to fix your status for all time in the minds and hearts of your teammates today. How you fight is what you will be remembered by. If any shirks, the Lord pity him. He will be downgraded in the hearts of the rest of you as long as he lives. Now is there any man here who will not fight every inch of the way? Will any man here disgrace himself and live in the contempt of his teammates the rest of his days?

McGugin's way of building his team's spirit must have worked—Vanderbilt proceeded to demolish Texas 20 to 0.

On November 5, Vanderbilt shut out Alabama 14 to 0 in Montgomery, giving Alabama fans their first real look at Wallace Wade. Little did they realize two years later he would return as their head coach. Xen Scott coached Alabama to a 5-4-2 overall record in 1921. The only blemish of 1921 was a 7-7 tie with Georgia, who finished 7-2-1 that year under Coach H.J. Stegeman. The Commodores finished 7-0-1 and won the Southern Conference championship.

Great success was expected in 1922. Lynn Bomar was back, and Jess Neely, who would go on to great coaching success at Clemson and Rice and end up in the College Football Hall of Fame, was the captain and a star player. Wade was back for a second year, and was starting to get credit for being primarily responsible for the stingy defense exhibited by Vanderbilt in 1921 and 1922.

Vanderbilt dedicated its new 20,000 seat Dudley Field on October 14. The new stadium was named after Dr. William Dudley of Vanderbilt, who had organized the Southern Conference back in 1894. The opponent for this game was mighty Michigan, still coached by Fielding Yost, who happened to be the brother-in-law of McGugin. The game ended in a scoreless tie, and it was to be the only blemish on either team's record for the year. Vanderbilt finished 8-0-1, and Michigan ended the season at 6-0-1.

Before the game with Michigan, Coach McGugin used a little southern pride pep talk. Just before the kickoff, he pointed to a nearby military cemetery and then to the Michigan team. "In that cemetery sleep your grandfathers," he said, "and over there are the grandsons of the Damn Yankees who put them there." Bomar played especially well in this game from his linebacker position on defense, and from his offensive back slot when Vandy had the ball. Bomar was a big boy for the times, at 6'2" and 210 pounds. A few years after this game, Wallace Wade would invoke the pride of the south into a talk to his Alabama team, and the Crimson Tide would deliver a blow heard across the United States.

On October 21, Vanderbilt again traveled to Dallas to take on the Longhorns of Texas. Since losing to Vanderbilt in 1921, Texas had not lost a game. Again the Commodores dealt Texas a loss in their home state, but Texas did score 10 of the 16 total points Vandy allowed in 1922. The only other team to score against the Wade-led defense was Tennessee, but Vanderbilt won in Knoxville over the Volunteers 14 to 6. After this 1922 win over in-state rival Tennessee, McGugin had won 11 games against the Volunteers and suffered only two losses with one tie. The tide would start to turn in 1926 upon the arrival of General Robert Neyland to Tennessee.

In another game, McGugin exhibited the ability to stoke a player's furnace. Although he was a successful lawyer along with being such a great coach, he probably could have also been a great psychologist. This short speech would fire up most players:

> With each of you boys there was a time — a time when you were two-months-old, or five-months, when your mother looked at you in the cradle, and she wondered, she asked herself, what kind of heart beat in that little body; of how this little boy, as he grew into a man, would meet his first test of courage; whether, when that time came, she could feel the pride that only a mother can feel for a son who is courageous — and fearless — or whether there might, perhaps, have to be a different feeling. She knew that such a time, such a day, would come. Today — she may be wondering.

The 1922 season ended with shutout wins over Kentucky, Georgia, and Sewanee. Another undefeated season, coupled with another Southern Conference championship, ended the only consecutive undefeated years in Vanderbilt football history. They had gone 15-0-2 for 1921 and 1922.

* * *

There can be no doubt of the great coaching ability of Dan McGugin, and Wallace Wade would forever admire and respect him. Coach McGugin was highly influential in college football circles and played a large role in recommending Wade for his next stop in his coaching career in Tuscaloosa, Alabama.

At the same time, Wade's imprint on the Vanderbilt program was huge. Not only did he, for the most part, refine and develop the great defenses of 1921 and 1922, he spent much more time coaching than McGugin, who would sometimes not arrive to practice until Wade had them out on the field for an hour or more. This was due to the fact that McGugin also worked as a lawyer. Wade had one job and that was as a year-round coach of athletics. Another innovation that Wade brought to Vanderbilt was a year-round conditioning program for athletes. If you were an athlete, you were either playing a sport or conditioning yourself to get ready for the next season. Although this is the norm today, in the 1920s this was not practiced by many.

* * *

At the end of the 1923 school year, Wallace Wade had gained a reputation as an up-and-coming star in the coaching ranks. At just 30 years of age, the best was yet to come. Another school in the Southern Conference, Kentucky, knew about Wade from having opposed his Vanderbilt teams and asked him to come for an interview.

Wade was a young man, who, despite not being the most talkative individual, had a fierce pride and determination in his ability to be a successful coach. He knew that he had what it took to lead teams to success. He also knew by the time of the Kentucky interview that the combination of his previous record, coupled with the endorsement of who was considered to be the best coach in the south, McGugin, that a head job was soon to be his at a good school.

After interviewing with a committee of Kentucky officials, Wade was asked to step out of the room so that the officials could discuss the results in private. Wade did so but was evidently left waiting longer than he liked. After waiting and waiting some more, Wade had had enough. He walked back into the room and told the startled gathering that he was tired of waiting and would not take the job even if offered. He added, "And furthermore, I will promise you that no football team of mine will ever lose to the University of Kentucky!" Wade kept his word. In 11 games against Kentucky at Alabama and Duke, Wade's teams won them all.

After Wade accepted the head coaching position at Alabama, the *Vanderbilt Alumnus* magazine had this to say about Wade:

> His promotion is deserved. His influence as a man has been of the best. He is clean, aggressive, as energetic as ever a coach was, a fighter. He worked to put iron in the souls of his men. His medicine was bitter to the lazy man, the quitter, and the lad who expected to have a "V" handed him on a silver platter. He was not coarse or brutal, but he was hard. That would be valuable training to any man. He is an indefatigable worker, and the Vanderbilt men have done more hard work in practice during the past two years than ever in the history of football here. We wish him the greatest success possible at Alabama.

CHAPTER FIVE

A Bear Arrives in Tuscaloosa

The Athletic Council of the University, which is the official body charged with the control of athletics, has endeavored to proceed with due caution in selecting a football coach. Naturally we share the desire to turn out winning teams.

We need only add that we strongly feel that, in solving the problems committed to us, we have not only preserved the high standards of the University in the matter of sound procedure, but have at the same time secured a man whose actual record of achievement will commend him to the mature judgment of all who desire to have our teams coached by men of expert knowledge, successful experience, outstanding personality, and above and beyond all else, of tested character.

The Council has, after most careful consideration, decided to appoint William Wallace Wade, director of athletics of Vanderbilt University, as head coach of our athletic teams.

Mr. Wade, in addition to holding the important position as director of athletics, is head coach of baseball and basketball and associate head coach of football at Vanderbilt. He is given credit by competent authorities in large degree for the enviable football record of Vanderbilt for the past two years, during which time he has been actively engaged in coaching the football team.

Mr. Wade is a southern man, a product of Brown University, where for three years he played on one of the greatest teams of the East, a team that defeated both Harvard and Yale. He was coached by Robinson, one of the outstanding coaches of America. No man whose name has been presented to us for consideration has been vouched for by a larger group of competent critics.

Wallace Wade during his Alabama years.
Courtesy of Duke Sports Information Department.

Mr. Wade's experience as a football coach has been brilliantly successful. He comes to us with the highest recommendations, not only from the Vanderbilt and Brown authorities, but also from many of the leading football experts of the south and indeed of the entire country. If we may rely on expert testimony, the University is fortunate in securing a man of Mr. Wade's character, experience, and achievements.

> Dr. Eugene A. Smith
> Chairman of the Athletic Council
> Of the University of Alabama

The hiring of Wallace Wade established Alabama as a storied name in national football circles. None other than the authority Bear Bryant said, "Coach Wade's teams got the ball rolling around here. There is no question about that. There is no doubt that his teams back then are more responsible than anybody else for the tradition we have. I hold all of those Alabama teams back then in reverence."

Wade, ever a modest man, later on said, "I would not go so far as saying we started tradition at Alabama, but I admit we had a solid hand in it." But Al Browning agreed with Bryant, writing, "Wade led Alabama to its thundering entrance to national acclaim, spawning Crimson Tide tradition as we know it." Keith Dunnavant, an Alabama football historian and writer, adds that Wade transformed the Crimson Tide into a national power. Wayne Hester, at one time sports editor of the Birmingham News, wrote, "A 'Bear' led Alabama football through its first great era and established the rich tradition of the Crimson Tide. No, not that Bear. This Bear was Wallace Wade. Some people call him the Godfather of Alabama football, but his players called him the Bear." Yes, there was a Bear on the Alabama campus before Bear Bryant. The first four conference championships and first three national titles in Alabama football history were earned under William Wallace Wade.

* * *

The University of Alabama was formally opened for the reception of students in 1831. Thirty-five boys made up the first student body under Dr. Alva Woods, the first president of the university. The school grew and prospered, adding a chapter of Phi Beta Kappa in the 1850s, making it the first such chapter in that part of the south.

During the Civil War, Alabama did not close its doors, because it offered military training. By the fall of 1864, however, the Confederacy was faltering with Atlanta being taken in September. General Ulysses S. Grant was tightening his grip on Richmond, while Robert E. Lee's army was at Petersburg. To help finish the war, Grant proposed sending a cavalry raid deep into Alabama, and selected General James H. Wilson for the job. On March 22, 1865, Wilson ferried 13,480 Union soldiers across a rain-swollen Tennessee River. On March 30, Wilson learned that no Confederate troops were in the vicinity of Tuscaloosa, home of the University of Alabama. Wilson, although at this point heading south to Selma to destroy a munitions work, decided to attack Tuscaloosa. He gave orders to General E. M. McCook to "detach one brigade of your division, with orders to proceed rapidly by the most direct route to Tuscaloosa, to destroy the bridge, factories, mills, university, and whatever else may be of benefit to the rebel cause."

General John Croxton was chosen to carry out this raid on Tuscaloosa. On April 2, Croxton moved his men, numbering around 1,500, across the Black Warrior River. Attacking Tuscaloosa late on April 3, the Union troops set fire to factories and roamed the streets for other buildings to destroy. About 12:30

a.m. on April 4, President Garland of the University of Alabama was seen running across the campus shouting, "The Yankees are in town!" The university cadets sprang from their beds, dressed quickly, and grabbed their muskets. Some professors even fell into line to protect their beloved university. Colonel James T. Murfee, a professor of mathematics and commandant of cadets at the university, assumed command. Murfee had shown a propensity for turning young, inexperienced young soldiers into accomplished military officers.

Murfee ordered a platoon to march toward Tuscaloosa to engage the enemy. Cadet James Cowan recalled that on the muddy road to town "the night was intensely dark and dreary, a thin misty rain was descending, and we did not know how soon we would come upon the enemy." Upon reaching town, the Union troops were seen. In the first encounter, three Federal troops were killed and Colonel Murfee and two of his cadets were wounded.

Back on campus, President Garland waited with no more than 300 cadets to defend the university against seasoned Union forces of 1,500. These young cadets were no match for the Federal forces arrayed against them. By the morning of April 4, the skies around Tuscaloosa were darkened with billows of black smoke, and by noon, most of the University of Alabama lay in ashes.

One heroic act out of many on the Alabama campus on this infamous day was performed by Andre Deloffre, a modern language professor. Deloffre approached a Federal officer and appealed to him not to burn the library, by then one of the finest in the south. When word was sent back to Colonel Croxton, he replied that his orders left him no alternative; all public buildings must be destroyed. Although the building was destroyed, some 1,200 of the 7,000 books that were stored in the library somehow survived; some still exist today, with charred edges that are a reminder of a time when people of the same great country destroyed lives and property of their fellow citizens.

After almost two days, the occupation of Tuscaloosa and the university left damage everywhere. Federal troops took many horses and mules and destroyed a university on the cusp of greatness. Also destroyed were a foundry, a tanyard, a Confederate hat factory, and two large cotton warehouses. Several stores and private homes were broken into.

On April 5, Croxton got word that Confederate General W.H. Jackson was headed to Tuscaloosa to engage the Union forces. Having accomplished his mission, Croxton ordered his men out of town before Jackson's troops arrived. Although he and his men evacuated, 23 of Croxton's men had been killed or wounded, while only one Confederate soldier died—Captain Ben Eddins. A few Confederates were injured.

* * *

The University of Alabama survived the Civil War, and today it is one of the finest institutions of higher learning in the country. One of the men most responsible for this is Dr. George Denny. Denny assumed the presidency of Alabama in 1912, serving until 1936, and again briefly in 1941. In 1912, there were only 400 students and nine major buildings on campus. When Denny retired in 1936, there were 23 major buildings and 5,000 students. Not only did enrollment increase dramatically, but also academics and athletics flourished under his leadership. President Denny was a strong advocate of athletics, and today the football stadium on the Alabama campus bears his name and Bear Bryant's. Bryant-Denny Stadium now seats over 90,000.

* * *

Football at Alabama began in 1892 under the leadership of William Little. Little had learned the game while at Phillips-Exeter Academy in Massachusetts as a student, but he was sent back to his home state of Alabama upon the death of a brother. After entering the University of Alabama, Little decided to organize a football team, and the first game was November 11, 1892. The game was played at Lakeview Park in Birmingham against a team of mostly high school players, and Alabama won 56 to 0. Little scored one of the touchdowns in this game. One of the players on this first Alabama team was William Bankhead, who went on to become Speaker of the House of Representatives in Washington, D.C. Another player, Bibb Graves, twice was elected governor of Alabama.

The following day, November 12, Alabama returned to Lakeview Park to play the more experienced Birmingham Athletic Club. Strangely, in 1892, a field goal counted more than a touchdown, and since the Birmingham Club scored on a drop kick field goal, worth five points, they defeated Alabama, who scored one touchdown worth four points. Another oddity to this game was a report that "Coach Beaumont of Alabama was the referee and Walter Winn, the umpire. Their decisions met with general satisfaction." Alabama played the Birmingham Athletic Club again in December and won this one, 14 to 0.

To get a better idea of what college football was like in the early 1890s, consider the following report by Fuzzy Woodruff, a noted college football historian. Woodruff wrote this in the 1920s:

> It was an era of beef and brawn, rather than speed and skill. The ideal football team was made up of linemen scaling above 200, a gigantic playing fullback, a couple of halfbacks capable of carrying a cow on their shoulders, and a quarterback who weighed about 100

pounds soaking wet. I have never yet understood the whys and wherefores of the pygmy quarterback.

Auburn had two notable midget quarterbacks in the early 90s in "Dutch," now Dr. R.T. Downey, and W. Reynolds Tichenor. I doubt if either weighed much more than 100 pounds, but each was the most notable ground-gainer of his team. Both, too, were deadly tacklers. Alabama had a pair in Will Walker, now a distinguished judge of Birmingham, and Borden Burr, now a great corporation lawyer of the same city.

In those days, the art of punting was practically unknown. The team with the ball had three downs in which to make five yards. The runner could be hauled and tugged. He could hurdle or he could crawl. The ball was not down until its progress, either backward or forward, had been stopped. Accordingly, scrimmages were frightfully rough. They lasted sometimes for several minutes.

It was the era of the flying wedge, a foundation in which only the center was on the line of scrimmage. The rest of the team formed a "V" behind him, as the apex, with the ball carrier in the middle. Nine times out of ten they smashed straight ahead.

The first football costumes were padded breeches, stockings, a tightly laced sleeveless jacket under which a jersey was worn, and a hockey cap. These were later added to with shin guards, nose guards, with the head bare except for a shock of hair in which every collegian took an abiding pride.

Football fields were primitive affairs. Matches were usually played in baseball parks or fair grounds. The playing field was sometimes roped off, but usually the spectators encroached on the sidelines and had to be shooed back throughout the contest.

On February 22, 1893 (yes, an odd time for a college football game), Alabama met its in-state rival, Auburn, for the first time. The Tigers of Auburn won 32 to 22. A very notable aspect of this game is that it drew over 5,000 fans, a huge number in the 1890s. This game served as a prelude to the intense fan interest citizens of Alabama had in their college football, especially Alabama and Auburn.

In 1894, Alabama had its first victory over Auburn, 18 to 0. Again, let's turn to Fuzzy Woodruff for a review of the game.

Poor, puny Alabama had lost to Auburn twice the year before, and Auburn's machine was far better this year. A remarkable crowd of 4,000 was at Riverside Park in Montgomery, an old state fair grounds field that was within a mile of a dirt track used for trotting horses.

On the far side of the field were the high seated traps and low slung victorias, the fashionable equipages of the day, and each conveyance was gay with colors and pretty femininity. The entire student bodies of both schools had made the journey to Montgomery and all the young men wore their hair in the exaggerated chrysanthemum shape that was then the mode.

Before the game the first charge of using ringers was made. Auburn charged Alabama was to use two players especially imported from the University of North Carolina for the game. If so, it was never proven because they didn't play. Collecting tickets and handling water buckets that day was a fellow named Champ Pickens, who promoted Alabama trips to the Pacific Coast 30 years later.

From the start of the game it was apparent that Auburn, despite its vaunted strength in the line, had nothing that could match the fury of the Alabama forwards. The attack was led by Jim Shelley, the halfback who repeatedly crashed over Frank Cahalan's tackle to lead an 18-0 victory.

In 1902, Auxford Burks made his debut for Alabama and became one of the Crimson Tide's first great players. Burks was described as "tall, rangy, and powerful, with the most baffling knee action imaginable as a halfback." After leading Alabama over Auburn in 1903, Auburn's coach, John Heisman, called Burks "the best running back the south has ever produced." Burks's prowess led to the following poem being written.

> Greatly to prosper and proudly to grow,
> While every hill and glen
> Sends our shout back again,
> B. Auxford Burks! Alabama! Ho! Ho!
> Long shall old Auburn,
> With groans and with madness,
> Remember our halfback who played them so fast;
> Long shall Sewanee, with wonder and sadness,
> Remember our onslaught of November last.
> Though this season ends his fight,
> Long shall the Auburnite
> Think of Burks's tackling
> With fear and with woe,
> Victory upon victory then,
> Echoes his praise again.
> B. Auxford Burks! Alabama! Ho! Ho!

Alabama and Auburn severed athletic relationships after their football game in 1907. The 1907 game ended in a 6 to 6 tie. In January of 1908 Alabama received from Auburn a letter enclosing its contract for the game that year, which was different from the previous season's. The number of men allowed on each team and expenses allowed per player changed. Auburn also requested that one of the officials be from the east. Another contention of Auburn was the so-called "military formation" used by Coach Pollard of Alabama, which it considered a trick formation. Ringers were also a point of conflict claimed by each side against the other. A compromise could not be reached, and Alabama would not meet Auburn again in football until 1948, when the Crimson Tide ran roughshod over the Tigers 55 to 0 with Red Drew as head coach.

Arriving on campus in 1911 as coach was D.V. Graves, a former coach at Blee's Military Institute in Missouri. Honest to a fault, Graves announced,

> I know nothing of Southern football nor how Alabama ranks in comparison. The team is rather green in the so-called rudiments of the game. We have some big linemen, slow and clumsy, who with lots of practice ought to be fair linemen by November.

But despite this assessment, Graves went 21-12-3 over the next four seasons.

William T. "Bully" Van de Graaf stepped on campus at the "Capstone" in 1912 and became Alabama's first All-American player in 1915. Van de Graaf was a great blocker and tackler and one of the best runners around, while also perhaps being the nation's best kicker. In a 1915 game against Sewanee, he ran an interception back 65 yards for a touchdown, kicked three field goals and two extra points, and punted out of his end zone 78 yards on one possession. This was just one of many games that demonstrated his all-around ability.

Alabama did not field a team in 1918 because of WWI, but resumed in 1919 under Coach Xen C. Scott. Scott had a sterling record of 29-9-3 from 1919 to 1922. Scott had been head coach of the Cleveland Naval Reserve team and also Western Reserve University, where his teams had won the Ohio Valley Conference championship twice.

Reportedly, Alabama became the Crimson Tide during the Scott era. Birmingham News Editor Zipp Newman said he got the idea one day while watching the tide pound a seashore, suggesting a force that kept pounding away at you. After using "Crimson Tide" in a newspaper article, the nickname stuck.

It is also thought that Alabama's famed Million Dollar Band got its name in 1919. After WWI, General John J. Pershing noted that regimental bands had been "worth a million dollars to the American Expeditionary Forces." When a U.S. military concert band played in Tuscaloosa after the war, Gen-

Alabama's Million Dollar Band in the 1920s. Courtesy of Anita Caldwell.

eral Pershing's comment was quoted. Some said that the university band was equally as valuable, and soon the Alabama band had a new name.

The 1919 team was lead by Riggs Stephenson from Akron, Alabama, who was a great triple threat running back. Stephenson's best sport, and first love, however, was baseball. Stephenson went on to become a great major league player, where he compiled a lifetime batting average of .336 in 14 seasons with the Cleveland Indians and Chicago Cubs.

Another football player on Scott's 1919 team was Joe Sewell, who also gained fame in major league baseball. The next year, 1920, saw Sewell serve as captain of the Alabama baseball team and end 1920 with the Cleveland Indians and helped them win a World Series title. Sewell could put the wood on the ball as well as any player in the history of baseball, only striking out four times in 608 at bats in 1925. Luke Sewell, who also played football for Scott, went on to become a long-time star catcher in the big leagues.

In 1921, Hank Crisp arrived at the Capstone (Capstone was coined by President Denny when he said that he wanted the university to be the capstone of education in the country). Crisp served as a key assistant to Scott, Wade, and Frank Thomas at Alabama, while also coaching other sports and serving as athletic director. As a farm boy growing up in North Carolina, Crisp lost his right hand in a silage cutting. Not letting it deter him, he played football at Virginia Polytechnic Institute, making the All-South Atlantic team his senior year.

After giving up coaching football in 1942, he coached again under Red Drew and J.B. Whitworth from 1950 to 1957. Few individuals have had a bigger impact on Alabama athletics than Hank Crisp. He is most remembered as the man who recruited Bear Bryant out of Arkansas to come play football at Alabama.

Coach Scott ended his tenure at Alabama in 1922, going 6-3-1, but a victory that year gave the Crimson Tide its first real national publicity. The Tidemen traveled to Franklin Field, the home turf of Eastern power Pennsylvania. Eastern teams still dominated teams from the south, so it was expected that this year would go the same route. But 25,000 stunned fans saw Scott's gallant southern boys win 9 to 7. Upon arriving back in Tuscaloosa, a big crowd welcomed the boys at the train depot. Al Clemens, a player that year, recalled, "They had three big flat-bed trucks pulled by horses. They hitched them together and we stood up on them and waved as they pulled us through the center of town."

The 1922 season ended with Scott's resignation. The players had noticed that he had been losing weight and his voice as the season wore on. Scott was dying of throat cancer, and a new coach was needed.

* * *

Wallace Wade became head coach at Alabama in 1923 at a time in the country called the Jazz Age. This was an exuberant era where convention and old-fashioned morality were tossed aside. New dances like the Charleston, the beginning of the movie industry in Hollywood, and just a general freer spirit seemed to take hold of Americans. Women bobbed their hair, smoked, shortened their skirts, and allowed their bosoms to show. In 1920 women started voting. Economic prosperity seemed to be abundant. Prohibition only drove "drunkenness behind doors and into dark places and did not cure it or even diminish it."

In the state of Alabama, remnants of this new age reached part of its population, but times were hard. Part of the state saw rapid change and prosperity, especially the urban areas. But much of Alabama was in poverty, lacking educational opportunity and access to decent medical care. In 1920, the illiteracy rate was 16.1 percent for people age ten or above. For blacks, the rate was 31.3 percent. Child labor was too high.

As the 1920s progressed, so did many of the living standards in Alabama. Child employment dropped, education spending improved, illiteracy rates dropped, and public health services increased. Manufacturing jobs went up as citizens found employment in textile mills, steel and iron mills, and other industries. By 1929, Alabama produced 9.1 percent of the nation's iron ore. Birmingham made 3.3 percent of the nation's steel production by 1929. Population in the state grew from 2.35 million in 1920 to 2.65 million in 1930. Birmingham, especially, boomed, boasting 260,000 people in 1930, at a time when Atlanta had 270,000. Most Alabamians remained on farms, growing cot-

**Wallace Wade Jr. (left) strikes a pose beside Coach Wade
shortly after their arrival in Tuscaloosa.**

ton and other agrarian products. For many, farm income dropped during this
time, and the so-called Jazz Age was just something they heard about but never
really experienced. One Alabama boy who did was Nathaniel Adams Cole,
born in Montgomery in 1919, later known as Nat "King" Cole, who contributed his great musical talents to his country.

* * *

Wallace Wade soon made his presence known on the Alabama campus.
Wade believed in doing things one way, and one way only: the right way. Hard
work, extreme dedication to a task, focus, total preparation, and respect for
the game of football were just some of the traits Wade taught and expected
his players to abide by. Whereas Coach Scott was outgoing with a pleasant personality, Wade could be crusty, blunt, and a perfectionist.

His pedigree as of 1923 certainly vouched for his track record and played a
large role in his confidence to get the job done. By this time he had attended
a very disciplined military prep school, played for one of the best college teams
in the country (Brown), participated in a world war, produced state championship teams at the high school level, and played a major role as an assistant

coach at Vanderbilt. Three of the most respected coaches in the country, Amos Alonzo Stagg, Edward Robinson, and Dan McGugin, had highly recommended him for the Alabama job. All of this had been accomplished by 1923 at the age of 31. His teams at Brown, Fitzgerald and Clark, and Vanderbilt, in his association as a player and coach, had won 49 games with ten losses.

Despite this early success and in recognition of his occasionally distant personality, Wade remained the most humble of individuals. In interviews during and after his career, he never accepted credit for much of anything except losses, for which he took the blame. He always attributed victories to his players and never made excuses. He also had a very kind heart underneath the rough exterior, exhibiting this many times in his life, to players, friends, and sometimes even strangers.

* * *

Alabama had finished 6-3-1 in 1922, and there is no question that Xen Scott and Hank Crisp had laid a solid foundation upon which Coach Wade could build. As the players took the field on September 10 for the first day of practice, the Wade system of football immediately became clear. There were no benches for resting, no water buckets for parched tongues, and constant activity was evident. Soon practices reached three hours in duration, with absolutely no horseplay allowed. Coach Wade was all about football being a serious business, as these Alabama players soon learned. The conditioning process was one never before seen at the Capstone.

Fundamentals were emphasized repeatedly for several weeks before any plays were even practiced. These are the days when Wade earned the moniker "Bear" from his players, but this was only uttered when he was not within earshot. Defensive play was so emphasized over offense in these early practice sessions that by the time of the first game, Alabama's offensive playbook options were few.

Al Clemens, a veteran from Scott's teams, was elected captain for 1923. Other key players for the team were "Shorty" Propst at center, Pooley Hubert, Grant Gillis and "Lovely" Barnes, both Grove Hill High School graduates in Alabama. Johnny Mack Brown from Dothan, Alabama, and Jimmy Johnston from Tuscaloosa High were expected to play key roles. Assisting Wade on the staff were Crisp and Russ Cohen. Cohen served as a key assistant under Wade until accepting the LSU head job in 1928, and was 23-13-1 through 1931.

In the first game as Alabama coach for Wade, the Tide won over Union 12 to 0. Due to the lack of practice time on offense and Wade's belief in defense first made for a lackluster performance when the Tide had the ball. Pooley Hubert ran for a touchdown and Ben Hudson caught a touchdown pass. Notably, in one of the most remarkable statistics in college football history, this was Wade's first shutout at Alabama. Over the course of his next eight years at the helm, opponents failed to score at all 47 times out of 77 games. Not only did Wade win 81% of his games while coaching the Crimson Tide, the other teams did not score a point 61% of the time.

After shutting out Mississippi 56 to 0, Alabama took a long trip to play Syracuse. After trailing only 3 to 0 at the half, Syracuse scored three touchdowns in the second half to win 23 to 0. This was considered to be a good showing, as Syracuse was part of the eastern teams that still looked down on southern teams as being vastly inferior. Syracuse would finish 8 and 1 in 1923. A great welcome home was extended, even though the team lost, and 2,000 people met the train. Classes were even excused so the student body could attend. Something else worth noting in this game is that the loss by 23 points, along with a 23-point loss to Tennessee in 1931 during his first year at Duke, were the worst defeats by point differential in Wade's entire career. In other words, none of his teams, in 230 games, was ever non-competitive right up until the last quarter of play. No team of his ever lost badly. When you played a Wade team, you knew you were going to be in a battle each and every game.

On November 3 in Atlanta, Georgia Tech held Alabama to a scoreless tie. Tech penetrated to the Tide's five-yard line on one occasion but could not cross the goal in four attempts. Though the game was played in a driving rain, 10,000 fans turned out. Georgia Tech had been a combined 15 and 3 in 1921 and 1922, and was coached by William Alexander, who from 1920 to 1944 won 134 games at Tech. Wade and Alexander would battle six more times while Wade was at Alabama, with Wade winning four.

Georgia was beaten 36 to 0 in Montgomery, as everything Alabama attempted seemed to work. Grant Gillis both ran for a touchdown and caught another for a score. Wade ended up 6 and 2 against Georgia while at Tuscaloosa.

Playing the Gators of Florida in Birmingham on a wet, rain-soaked field in late November, the Wade men lost the final game of the season 16 to 6. For the season, Alabama finished 7-2-1, and a new optimism reigned on campus that even better days were ahead. The optimism was well founded, as the next three years of Alabama football would produce a stretch of greatness to rival any in the long storied tradition of Tide football. A magical ride of 27-1-1, two national titles, and three Southern Conference championships was about to begin. Alabama football would never be the same.

CHAPTER SIX

THE TIDE STARTS TO RISE

By 1924, over 2,000 students were enrolled at Alabama. Football certainly helped increase publicity for the university, and by 1930, enrollment would dramatically go up. The desire of some young Alabamians to come to Tuscaloosa was admirable, such as indicated in this letter to President Denny in 1924 from Boaz, Alabama.

Dear Sir,

I am without means to obtain a college education. I say without means; I mean I have a brain and a good body. I am expecting them to tide me through. I do not mind hard work. In fact, that has been my hobby since the days of my early remembrance. When at the age of four my father died. Then after three years of hard struggle my mother passed away, leaving four children. So you see that since the age of seven I have been thrown almost completely upon my own resources. I will be eighteen in June.

Is it possible that I can work my way? Have you any encouragement for me? I do not mind any kind of work. I am not above the lowest. I want an education. To obtain it I will give anything. I am willing that it may be ground out of me. I suppose that I can do any kind of common labor.

Now Dr. Denny, is it possible that you can help me, or are my dreams in vain? If you will be so kind and generous as to let me know some answer to these questions I assure you that I shall be thankful beyond measure.

Truly,
George Elliott

This letter epitomizes the kind of young men Wallace Wade would enjoy coaching: hard working with an intense desire to do well at whatever task he undertakes. In fact, many of Wade's players had these characteristics, and Wade looked to 1924 with the knowledge that he had the makings of a good team.

Allison T.S. Hubert, better known as Pooley, was elected to be captain. Johnny Mack Brown would be returning at halfback, Hoyt "Wu" Winslett at an end position, Ben Compton and Shorty Propst at guard and center, Bruce Jones at a guard spot, Grant Gillis at quarterback, and Herschel Caldwell at end.

The season opened with easy victories over Union, Furman, and Mississippi College. On October 18 they defeated Sewanee 14 to 0, with Pooley getting huge yards on line plunges and end runs. Alabama's student paper, *The Crimson-White*, reported, "It is universally known that no one man can stop Pooley. Sewanee knows no two can. It took three Sewanee men to stop this line-smashing terror. Even the Sewanee backs, playing up close behind the line waiting for him, failed to stop him, being carried back yard after yard clinging on." October 18, 1924 was a day to remember in college football history, and not for the Alabama-Sewanee game. On that day in Champaign, Illinois, Red Grange had what many say is the greatest individual performance of any collegiate player. Playing for Illinois against Michigan, Grange ran for 402 yards, completed six passes for 64 yards, ran for five touchdowns, and passed for one touchdown. Highly-regarded Michigan was defeated 39 to 14. A side note to this game is that a backup runner to Grange for Illinois was Gerry Gerard, who Wade hired later at Duke, and Gerard later became basketball coach at Duke.

Grantland Rice, the most famous sportswriter of the era, pinned on Grange the immortal designation "Galloping Ghost." Rice also waxed poetic after hearing of the great performance on October 18:

> There are two shapes now moving
> Two ghosts that drift and glide
> And which of them to tackle
> Each rival must decide.
> They shift with special swiftness
> Across the swarded range
> And one of them's a shadow,
> And one of them is Grange.

Rice also wrote,

> Grange runs with almost no effort, as a shadow flits and drifts and darts. There is no gathering of muscle for an extra lunge. There is only the ghostlike weave and glide upon effortless legs with a body that can come to a dead stop and pick up instant speed, so perfect is the co-ordination of brain and sinew.

Wade was able to see Grange run after his college days were over and Grange was on a barnstorming tour through Alabama with his pro team. "No doubt,

1924 Southern Conference champions. Courtesy of Anita Caldwell.

Grange was one of the best to ever play, he had great speed," Wade said, but he also always claimed that his former teammate at Brown, Fritz Pollard, was Grange's equal.

On the same day that Grange ran wild, Notre Dame beat Army 13 to 7 at the Polo Grounds in New York. Rice attended that game in his capacity as reporter for the *New York Herald Tribune*. After the game Rice typed the most famous lead in the history of sports journalism:

> Outlined against a blue-gray October sky the Four Horsemen rode again. In dramatic lore they are known as famine, pestilence, destruction, and death. These are only aliases. Their real names are Stuldreher, Miller, Crowley, and Layden. They formed the crest of the South Bend cyclone before which another fighting Army football team was swept over the precipice at the Polo Grounds yesterday afternoon as 55,000 spectators peered down on the bewildering panorama spread on the green plain below.

After its first six games, Alabama had scored 219 points and had allowed zero. That's right, 219 to 0. By this time, news of Alabama's run had started to spread around the country. *The Boston Post* carried a headline story, in part reporting,

> If the figures above sufficed [meaning the 219 to 0], Alabama has the best team in America right now. She has rung up 219 points to a large, fresh farm-laid goose egg for the opposition. Her great feat was the defeat of Georgia Tech. The previous week the Yellow Jackets scored two touchdowns and a field goal, beating Penn State 15 to 13.

Centre College must not have believed the press clippings on the might of the Crimson Tide, as it beat Alabama on November 15. Possibly, overconfidence and the fact that the game was not a conference affair kept the Tide from playing to its potential. Alabama did go on to win the 1924 Southern Conference title.

November 15, 1924 was the last time Alabama would lose a game until October 15, 1927, a stretch of almost three years. The Crimson Tide was about to embark on a 24 game unbeaten stretch in which it would score 656 points while allowing only 53. The Wade system was fully installed, and teams from across the landscape of college football were about to realize its devastating force. 1925 and 1926 would be the years that once and for all established Alabama football as one of the greatest programs ever.

CHAPTER SEVEN

THE SOUTH RISES AGAIN

As the 1925 football season neared, America was still celebrating the Jazz Age and the Roaring 20s. H.L. Mencken, in his widely read newspaper columns, helped to define the era. Mencken once described puritanism as the "haunting fear that someone, somewhere, may be happy." Well, optimism and wealth during this time tended to make many people happy. Many Americans found they had more money to spend and more time to spend it. It was an era of radios, flappers, the national appearance of automobiles, the rise in women's hemlines, a carefree feeling for men, and a flourish of sports heroes and great literature. F. Scott Fitzgerald published *The Great Gatsby* in 1925, and Ernest Hemingway wrote his first novel, *The Sun Also Rises*, in 1926.

In the sports world, the immortal Babe Ruth whacked baseballs out of the park and the nation fell in love with him. Jack Dempsey, the Manassa Mauler, knocked out opponent after opponent, and Bobby Jones ruled the golf courses.

The prosperity of the 1920s barely touched some Americans, however. Nowhere was this pain felt more than in the rural south, including most areas of Alabama. Many farmers could not find adequate markets for their crops and looked for work in towns or wherever they could find it. The south received much attention, mostly negative, during the summer of 1925 during the Scopes Monkey Trial in Dayton, Tennessee, where schoolteacher John T. Scopes was found guilty of illegally teaching the theory of evolution. The Ku Klux Klan was a force in Alabama, spreading its doctrine of hatred.

* * *

The Alabama football team had its minds focused not so much on the Roaring 20s, but on the upcoming football season of 1925. They had few choices in this matter. Wallace Wade simply demanded total dedication, and he insisted that his players go to class and do their very best, then come to the football field and get the job done. Wade's iron discipline put fear into the hearts of his players. Frank Howard, who played for Wade at Alabama, said, "I was scared to death of Coach Wade at Alabama. Heck, I'm still afraid of

Athletics at Alabama rose to championship levels under Wade.
Courtesy of Anita Caldwell.

him"; this, after a legendary coaching career at Clemson. Howard Pill, of the
Birmingham News, had even written "The spirit of Wallace Wade is already
an institution around the Crimson stronghold," and he wrote this in 1923 before Wade coached his first game in Tuscaloosa. Wade drove his players hard.
He believed in the "all or none" football mentality. A player either gave everything he had or that player simply did not play and in some cases no longer
remained a member of the team. Another example of the fear and respect that
players had for Wade was shown during one practice when Wade was called
from the field for an important long-distance telephone call. After the call,

Wade was so absorbed by the message that he forgot about practice and went home. Meanwhile, the assistant coaches and players continued to practice, not daring to stop until Wade uttered his familiar signal that practice was over, "All right, that'll do." Finally, after a couple of hours, a coach called Wade at home. Wade paused and said, "Yes, well, let them go in. It's dark now."

Although he was not the affable, slap-you-on-the-butt type of coach, his players had the utmost respect for him. In over 40 interviews and written correspondences with former players of Wade, I never once heard or read an unkind word about him. Words like tough, stern, and unbending were used, but they were always followed by words such as fair, respected, motivating, and winner. The best way to motivate a team was to win, and to a large degree, Wade's teams stayed in a good frame of mind and played confidently because Wade won with such consistency. In 28 years of coaching, Wade only had one losing season, 1946, when Duke was 4-5.

A good insight into Wade's philosophy comes from his comments, "Football is a lot like war," and, "Nobody ever got back-slapped into winning anything." In a 1927 newspaper article written in the *Birmingham News*, further evidence of his motivational techniques were given: "Coach Wade is one of the most modest of men; he is very reticent about himself—just as we'd been told—but he is ever ready to talk about football and about the Crimson Tide, which is the pride of his life." In the same article, Wade said,

> What I try to do is get the very best out of every boy who becomes a member of the Crimson Tide team. I try to impress upon boys that I am fair and square with them; I never try to appeal to their sentiment. I never ask a boy to try to win a game for my sake, but on the other hand put him on his mettle to do his level best and failing, he feels the discomfort of not having done his duty, measuring up to the best that is in him. A coach gets or fails to get results on account of his ability to handle boys; he must inspire them with confidence and enthusiasm, which is far more important than his technical training.

* * *

As summer green turned to fall foliage on the Alabama campus, Tuscaloosa was a good place to be. Young people attended lectures and cast admiring glances at the opposite sex, while Tuscaloosa merchants vied for their attention. The Harris Hammer Company advertised itself as "The Co-Ed's Gift Shop" with bloomers, chiffon hose, pearl choker necklaces, silk parasols, and hatboxes. Black's Store promoted a former Alabama football star, "Big" Ben Compton, as a new sales clerk ready to greet customers.

Coach Wade at practice in 1925. Courtesy of Anita Caldwell.

Meanwhile, football season was ready to start. Johnny Mack Brown, Pooley Hubert, and Grant Gillis returned to form an offensive backfield to rival any in the nation. Zipp Newman, of the Birmingham News, wrote,

> Alabama will have the greatest collection of smart running backs in the south; they will have the class of the southern backfields with Mack Brown, brilliant broken field runner; Pooley Hubert, one of the greatest all-around backs in America; Grant Gillis, a cool and steady punter; Red Barnes, a punter and broken field runner; Jimmy Johnston and "Red" Pepper, a 200 pound fullback; and "Little Dave" Rosenfeld, Herschel Caldwell, and Red Brown, the flashy brother of Mack.

An Alabama game at Denny Field in Tuscaloosa. Courtesy of W.S. Hoole Special Collections Library, University of Alabama.

Guard Bill Buckler had been chosen All-Southern Conference in 1924 and was back. Hoyt "Wu" Winslett and Bruce Jones returned as key players. With the addition of former player Shorty Propst to the coaching staff to help Hank Crisp, Russ Cohen, and "Bully" Van de Graff, Wade was sure his 1925 outfit was a team to be reckoned with.

The first two games were easy, a win over Union 53 to 0, and then Birmingham Southern fell 50 to 7. On October 10, LSU, playing at home in Baton Rouge, was expected to challenge the Tide but was shellacked 42 to 0 before 8,000 fans. Mike Donahue, who had won 99 games at Auburn before going to LSU in 1923, coached LSU at this time. Hubert scored three touchdowns, and Caldwell scored two on end runs. Bill Buckler converted all six points after touchdowns.

Sewanee provided the opposition in the next game, played in Birmingham. Alabama won 27 to 0; this game should have warned upcoming foes that not only did Alabama have a devastating running attack, but also it could pass with efficiency. Operating out of the single wing formation, which Wade emphasized all of his career, this game featured a 35-yard touchdown pass from Grant Gillis to Herschel Caldwell, and another 38-yard pass for a completion to the Sewanee 2-yard line, where Pooley Hubert then ran the ball in for a touchdown. Alabama clearly exhibited the ability in this game to utilize the forward pass, which would reveal itself again and again as the season wore on.

Journeying to Atlanta on October 24, a wet field greeted Wade and his men. A huge crowd of 20,000 was on hand. Tech entered the game 4 and 0, just like Alabama, and had beaten Penn State and Florida already. The Tide prevailed, scoring its only touchdown on a spectacular run by Johnny Mack Brown. Receiving a punt on the Alabama 45, and with great blocking, Brown scored. In later years, Brown remembered looking back after he scored and seeing that all eleven Tech men, and the referee, were on the ground, having been put there by his teammates.

After a Homecoming Day win over Mississippi A&M 6 to 0, with Hubert tossing a touchdown to Winslett, Kentucky was next. The Wildcats went down 31 to 0, with Johnny Mack breaking loose on a 79-yard touchdown run. In Montgomery, the Florida Gators were shut out 34 to 0. Hubert passed for three scores and ran for another.

The last game, or what was thought to be the last game, took place in Birmingham on November 26 against Georgia. Georgia had impressive wins over Vanderbilt and Auburn earlier in the season but had lost to the eastern power Yale by 35 to 7. But this was the Crimson Tide's day, as it rolled 27 to 0. A little "trick" play was used by Wade, as Hubert handed the ball to Winslett, who then passed for a touchdown to Gillis.

Before the game had started with Georgia, Coach Hank Crisp used some rather unusual psychology on two stars of the team. Right before kickoff, Crisp told Winslett, "We've been keeping you around here for four or five years, and you haven't done a damn thing yet. We're giving you one last chance!" On Hubert, Crisp actually used another ploy, telling him, "Pooley, your mama's sick in bed, over there in Meridian [Meridian, Mississippi, Hubert's hometown], listening to the radio and hoping you'll do something good." After Pooley expressed concern, Crisp shouted, "All right, let's go beat the hell out of Georgia!"

Alabama finished as Southern Conference champions for the second year in a row. Pooley Hubert was voted the conference's most valuable player, and the *International News Service* selected him as the best back in the south in ten years. Hubert, Brown, and Winslett made the All-Southern team, and Hubert and Winslett were selected as All-Americans. The Tide had outscored its nine opponents 277 to 7.

After the season, Alabama signed Wade to a five-year contract that would keep him through the 1930 season. Two Pacific Coast Conference schools, Oregon and Washington State, had come after Wade, but the new contract kept him in Tuscaloosa. His alma mater, Brown, had also expressed interest in bringing him back to Providence. "We are indeed gratified that Coach Wade has seen fit to sign a five year contract at Alabama," said Borden Burr, a prominent alumnus who handled negotiations. "He has made us an ideal coach from every angle, and we know he is the man for Alabama. A long time contract will give him an opportunity to further install his system which has worked so successfully for three years." Russ Cohen expressed his happiness that Wade signed the new contract, saying, "Wherever Coach Wade goes, I go." Cohen, however, did eventually leave Wade in 1928 after becoming head man at LSU.

Coach Wade looked to the future with eagerness. After three years, his teams were 24-3-1. Also boding well for the next few years was the performance of Coach Van de Graff's "Baby Tide" team, the freshmen. From 1923 to 1925, the Baby Tide had not lost a game. Not only had Van de Graff proven himself to be one of Alabama's all-time best players, he now was showing his coaching prowess as well. It would not be long before Van de Graff, too, was offered head coaching positions, and he accepted the job at Colorado College in 1926.

Everyone connected with the Alabama football program naturally assumed after the Georgia game that the season was over. There was only one bowl game in the postseason, and that was in far off California, and besides, the Rose Bowl never showed interest in the "inferior" brand of football played in the south.

Banquets feting the team were held around the state, with more than 900 attending in Birmingham. A highlight of this banquet was the appearance of eight of the members of Alabama's first team, back in 1892. The Champ Pickens Cup, emblematic of the Southern Conference Championship, was presented to the team. Mr. Pickens was a long-time promoter of Alabama football. Birmingham alumni presented graduating members of the team handsome gold watches. Also lending a hand to the festivities was the Million Dollar Band. It was announced at the banquet that Pooley Hubert had been named the most valuable player in the entire south, beating out Peggy Flournoy of Tulane. Pooley received a super-heterodyne radio set as a gift.

The day of the banquet, Zipp Newman wrote about the Rose Bowl in his Birmingham News column:

> While a semi-official report says that Colgate will be invited to the Tournament of Roses as Washington's opponent on New Year's Day, it is a lead pipe cinch that the coast has heard of Alabama. All of the coast papers, from Seattle to San Diego, have been full of copy about Alabama's great undefeated and untied eleven. The names of Hubert and Mack Brown are just as well known on the coast as the names of Nevers and Wilson are known in Dixie. Alabama has received plenty of publicity throughout the nation and were she an eastern eleven,

would have been the first invited. However, being a southern eleven, she is handicapped as the coast wants an eastern team.

Reports also circulated that Dartmouth and Yale were being considered. When one Rose Bowl representative was approached with the idea of inviting Alabama, he replied, "I've never heard of Alabama as a football team and can't take a chance on mixing a lemon with a rose."

In early December, however, the Rose Bowl spokesman, Jack Benefield, issued an invitation to Alabama. News of the game hit the Alabama campus, and celebrations erupted. It was the first appearance for a team from the south, but the arrival of the southern boys of Alabama would forever change the way people across the nation viewed southern football.

CHAPTER EIGHT

1926 ROSE BOWL

Hardly anyone gave Alabama much of a chance against the Washington Huskies. Ed Danforth, of the *Atlanta Georgian*, thought that perhaps "Alabama would travel all the way out there, get spanked, and come home with a good record dented." Disdain for Alabama was shown in a description of the Tide team as "swamp students," and the famous Will Rogers labeled the team from Tuscaloosa "Tusca-losers."

Washington came into the 1926 Rose Bowl undefeated. Since 1922, the Huskies were a combined 34-3-3 under Coach Enoch Bagshaw. This team had tradition and plenty of it. From 1908 to 1916, Washington went 58-0-3 under Gil Dobie. The 1926 team was led by All-America halfback George "Wildcat" Wilson, who had already turned down a then incredible $3,000 salary to turn pro.

Coach Wade had been asked to write a series of articles on athletics earlier in the 1925 year. In one of these he wrote about how football in the south compared to other sections of the country. This column ran in newspapers well before the Rose Bowl game with Washington.

> Sectionalism in football is rapidly disappearing, due to the interchange of coaching ideas. Coaching schools are being held and attended by coaches in all parts of the country. Coaches are coming into the south from other sections; also coaches are carefully studying the football books put out by the leading coaches of the west and east. More men are devoting their entire time the year round to the study of football. This and many other conditions are putting the standard of football of the south on a plane with that in other sections.
>
> Southern football has also retained certain technical characteristics. The forward pass has come to be used as a scoring weapon in the south, while in the east, particularly, it is still largely used as a threat to make the running attack more effective. The north has come to use the long scoring pass and the dangerous pass into flat territory with deadly effect. Not many years ago, passes were only employed when

the running attack had failed. Now all good teams in this section are using the pass on first down and at times least to be expected.

The greatest improvement made in southern football during the past few years has been in defense. One of the first outstanding defensive teams was the Vanderbilt team of 1922. This team held the powerful Michigan team scoreless and had only one touchdown scored on it by southern teams. During the past two years, Georgia Tech has been one of the hardest teams in the country to score on. Mike Donahue of Auburn and Louisiana State has always turned out teams strong on the defense.

Increased interest in football throughout the south has helped to make it compare more favorably with that of other sections. Seating capacities are being increased and playing fields made better. Many times during the past season, crowds ranging from 15,000 to 30,000 collected together. The newspapers are doing a great work to increase interest in football, giving much space to the accounts of games written by trained experts and by reproducing important plays for their readers with action pictures.

Such was the state of football in the south; it was catching up with the rest of the country, but a stigma of inferiority was the general perception. Not only that, but the south had a historical legacy of military defeat, poverty, and cultural alienation from the rest of America. As the train carrying Alabama's team left Tuscaloosa on December 19, the hopes of an entire region traveled with it. President Denny realized what they were up against, saying,

> Our team will strive to represent worthily our great commonwealth and our great section. We recognize the difficulties and the handicaps of a long trip to the distant region in which we shall be strangers, both to the climate and to the people. We recognize we shall meet the champions of the Pacific Coast, one of the greatest teams in the country, one of the most powerful America has produced. Such is the colossal task to which our boys have set their hands. Win or lose, this trip means more widespread and sustained publicity for Alabama than any recent event in the history of the state.

Coach Wade took no chances. He ordered that drums of Alabama drinking water be brought on the train to decrease the possibility of water-borne disease. He had learned this from his old Brown coach, Edward Robinson, when Brown had played in the 1916 Rose Bowl. Also, as the team journeyed across the vast expanse of America, Wade held briefings with his team twice a day on

Cowboy Tom Mix holds Coach Wade's children, Wallace Wade Jr., left, and
Frances, right. Coach Wade is standing beside Frances. Alabama is in
Pasadena for the Rose Bowl. Courtesy of Anita Caldwell.

the game plan and scouting reports. Zipp Newman, with the team, wrote
"There isn't a player on the train who can't tell you the name, weight, disposition, and a few other little things about every player eligible on the Washington team." Wade had told his team before departing, "Now, this is to be a
trip to go win a football game. We're not going out there to make an appearance and enjoy the scenery. I want your minds on Washington." Knowing full
well the value of physical conditioning, Wade had his players off at every stop
to do some running and "limbering up" exercises. The team was allowed to
stop at the Grand Canyon for a tour. In Williams, Arizona, the team held a
formal practice at a local high school field.

The Alabama squad arrived in Pasadena on Christmas Eve, but Coach Wade
was in no mood to be Santa Claus. His Christmas present to his team was a
long, hard practice, with talk of Huskies instead of reindeer. Coach Wade was
not the complete Scrooge, allowing sightseeing tours for a couple of days in-
between his practices. But days before the game, he had had enough. "In order
to get in the right mental attitude, no more entertainment will be indulged
in," he declared on December 28.

Pooley Hubert and Johnny Mack Brown seemed to garner a large part of
the press' attention. In fact, Newman wrote "Hubert and Mack Brown will

have enough experience posing for the cameramen to enter the movies after their stay here." Little did Newman know that Brown, sure enough, became one of the premier cowboy movie stars of the 1930s and 1940s. Brown's great personality and striking good looks helped his entrance into celebrity status. Interestingly, Washington had a future movie star also. Herman Brix, who would win a silver medal in the shot put at the 1928 Olympics, played the title role in *The New Adventures of Tarzan* in 1935. Using the stage name of Bruce Bennett, Brix appeared in over eighty feature films.

As the game neared, the press continued to advertise the game as one of the largest intersectional conflicts since the Civil War. Alabama started to feel the pressure of not just winning the game, but of representing the entire south. Washington was cast into the role of the Yankees, even though its ancestors had fought more Indians than Confederates. Coach Wade was not opposed to this territorial pride building, as he realized it would probably only serve to further motivate his "southern boys." In later years, he would sometimes refer to his old Brown teammates as "Yankee boys," but in a teasing, friendly way.

* * *

As New Year's Day 1926 arrived, crowds of Alabamians gathered in theater auditoriums and in offices to follow the play-by-play account of the game over a special Associated Press wire. The Grand Theater in Montgomery was filled to standing room capacity, and hundreds more could not get in. The police decided to rope off a block of Dexter Avenue, the main downtown Montgomery street, for those who stood outside in cold winter weather to get reports of the game. There were similar gatherings around Alabama and throughout much of the south. Huge throngs of people did this despite the fact that several radio stations in Alabama were broadcasting a re-creation of the same wire transmissions, but they chose to gather to show their collective support for "their boys." At Auburn University, students packed the campus auditorium to cheer their rivals on.

The game started badly for Alabama. On Alabama's first possession, Wilson stopped them cold. The Tide marched to Washington's 15-yard line. On the next play, Wilson hit Johnny Mack Brown and threw him for a two-yard loss. On the very next down, Wilson crashed through the offensive line to sack Emile Barnes for an eight-yard loss. Wilson, whom Winslett had described as looking like "a bale of cotton" because of his huge size, then intercepted an Alabama pass. Patton scored a touchdown for the Huskies, but the point after was missed.

Early in the second quarter Wilson threw a 20-yard touchdown pass to Cole for a 12 to 0 lead. Wilson was unstoppable on offense and defense. The Alabama players were stunned at the speed, power, and ferocious spirit of this man called "Wildcat." The Huskies had scored two touchdowns in less than a half, compared to only one touchdown that had been scored on the Tide in nine regular season games all year. It looked as though the prognosticators had been correct; West Coast football was still very much superior to the brand of football played in the south.

Not only was Wilson dominating play, he decided to get a little dirty with Alabama. On a tackle against Johnny Mack Brown, Wilson viciously twisted Brown's leg well after he had him on the ground. This unnecessary roughness can be seen clearly on game film. This was a mistake, as the Alabama teammates were tremendously loyal to each other, and to see Wilson try to injure one of their own literally incensed them. This tackle, combined with an outburst from their leader, Pooley Hubert, really got their fighting spirit up. Hubert was so disgusted with his teammates' play at one point in the first half that he called all of them over during a timeout and screamed "All right, what the hell's going on around here?"

Back in Alabama and around the south, sad crowds had not given up hope, but certainly prospects did not look good. The crowd on Dexter Avenue in Montgomery walked about, their hopes seemingly dashed. In the front window of the Rosemont Gardens Florist Shop, some of the fans looked at the Alabama team photograph, which was displayed inside a horseshoe-shaped arrangement of red roses. Meanwhile, in Court Square of Montgomery, where a wild celebration had taken place 65 years earlier when news of the fall of Fort Sumter had come, a stockpile of fireworks awaited the big display that had been so hoped for after the boys of Alabama defeated the "Yankees" of Washington. Across the south, despondent fans worried that what most people around the country had predicted was about to come true, that Alabama had not deserved to be invited to the prestigious Rose Bowl.

Back in the clubhouse at the Rose Bowl, the Crimson Tide players were getting "riled up," to use an old expression. They were "mad as hell," according to Coach Wade, over the fact they had played so poorly in the first half. They were upset at Wilson for his rough handling of Brown, and they felt they had let their field general, Hubert, down. They had seen the fire in Hubert's eyes, the man Wade, in retirement, called "the best field general I ever coached, he could lead men like no other player I ever had."

The team gathered together expecting Coach Wade, Coach Crisp, and Coach Cohen to "lay into us," as one player put it. Wade knew his team, knew the pride it had in itself. He knew their faces and what he saw pleased him to no end. There was no look of despondency, there were no drooping shoulders, and they did not look like a team who was literally being dominated. No, instead there was a tensing of muscles, a ramrod posture, and a look in the eyes that had a fierceness about it. Wade, at that point, calmly made an adjustment to his lineup that would have a profound impact on the game. Most of Washington's big yardage plays in the first half had been made through Alabama's ends. He inserted two heavier players at these spots for the second half, and this move cut down the running attack for the Huskies dramatically.

Abraham Maslow, a famous psychologist, coined the term "fight or flight" for people who are under a lot of stress. Wade, from looking at his boys, knew that his team, every single one of them, was now confronted with the choice of fighting or quitting, and he had absolutely no doubt they had chosen. To put them over the edge, he walked in and said in a rather low voice, "They told me boys from the south would fight." Then he left. The game was now over, those "damn Yankees" were about to experience the beating of their careers.

* * *

Another change Wade had made at halftime was to tell Hubert to start running the ball more. On the Tide's first possession of the second half, Hubert exploded up the middle for 27 yards. He then carried the ball four more times in a row, plunging over the Washington goal from the one-yard line. Five carries in a row for a total gain of 42 yards, on runs of 27, 10, 1, 3, and 1, by Pooley made the score 12 to 6. After the point after, it was 12 to 7. On Alabama's next possession, the ball was snapped to Grant Gillis, who threw the ball at least 50 yards to Johnny Mack Brown, who made a spectacular catch and scored on the 63-yard play. With the PAT, it was now Alabama 14, Washington 12. Pandemonium started to break out back home in Tuscaloosa, Montgomery, Birmingham, Dothan, Auburn, Meridian (hometown of Hubert), Atlanta, New Orleans, and all across the south. But the game was far from over.

The Tide held on defense. George Wilson was on the bench, having been knocked unconscious on an earlier play, which was delivered courtesy of the enraged Alabama players over the tackle Wilson had put on Brown. With the ball again, and up by two, the Crimson Tide went to the air again, this time Hubert passing to Brown, who caught the ball over his shoulder, side-stepped to get by one tackler, then stiff-armed another to score. The point after was missed, but now Alabama was up 20 to 12. Alabama had erupted for three touchdowns in seven minutes of play in an era where offensive explosions were not the norm. But plenty of time remained, and Coach Enoch Bagshaw of Washington and his Huskies had no quit in them. A still dazed "Wildcat" Wilson came back in the game, scored a touchdown in the fourth quarter to make it 20 to 19. Time still remained, and the hopes of the south were in the hands of the boys from Alabama.

With Wilson running and passing, the Huskies drove deep into Alabama territory late in the game. Brown made a key tackle of Wilson on this drive, and an interception ended the hopes for a Washington comeback and lifted the hopes and spirits of southern football fans everywhere. This victory put Alabama on the national football map. Alabama had its first national championship, of which many would follow. The victory today is known by most scholars and historians of the game as the biggest victory in the history of southern college football.

* * *

Even the fans of the Rose Bowl, who had begun the game firmly in favor of the West Coast Huskies, had gradually seemed to shift their allegiance to the underdog Alabama team. By the time the game ended, there was a thunderous roar for the Tide. Fans actually ran on the field to get close to this team who had proven all the experts wrong. They knew they had witnessed and had been a part of something historic. David had truly slain Goliath once again.

As "Alabama Wins" flashed across the wires back in Alabama, pandemonium erupted in the packed streets, theaters, auditoriums, and offices across the state. Southern honor had been vindicated.

CHAPTER NINE

AFTER THE GAME

All the way along the route home, people gathered to shout and cheer the Crimson Tide. There was a huge celebration in New Orleans, led by William Little, the man who had started Alabama football back in 1892. Large iced cakes and dressed turkeys were presented to the team. Speeches followed and a band played. Hip, Hip, Hip, Hurrahs for the players and coaches never seemed to stop. The train stopped in the Alabama towns of York, Livingston, Akron, and Boligee. More speeches and bands, more gifts as tokens of appreciation for the great victory.

All of Tuscaloosa turned out to meet the team when its train arrived at the depot, and people from around the state came. Some fans even climbed up on the depot's roof to get a better look. It was with much difficulty that a passageway was made for the team to reach the decorated wagons waiting to pull them through the crowded streets of Tuscaloosa. The Million Dollar Band paraded ahead of the wagons to the intersection of Broad and Greensboro Avenue, where Governor Brandon voiced an eloquent welcome home and thank you on behalf of the state. So many people came to see the team that it took an hour to inch along the three-quarter mile route from the depot to downtown. One speaker told the happy gathering, "When the band plays Dixie over this team, it can whip eleven Red Granges." Wade and Denny made speeches also, and particularly loud cheers were given to them, Hubert, and Brown. The parade formed again and proceeded to the university, where more speeches, band playing, and general merriment ensued. The Tuscaloosa Chamber of Commerce presented each player and coach with gold watches and other gifts.

* * *

Praise flowed in for the Crimson Tide from all over the country. The *Birmingham News* summed up the victory this way:

> For all the last stands, all the lost causes and sacrifices in vain, the South had a heart and a tradition. But the South had a new tradition for some-

**A welcome home for the national champions in Tuscaloosa.
Governor Brandon, left, Coach Wade, middle, and President
Denny, right. Courtesy of Nancy Wade.**

thing else. It was for survival and victory. It had come from the football
field. It had come from those mighty afternoons in the Rose Bowl in
Pasadena when Alabama's Crimson Tide had rolled to glory. The South
had come by way of football to think in terms of causes won, not lost.

The *Atlanta Georgian* called the win "the greatest victory for the south since
the first battle of Bull Run." The *Atlanta Journal* carried the headline "Dixie
Acclaims Her Heroes." The *Birmingham News* claimed that words on
newsprint could not do justice to the "miracle at the Rose Bowl," instead the
victory should be proclaimed to the world on "a ten league canvas with
brushes of comet's hair."

The many references to "a victory for the south" were in large part due to
the still felt sting of defeat in the Civil War and the effects of Reconstruction.
Many southerners held the belief that one Confederate soldier was worth several Yankees in battle, and Alabama's victory helped to validate that opinion.

Thousands turned out at the Tuscaloosa train depot to cheer the triumphant Crimson Tide team. Courtesy of Duke Sports Information Department.

Much of the south in 1926 still held special holidays and celebrations to commemorate the war and many towns had Confederate monuments displayed proudly in courthouse squares. Leaders in Tuscaloosa had even decorated the city's lampposts with American, Alabama, and Confederate flags for the welcome home ceremony for the Tide team.

But this victory did much more than just lift spirits. It lifted the profile of the south, especially Alabama, across the nation as a region that was on the move, a section of America that was catching up, an equal. A speaker introduced Wallace Wade sometime after the victory as "a man who has advertised Alabama more in the past three years than any other man in the past fifty years." Zipp Newman perhaps summed up the importance of the victory best, writing, "No victory in football ever changed the destiny of one section of the country like Alabama's furious seven-minute comeback against Washington.

Johnny Mack Brown came back to Tuscaloosa after the Rose Bowl. Brown had finished his playing career and needed to take his next step in life. He had known nothing but success, even earning the "most handsome" senior award at Dothan High School in Alabama. After choosing Alabama over Auburn for college, helping to lead the Tide to unprecedented glory, and earning the nickname "Dothan Antelope," he now faced the prospect of life without football.

Johnny Mack Brown the movie star. Courtesy of Anita Caldwell.

He was good enough to play professionally, but in 1926 professional football was not the high paying game it is now. He had previously worked as a clerk at Charles Black Company in Tuscaloosa. He decided to enter the insurance business, married Cornelia Foster, and helped Coach Wade with some coaching. After going with the team to the 1927 Rose Bowl, Brown was given an audition and soon signed a contract to make movies for MGM. Brown ended up starring in over 160 films, mostly as a cowboy. He played in Billy the Kid in 1930, which held its world premier at the Bama Theater in Tuscaloosa. He would appear alongside John Wayne, Greta Garbo, and Joan Crawford. Brown continued to love Alabama throughout his life, even helping to scout Stanford for Frank Thomas as the Alabama head coach in 1935 prepared to face them in the Rose Bowl that year. He ended up in the College Football Hall of Fame for his exploits at Alabama and also received a star on the Hollywood Boulevard Walk of Fame. Brown passed away in 1974.

* * *

**Pooley Hubert. Courtesy of W.S. Hoole Special
Collections Library, University of Alabama.**

Allison Thomas Stanislaus Hubert, better known as Pooley, always remained one of Wallace Wade's favorite players. Wade injected Hubert into dis-
cussions of football throughout his life. In a taped interview in 1985, at the
age of 93, Pooley was discussed in various ways: "great field general," "tough-
nosed ball player," "all the other boys looked up to Pooley and had great respect for him," a real leader of men," "could have played for anybody anytime,"
and "tough as nails."

Hubert graduated from high school in Meridian, Mississippi. After a cir-
cuitous route to Tuscaloosa, Hubert became one of the most storied players
to ever don an Alabama uniform. It was Hubert who had got the Tide rolling
against Washington, scoring Alabama's first touchdown and getting his teammates fired up with his infamous line, "Now, just what the hell's going on
around here?" Also during that game, Jeff Coleman, the longtime business
manager for the athletic department, recalled that Hubert, not the least bit intimidated by the great All-American George Wilson, pointed directly at "Wildcat" and said, "We're coming right over you," and so he did.

Hubert went on to play professional football with the New York Yankees, where he played with the immortal Red Grange. In 1931, with Wade's strong endorsement, Hubert was selected as head coach at Southern Mississippi, where he went 26-24-5 from 1931 to 1936. He moved to Virginia Military Institute in 1937 and was 43-45-8 until 1946. In his first four years at VMI, they beat Virginia Tech three years in a row and were 3-0-1 against Virginia. In 1939 VMI hosted Duke, which was then coached by his old mentor, Wallace Wade. It was a joyful reunion for both, even though Duke won the game 20 to 7. Hubert coached Joe Muha at VMI, who went on to an All-Pro career in the NFL. Another All-Pro NFL player who played for Hubert at VMI was Bosh Pritchard.

There was quite an Alabama connection at VMI. Russ Cohen was VMI's assistant and formerly an assistant at Alabama during the Hubert years. Other assistants were Albert Elmore and Carney Laslie, who were on Wade's 1931 Rose Bowl squad, and Jimmy Walker, captain of the 1935 Alabama team. One other person from Alabama was thinking seriously of coming to VMI as an assistant, but at the last moment Paul "Bear" Bryant accepted a position at Vanderbilt. Years later, Hubert said, "Bear and I would have made a good team. We might not have had the best football team in the country, but I guarantee you there wouldn't have been a meaner team."

Hubert eventually moved to Waynesboro, Georgia, coached at Edmund Burke Academy, and also grew peaches. Hank Crisp, the longtime coach of Alabama, said that "Pooley was the greatest player I ever helped coach in over 40 years," and to football fans of Alabama, Pooley Hubert will forever represent what it means to wear the Crimson colors.

* * *

Another footnote to the 1926 Rose Bowl, as noted earlier, is that it was the first football game Bear Bryant ever listened to. The Crimson Tide of Alabama remained in young Bryant's heart from that moment on. He recalled many years later,

> I never imagined anything could be that exciting. I still didn't have much of an idea what football was, but after listening to that game, I had it in my mind that what I wanted to do with my life was to go to Alabama and play in the Rose Bowl like Johnny Mack Brown.

The following is from Allen Barra's book *The Last Coach*:

> Although Bryant never played for Wallace Wade, he was acutely conscious of how much he owed him. The first football game he ever lis-

tened to was Alabama's victory in the 1926 Rose Bowl, and Wallace's image still dominated Alabama football when Bryant arrived in 1931. Bryant, who would become as awe-inspiring as any coach to ever step onto a college field, never got over his awe of Wallace Wade.

In 1976 Bryant invited Wade to attend spring practice in Tuscaloosa, after which the coaches went to a party at the Tutwiler Hotel in Birmingham. Clem Gryska, one of Bryant's assistants, recalls that the two Bears went off in a corner to talk. Wade asked Bryant how he thought the team would do that season. "It could be good, but to be honest, Coach," said Bryant, "I need a fullback." "Well, Paul," said Wade (Gryska could recall few people who ever addressed Bryant by his Christian name), "Did you not know when you were out recruiting this winter that you'd be needing a fullback?" Bryant, who towered over the older man, replied in a quiet voice, "Yes sir, Coach, you're right. I should have done something about that."

Edwin Hardy Foster wrote the following poem about Johnny Mack Brown after the 1926 Rose Bowl. Excerpts from it are:

> O, Johnny Mack Brown is come
> Back from the west!
> Through all the wide border
> His speed was the best.
> 'Mong fleetest of athletes
> He rival had none.
> He dashed like a meteor
> And shone like the sun.
> And the whole 'Bam' team,
> Now famed near and far,
> As national champions,
> With this Lochinvar.
>
> So stately his form,
> And so beaming his face,
> There never a field such
> A half back did grace.
> And purple fans whispered,
> "Twas better by far
> To have wagered like Champ
> On this young Lochinvar."
>
> One look to Jones, captain;
> One word in Holmes ear;

Pooley tossed the ball back,
And Grant Gillis stood near.
So light through the azure
The leather Grant flung,
So light through the
Rose Bowl before it Mack swung,
It is won! He is gone
Past Cole, Brix, Schuh, Tesreau!
"They'll have swift wings that follow,"
Laughed back Lochinvar.

There was racing and chasing on
Pasadena's Bowl;
But the Crimson in glory
Flashed over the goal.
So dauntless and valiant in gridiron war,
Have y'e'er heard of half back
Like the South's Lochinvar?

This poem, "The Battle of Pasadena," was written by Clyde W. Ennis of Ensley, Alabama. Its beautifully written and nostalgic lines just may, for a moment, have you thinking you were there the day the Crimson Tide captured the nation's attention.

The Battle of Pasadena

The day was fair and balmy
With scarce a breeze astir,
Men left home their overcoats
And the women came sans fur.
The Rose Bowl's sides were awful full
Of fans come out to see
What the south could show to them
Of football artistry.
The playing field was emerald green,
A meadow smooth and true;
The white lines glimmered in the sun,
The goal sticks glimmered, too.
The starting time at last came round,
They popped the opening gun,
Then the clash was on between

Alabam' and Washington.
The ball sailed down to Lovely Barnes,
He dragged it back a mile,
And then the tide began to roll
We cry a while then smile.

On and on the Crimsons came,
The stands were wild with glee
As Gillis, Hubert, and Mack Brown
Climbed up the glory tree.
Then came a mighty jolting blow,
That Fate stepped up and dealed
George Wilson snagged a Bama pass
And scampered up the field.
The Huskies then began to surge
Our hearts within us dropped
Those terrific, plunging, driving rams
It seemed could not be stopped.
On they swept across the line
With Wilson in the lead
George, the Great, they called him there,
A gent of drive and speed.
Then once again the purple horde
Stormed its way across
Our fingernails and peace of mind
Both became a total loss.

Then came the ending of the half,
But e'en before twas o'er
The gallant Tide had hit its stride
And was bidding for a score.
As our brave boys in Crimson clad
Trooped slowly off the green
The place was filled with mighty cheers
For the plucky red machine.
Their blankets spread, they rested,
Tired but full of fight
And all the while the mammoth crowd
Cheered them with all its might
In quiet but true inspiring tone
Spoke their chieftain, Wallace Wade,

"We'll win this game, my boys," he said.
The rest of us all prayed.

That next quarter is now history,
And it will oft be told
How that Crimson Tide from Dixie
With a fighting heart of gold
Swept aside its mighty foe
And rambled swiftly down
That studded path of glory
On the flying feet of Brown.
On the flying feet of Brown and
On Hubert's hefty crash,
On Gillis' good throwing arm
On e'er famous southern dash
On Buckler's businesslike big toe
On Barnes' swishing steam
On the dogged fighting will
Of the WHOLE DAMN TEAM!!!

When Pooley ploughed across the line
For Alabama's starting score
The whole darn multitude arose
In one spontaneous roar
They were roaring still as Buckler
Toed the ball across the stick
And kept it up until the Tide
Lined up for the next kick.
Twas but a moment later
When Gillis took dead aim
And hurled himself and Johnny Mack
Into the hall of fame.
The distance of that timely toss
Is still argued everywhere,
But nobody thought of distance
As Mack took it from the air.

Took it from the air, I mean,
And took it on the run
And then began the sinking of
the good ship Washington.

Bill Buckler did his stuff again,
He drew a deadly bead
On the yawning goal posts
And we were in the lead
No one had even yet sat down
When Papa Hubert threw
Another toss to Johnny Mack
Lightning fast and true
Just as he had done before
Mack took it to his breast
Alabam' could then have had a deed
To the whole darn Golden West.

Who cared if Buckler's boot was blocked
The Tide's count then was twenty
E'en though the Huskies rallied strong
Alabama sill had plenty
And when that final pop-gun cracked
And we knew that we had won
That Alabama's Crimson Tide
Had engulfed Washington.
It seemed that the entire west coast
Had gone crazy as had we
While other southern folk there, too,
Jumped here and there with glee.
Up on the shoulders of the crowd
For a sweet, triumphant ride
Went then the boys who fought and won,
The gallant Crimson Tide.

CHAPTER TEN

1926 — NATIONAL CHAMPIONS AGAIN

There is no question, and Bear Bryant strongly supports the notion, that Wade-led Alabama made the Crimson Tide a storied name in national football circles. Wade led Alabama to its thundering entrance to national acclaim, spawning Crimson Tide tradition as we know it today. — Al Browning

Alabama's first national championship, earned in the 1926 Rose Bowl, permanently stamped the Tide as a force to be reckoned with. Eleven more national titles have followed since. One well known national publication in 2005 chose Alabama as the fourth-greatest college football program of all time, behind only Notre Dame, the University of Southern California, and Oklahoma, with Nebraska fifth. Of course, Alabama fans and supporters will passionately say the ranking is too low and with legitimate reasoning. But there is no question that Wallace Wade's 1926 national champions "got the ball rolling around here," as Bear Bryant said.

Much of the success at Alabama has been due to its tradition. Even Coach Wade realized this, saying,

A lot of the success Alabama has enjoyed through the years is related to tradition. Prestige and that sort of thing makes good boys want to come here and play on good teams. That helps along with good coaching and leadership. Tradition is a rich asset for Alabama football, no question.

* * *

Certainly the Crimson Tide was rising high as the 1926 season arrived. With an 11 game winning streak, Alabama had high hopes for the upcoming schedule. The football team's success had also contributed to the university receiving much favorable publicity. The Roaring 20s continued unabated, and good times and growth were experienced in and around Tuscaloosa.

One interesting event held on the campus occurred in February of 1926. Coach Wade, acting more as athletic director than football coach, and Champ Pickens scheduled the "fastest man on earth" to give an exhibition and lecture. Charles Paddock had agreed to run against Johnny Mack Brown and also Bob Hussey of Alabama's track team. Races were held at Denny Field, and the lecture took place in Morgan Hall on campus. Wade was always a coach who emphasized speed and quickness over brawn, so no doubt he was happy to have his athletes learn a few pointers from this great sprinter. The big day of sports was capped by Alabama's annual spring football game.

Regarding Champ Pickens, here was a man, as publicity director of the Crimson Tide, who did much to bring Alabama football to the nation's attention. The Pickens Trophy was given in his honor to the Southern Conference champion each year, and he promoted many other sporting events. For example, he promoted the appearance of Red Grange in 1926 in Birmingham, where Grange played an exhibition game with his new pro football team, the New York Yankees. Also helping to draw fans to Birmingham, and Wallace Wade, was the chance to see one of their own, the beloved Pooley Hubert, who was now playing in the same backfield with Grange.

* * *

Wade continued to write his syndicated column on athletics. In the following one, written before the start of the 1926 season, much about his football philosophy and beliefs can be gained.

> Coaches are often asked how a football star is made. A football star is not made by the coach, but a player makes of himself a star.
>
> Proper qualities of character are just as important as physical abilities, and traits of character can be improved by intelligent and systematic exercise. In fact, the development of these characteristics is the way in which football is most beneficial to young men. In order to become an outstanding football player, a boy must have and develop ambitious determination, loyalty, unselfishness, a spirit of cooperation, alertness, intelligence, and poise.
>
> Players do not drift into being stars. They must have the ambition to be outstanding, backed up with sufficient determination to keep trying at the task of becoming an outstanding player in spite of failures and disappointments. There are thousands of football players in the country with first-class physical ability who have the ambition to become outstanding. However, the small number who become great is composed of those who, in addition to physical ability and ambi-

tion, have sufficient determination to keep trying until they accomplish their purpose. A football player who succeeds is one who makes the effort that is required to accomplish his purpose.

Football is a team sport and a player can never reach his supreme height until he has devoted himself and his ability to his team and to the cause of his institution. I have never known a really great football player who was selfish; however, I have known a few who probably would have been great if they could have forgotten themselves long enough to give their team the benefit of their full cooperation and loyalty.

A player must learn how to accept victory and how to take a licking. No player will be great until he overcomes a disposition to shirk the responsibility for failures. A boy should learn to accept defeat as an indication that the opposition did a better job on that occasion and to resolve to be prepared and able to make a better effort next time.

Balance is probably the most important fundamental in both blocking and tackling. Blocking is probably one of the hardest things to learn in connection with football. A player who likes to block is a jewel. Good punting probably requires more practice time than any other attribute of football. A punter must have remarkable poise and timing. First of all, a punter must be able to get his kick away quickly, then must either be able to kick for exceptional distance or with exceptional accuracy.

There are two kinds of outstanding ball carriers. One is the type who is very elusive in the open field. The three best open field runners that I have known were Pollard of Brown, Grange of Illinois, and Johnny Mack Brown of Alabama. Another type of runner who is just as valuable is the line plunger. In ball carrying, speed is not so important as quickness. This applies to ability to start, stop, get up speed, turn, or dodge suddenly.

* * *

As the 1926 season neared, college football was experiencing a tremendous growth in popularity. Schools were building huge stadiums to accommodate the increased popularity of the sport. Newspaper and magazine coverage contributed mightily to the rise in popularity, as the likes of Grantland Rice, Zipp Newman, and Damon Runyon graced sports pages with captivating prose. Red Grange made a football feature film called *One Minute to Play* in 1926. The *Saturday Evening Post* ran three football covers in 1926. NBC Radio scheduled weekly college football radio broadcasts in 1926. On this note, Wade was one of the first coaches in the country to have his own radio show, aired on WAPI in Birmingham. The 1927 Rose Bowl game, involving Alabama, would be the first nationally broadcast football game on radio, covered by Graham McNamee.

There were still many opponents of big-time football, or what was commonly called King Football, during this time. E.K. Hall of Dartmouth, chairman of the football rules committee of college football, wrote eloquently against too much emphasis on the game and winning.

> One of the tendencies that I see creeping into the game is the increasing insistence, by undergraduates and graduates alike, for a winning season, a winning team. Because football is a game that calls for playing to win, and it is not a game unless you do play to win, we have jumped in an illogical sort of way to the idea that the winning of games is the purpose of football, and if we lost most of the games in a given season, the season is mostly wasted.
>
> What we have to do is to readjust our perspectives and our propositions, and look at this thing in a proper sense of proportion and perspective. It is not whether you win or lose, but it is how you played the game.
>
> Football is an incident of college life, not the purpose of it. The real values of football are too big and too intangible ever to be reflected in scores. It cannot be done.

Wallace Wade hated to lose, and after five years of college coaching, including his two years at Vanderbilt, his teams had only lost three games in 46 played. In fact, if you include all of Wade's coaching career through the 1927 Rose Bowl, including his two years as a high school coach, Wade had an amazing record of 66 wins with only six losses and three ties. Not a bad way to start a career. By the age of 35, he earned two national championships, four Southern Conference titles, and a state high school championship, and he had played and coached in three Rose Bowls.

But to some degree Wade agreed with what Hall wrote. In an interview, Wade stressed that

> college football is primarily intended to be an institution to build character and to develop young men. We should not forget that and get carried away with our enthusiasm for successful games. At Alabama, we take a boy, train him, and make something out of him. Hopefully, this will enable him to face life better after football. My idea is to conduct my football program in a way beneficial to the boys who played. You know, we got started in this game of football as an exercise to develop boys into capable men.

Herschel Caldwell as a player at Alabama.
Courtesy of Anita Caldwell.

* * *

Key returnees for 1926 were Fred Pickhard at tackle, Herschel Caldwell in the backfield and at end, Hoyt "Wu" Winslett at end, Gordon "Sherlock" Holmes at center, "Red" Brown (Johnny Mack's brother) at running back, Ellis "Dumpy" Hagler at guard, and Emile Barnes in the backfield.

Herschel Caldwell, after his stellar playing career under Wade at Alabama, coached at Sidney Lanier High School in Montgomery, where his teams lost only two games in his three years there, 1927 through 1929. Sidney Lanier won the state championship in 1928. After accepting the job at Duke in 1930, Wade sent Caldwell, along with Hagler, to Duke to start implementing the Wade system of football. Caldwell coached at Duke from 1930 to 1972, compiling a sterling record as freshman football coach, along with assisting Wade with the varsity. Hagler went on to an outstanding coaching career at Duke also after playing and coaching at Alabama. Not only did he coach football during the heyday of Duke football, he also became Duke's golf coach where he won 13 Southern Conference titles and 5 ACC titles. Hagler is now enshrined in the National Collegiate Golf Coaches Hall of Fame. Dumpy Hagler, from Blue Springs, Alabama, got his nickname in a game against Vanderbilt, when after the game, a reporter referred to him as "a dumpy little guard from Alabama."

* * *

Alabama opened with Millsaps in Tuscaloosa at Denny Field, winning 54 to 0. Red Brown scored three touchdowns, and Herschel Caldwell scored a touchdown and made five points after touchdowns. In the second game, Alabama went to Nashville to play Vanderbilt and won 19 to 7. It was the first time Wade coached against his old mentor, Dan McGugin. Winslett threw for two touchdowns to Caldwell. This win further solidified the reputation of Alabama as the dominant power in southern football, winning over Vanderbilt who had held that distinction for most of the early 1900s.

The Crimson Tide defeated Georgia Tech on October 16 in Atlanta before 18,000 people by the score of 21 to 0, holding Tech to only two first downs. Morgan Blake, of the Atlanta Journal, after the game obviously was impressed with Alabama and Herschel Caldwell. Blake affixed another nickname to Winslett, calling him the Dadeville Demon, to go with his "Wu" that his teammates had given him for his supposed Chinese eyes. About Caldwell, Blake wrote, "he takes passes from the air in all conceivable positions." Blake also waxed poetic about the Tide.

> From the plains of Alabama,
> From the land of iron barons,
> Flaming steel and smoking turrets,
> Come the Tuscaloosa Terrors.
>
> Cunning, nimble, very daring,
> Keen of brain and strong of muscle,
> Proud they are, befitting champions,
> Merciless they are, and cruel,
> Ready to destroy the Jackets,
> Cut their title claims to ribbons,
> Making vain their hopes and longings.

Sadly, someone defaced the walls of the Georgia Tech stadium with red paint after the win over the Jackets. Coach Wade was deeply disturbed about this lack of sportsmanship and wrote a letter to Alabama's student body:

**The Alabama team lines up to practice plays before a game
at Denny Field. Courtesy of Anita Caldwell.**

It has been called to our attention that following our recent game with
Georgia Tech in Atlanta, someone very seriously damaged the appearance of the Georgia Tech stadium by painting some signs on the
walls of this splendid building. It seems to me that the person who did
this not only violated the law but showed very poor taste in his manner of celebrating an achievement of the University of Alabama students. I believe that the students of the University of Alabama have a
right to feel proud of the way in which the majority of the students
have conducted themselves on our many football campaigns away
from home. We also should realize that it is more important that we
should have and deserve a reputation for clean sportsmanship and
proper conduct on the part of our students than to have the reputation of a winning football team. I will greatly appreciate any information that anyone will be kind enough to furnish in regard to this un-
sportsman-like act.

In Birmingham, Alabama barely won over the Sewanee Tigers 2 to 0. Nothing on offense seemed to work, due to sloppy play and the good defense of

Alabama team after a practice. Courtesy of Anita Caldwell.

Sewanee, but once again, Wade's defense saved the day. Against Kentucky, the Tide won 14 to 0. According to the *Crimson-White*, Alabama's student paper,

> Hoyt Winslett called signals and ran the team, punted, passed, gained consistently with the ball, making two touchdowns and in addition to this, played an outstanding game on defense. Ben Enis got a good game out of his system, throwing the Kentucky boys for numerous losses and stopping every end run that came his way.

Wade, throughout his career, was known as an extremely hard worker, a man who would keep his teams out on the field long hours and practice plays over and over to achieve the execution and precision he desired. But obviously, from this report from the *Crimson-White* after the Kentucky game, he tried to relax now and then:

> The Alabama varsity squad took a holiday Monday afternoon, the first holiday in many weeks and the only one during the season thus far. Coaches Wade and Crisp took to the woods and followed the trail of the shy and crafty deer, but no definite reports were obtainable regarding their success.

After beating Florida 49 to 0 in the Cramton Bowl in Montgomery, Alabama dominated Georgia 33 to 6 to end the regular season 9 and 0. The only solace for the Bulldogs was that they scored on Alabama for the first time in four years, but the Tide wrapped up its third consecutive Southern Conference title with the victory. It was the 20th straight win for Alabama. It was a streak of dominance rarely seen in the history of college football, with the Tide outscoring its opponents 571 to 46 in those games. The Rose Bowl invited Alabama back. Mighty Stanford and Pop Warner awaited them.

* * *

Before the Rose Bowl game with Stanford, however, it was time to celebrate the season past. A banquet was given by the Birmingham alumni at the Birmingham Country Club on December 1st. More than 1,200 paid tribute to the Crimson Tide team. Morgan Blake was on hand to present the Champ Pickens trophy, emblematic of the Southern Conference championship, to Captain Barnes. Borden Burr presented each of the graduating seniors with a gold watch. Captains and coaches of local high school teams were introduced. Telegrams were read from Dan McGugin, congratulating his old pupil, Wallace Wade. University president Denny lauded the team and coaches for their great effort, and Fred Pickhard was elected captain for 1927. Over 300 people attended a banquet given in Montgomery on December 8th. Wade, it was announced, had been chosen president of the Association of Southern Football Coaches for 1927. Wade, whose coaching school at Alabama was one of the first of its kind in the nation, was also chosen to conduct a summer school for coaches at Southern University in Lakeland, Florida, in August of 1927.

The coaching school at Alabama, in which high school and college coaches came to Tuscaloosa to hear lectures and participate in demonstrations about football, opened up a new avenue of recruiting to Alabama. Wade was able to sign most of the best players from Alabama during his time in Tuscaloosa. He also worked very hard to get his former players positions coaching high school sports, which certainly aided his ability to get good players. For example, Herschel Caldwell and Ben Enis both were hired after the 1927 spring term to coach at Sidney Lanier High School in Montgomery. This eventually paved the way for All-American Johnny Cain to come to Alabama to play football for Wade. Paul Burnum of Tuscaloosa High School and Wade had a close working relationship, one that eventually landed Burnum on Wade's staff at the Capstone. The Tuscaloosa High Black Bears were one of the most successful teams in the country during the 1920s.

* * *

Stanford would be a tough task indeed. Coached by legendary Glenn "Pop" Warner, Stanford had gone 10 and 0 in 1926, defeating such teams as Southern

California, Washington, and California. From 1924 to 1932 at Stanford, Warner would go 71-17-8. Warner was the inventor of the single wing offense, in which Wallace Wade was a firm believer; Wade had used it in devastating fashion in his four years at Alabama. Also coaching at Georgia, Cornell, Carlisle, Pittsburgh, and Temple during his career, Warner won 319 games in a tenure that stretched from 1895 to 1938. He had coached the immortal Jim Thorpe at Carlisle, even though he maintained that Ernie Nevers, his great back at Stanford, was perhaps better than Thorpe. Luckily for Alabama, Nevers was no longer at Stanford. But Stanford was still loaded with good players, such as Biff Hoffman at fullback and Ted Shipkey and Ed Walker at end, both All-West Coast.

The team left by train from Tuscaloosa on December 21st, having received a roaring sendoff at the A.G.S. Depot by local supporters. With stops in New Orleans, San Antonio, El Paso, and Tucson, the team took advantage of every opportunity to get off the train and run and loosen up stiff muscles. A special chin-up bar had been placed on the train to help the players maintain their conditioning. Arriving in Pasadena early on Christmas Day, Wade had his team out practicing, as he had the year before. The players were allowed to attend some Christmas festivities later in the day.

On the eve of the game, Governor William Brandon of Alabama sent a message to the team, which read in part:

> Alabama's glory is in your hands. Alumni and citizens depend on your repetition of last year's game. You have made history for your state and the university. May each member of the team turn his face to the sun-kissed hills of Alabama and fight like hell as did your sires in bygone days.

Regional pride still resonated among southerners, and after the great win over Washington, they wanted more. Another testament to this was a letter sent to the *Alabama Alumni* magazine from 1921 Bama graduate Percy Gellert, who was then living in New York. Gellert wrote,

> I would indeed be glad to hear from my old friends in and about Tuscaloosa so that I could share with them the pleasure in the doings of the Crimson Tide. It certainly gives me a kick to know of their achievements, and I am wondering if you couldn't get Wally Wade to bring his gang up and lick a few Yankee teams.

* * *

The teams were ready. Warner had personally scouted Alabama in its last game against Georgia, and Tide assistant Shorty Propst saw Stanford beat Cal-

Alabama plays Stanford in the 1927 Rose Bowl.
Courtesy of Duke Sports Information Department.

ifornia. Having been impressed with Alabama's speed, Warner had ordered silk pants for his team, which reportedly only weighed a pound-and-a-half.

Alabama's showing in 1926 had boosted interest for 1927. Tickets were being scalped at $50 a pair, and the Rose Bowl added 4,000 additional seats. Game attendance was 57,000, and gross receipts of $218,000 were a record.

The game was a defensive struggle. Four times Stanford moved inside the Alabama ten-yard line but scored only one touchdown, an 18-yard toss from George Bogue to Ed Walker in the first quarter. Time after time the Tide players pulled themselves together with the shadows of their goal post crossbars on their backs. On offense, Alabama was unable to move the ball much at all throughout most of the game. The hot sun had most of the crowd in shirtsleeves, and it wore down both teams as the game progressed into the fourth quarter with Alabama still trailing 7 to 0.

Forced to punt from its 42, Stanford's Frankie Wilton had his kick blocked by Babe Pearce of Alabama. The ball rolled to Stanford's 14, where it was downed. Wade, at this point, sent in Jimmy Johnston, who had been injured with a dislocated shoulder and had not played the entire game. Something about the moment just convinced Wade that now was the time to use him. Less than four minutes remained.

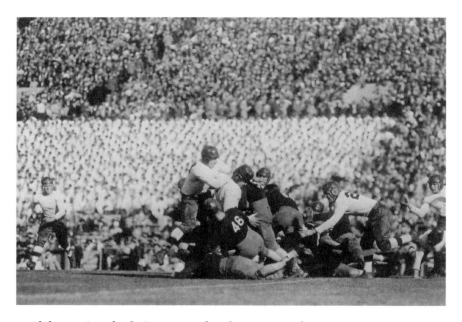

Alabama-Stanford. Courtesy of Duke Sports Information Department.

On the first play from the 14, Hoyt Winslett ran for three yards to the 11. Then Johnston bucked through the weakening defensive line of Stanford for seven more yards to the four. Winslett then ran straight into the forward wall of the Cardinal defense twice, but could only get the ball to the one. On the next play, Johnston scored on a run behind his right guard. Stanford led 7 to 6. As the shadows lengthened in the Rose Bowl, Alabama needed the point after conversion to tie Stanford. In 1927, a two-point conversion was not used.

Wade had practiced a certain play for just such an occasion as this. After lining up for the kick, Emile Barnes began to call his signals. Suddenly, he stood up and called "Signals off." At this, Stanford's players relaxed just a bit, anticipating another signal sequence. At that moment, Sherlock Holmes snapped the ball to Winslett who placed it down for kicker Herschel Caldwell, who sent it through the uprights. Stanford was completely fooled, as not one player recovered in time to penetrate the offensive line. Hoffman, of Stanford, returned Alabama's kick-off to his own 22, and two plays later the game was over, tied 7 to 7.

* * *

Judge James Mayfield had been listening to the game, which was the first national radio broadcast of a football game. Sadly, he collapsed and died while listening. A former Alabama Supreme Court Justice, Mayfield had graduated from Alabama in 1885 and was a passionate fan of Crimson Tide football. A memorial granite boulder now rests on the university campus to honor him.

Pop Warner applauded Alabama's effort after the game. In a newspaper column he wrote,

> Alabama, trailing by seven points and with the game well into the final quarter, refused to concede anything. Alabama made the big break and then followed up its advantage with a great exhibition of line-plunging that earned them an even break at the final whistle. The Alabama backs are not big fellows, but they hit with great force. Winslett at end played a fine game, and we had our eyes on him from the beginning. He enjoyed greater advance publicity, but his teammate on the other wing was just as good today. Pickhard at tackle was a constant torment and Pearce at center played a great game. Our supporters are undoubtedly disappointed at the final outcome, but so far as players and coaches are concerned, we have no regrets—except for the kick that was blocked. But if you take things like that out of football, where would be the thrills?

Everett Strupper officiated the game. He afterward commented that "Alabama made a nice rally in the last period, and the Tide's defense when Stanford was within scoring distance was really wonderful. Stanford made lots of yardage in the middle of the field but was stopped when a scoring chance came."

Braven Dyer of the *Los Angeles Times* wrote that "things were certainly gloomy for the Dixie boys when young Mr. Pearce, who carries 215 pounds of meat and muscle on his ample frame, crashed through the middle of Stanford's line and right on into the swinging hoof of Wilton." Paul Lowry of the same paper alluded to the Civil War,

> The battle spirit of the men from Alabama—the same spirit that kept the Civil War going—was all that saved the Crimson Tide from defeat at the hands of Stanford in the twelfth annual New Year's Day classic. A flashing figure in a red jersey who catapulted through the Stanford line in the last minute of a hectic game gave Alabama its lone touchdown. Johnston shot through a hole over his right guard so fast that he tripped and rolled over the turf for ten yards from the force of his own momentum.

Zipp Newman of the Birmingham News wrote: "Alabama thy name is courage—unyielding valor in all its splendor! Flow on Crimson thou hast brought honors aplenty to Dixieland in twice sweeping the Pacific Coast off its feet with two comebacks that will ever live in gridiron history."

* * *

Headed by the Million Dollar University Band, the entire student body, and most of Tuscaloosa, the team was welcomed home at the railroad depot. Tuscaloosa and the university pretty much declared a holiday (as all stores in town were closed and classes at Alabama were suspended) so that Wallace Wade and his team could be honored. Merchants decorated their window displays with pictures and other items related to the team. As in 1926, American, state, and Confederate flags could be seen all around town. A parade ensued, speeches were given, and parties erupted around town and campus. A second national championship had been won, and Tuscaloosa, Alabama, was now sitting on top of the college football world.

* * *

Wu Winslett gained All-American status for the 1926 season. Shortly after the Rose Bowl, he took a job with Protective Life Insurance and eventually retired from that business. "That was the only job I ever had," he said after retiring in Tuscaloosa.

Winslett attended Tallapoosa High School in Dadeville, Alabama. "Dadeville was War Eagle country in 1922," Winslett recalled. "They took it for granted I was going to Auburn and didn't do much. Later, when I decided to go to Alabama, I got a nasty letter from Mike Donahue, the Auburn coach."

Alabama had recruited Winslett hard, with Hugo Friedman, the graduate manager of athletics, driving Wu around Tuscaloosa. One of the sights, according to Winslett, was the local country club, teeming with pretty girls. "I didn't see that country club again until I joined it in 1932," he remembered later in life with a chuckle.

Winslett remembered Wade as "very thorough, very tough. He didn't take any foolishness. He knew football and he planned it well. He was cool and calm under all conditions." As for his nickname, Wu, here is his account.

> Pooley Hubert started it. He called me Chink or Chinaman. He said I had slant eyes and looked like a Chinaman. One time a stage play came to Tuscaloosa, and it was named Mr. Wu. Pooley started calling me that and the papers took it up. Nobody ever calls me Hoyt now except two or three people over in Dadeville.

CHAPTER ELEVEN

1927

As the 1920s roared on, it seemed a good time to be not only an Alabama football fan but also an American. Optimism reigned. Charles Lindbergh became a hero as the first man to fly solo across the Atlantic in his airplane, The Spirit of St. Louis. The 3,600-mile flight began on Long Island, New York, on May 20, 1927 and ended 33 hours later in Paris. Lucky Lindy became a symbol of American daring and creativity. The economy seemed to be performing well. Herbert Hoover, about to become President, said in 1928, "Our American experiment in human welfare has yielded a degree of well being unparalleled in all the world. It has come nearer to the abolition of poverty, to the abolition of fear of want than humanity has ever reached before." Sadly, the Great Depression was around the corner.

In the world of college football, attendance was booming. Over ten million people were attending games on an annual basis by the late 1920s. Colleges themselves were experiencing big increases in enrollments due to the return of veterans from World War I and also because the prosperity of the 1920s made it possible for more young people to attend college. The job market beckoned college-educated workers, too.

On campus in Tuscaloosa, the success of Wallace Wade's football teams raised the spirits of students, faculty, alumni, fans, and most everyone connected to the University of Alabama. President Denny, acting in large part due to the national attention the team had garnered, placed advertisements in Northeast newspapers, touting his university, emphasizing the warm weather and reasonable tuition fees. Northern students started enrolling at Alabama in large numbers, many of them Jewish. Don Noble, an Alabama English professor, wrote about this increase in interest:

> The administration decided to capitalize on this fame [Rose Bowl teams] and advertised the school in the metropolitan New York City newspapers. The university could boast of the championship football team, low out-of-state tuition rates, mild winters, and no "quotas," and it was quotas that were keeping many Jewish students in the

Northeast out of some of the more prestigious schools. Jewish students came, four hundred in 1926 and eight hundred in 1927.

Noble wrote the preceding words in his introduction to *Mud on the Stars*, William Bradford Huie's account of his life and others at the university in the late 1920s and 1930s. Huie, in his book, also wrote about the increased interest in Alabama that the football team initiated.

> But in that year [1925] the university discovered the publicity magic of Rose Bowl football teams and straightaway resolved to become a great national and cosmopolitan factory of learning. With low tuitions and nominal out-of-state fees; with sunshine and beautiful, drawling women; and with living costs, which looked like Southern hospitality to metropolitan New Yorkers, the university issued invitations to all and sundry to come and drink at its Pierian springs. And the modern Children of Israel, chafing under "restrictions" and "quotas" at the Eastern colleges, accepted with all the enthusiasm with which Joshua's Band blew the trumpets and took Jericho.

This influx of strange newcomers, for sure, made for some getting-used-to moments. Huie described one incident in his book:

> I despised the New Yorkers as a group. Not because they were Jews, but because I thought they were a garish, indecorous lot of magpies. During my first week at the university, when everything was strange for me, I went one night with a group of freshmen to "listen to the kikes." We were like little boys going to the zoo. We were approaching a great curiosity for the first time. We walked a mile to enjoy the sensation of sitting outside the dormitory known as "New Jerusalem" and doing nothing else but listening to the noises which came from that building.
>
> "They don't sound like folks," remarked one freshman as rural as I. "They sound just like a bunch of guinea hens who've seen a chicken snake."

A headline in the *Alabama Alumni News* in 1927 proclaimed, "University Enrollment Still Breaking Records." From 1926 to 1927, enrollment increased from 2,205 to over 2,750. There is no question that football played a huge role in this.

Hugh Bradley returned to campus and accepted a job in the extension department, after having spent three years at Oxford as a Rhodes Scholar. Bradley had graduated from Alabama in 1923 as a Phi Beta Kappa. Another joyous occasion was a quadruple wedding, with three of the grooms and two of the brides being Alabama graduates. The newlyweds, such as Otis and Mary Evans, had met in college.

Not all news was good in 1927; Dr. Eugene Smith died. Smith was a beloved figure on campus. He had graduated from Alabama in 1862 and served as an instructor of tactics at the university until April 1865, when Union troops had burned the campus. Returning in 1871 as professor of geology, he remained in that capacity until 1913, when he became professor emeritus. He also served as an Alabama state geologist for many years.

While football at Alabama was fueling much growth on campus, it was a different story at Auburn. The football team would finish at 0-7-2 in 1927, and a combined 13 wins with 29 losses and three ties from 1925 to 1929. President Spright Dowell of Auburn had de-emphasized football during his tenure, while Denny did everything possible to build the athletic program at Alabama. Prior to the 1927 season, Auburn quarterback Frank Tuxworth was caught sneaking into a women's dorm. Dowell was very distraught, calling the action a "most unwholesome fraternization between the sexes."

* * *

Alabama opened the 1927 season by beating Millsaps and Southwestern Presbyterian. On October 8 in Birmingham, LSU held the Tide to a scoreless tie in a driving rain. On October 15, Wade took his men to Atlanta to face Georgia Tech. It had been November 15 of 1924 since Alabama had lost a game, a 24-game unbeaten streak. But on this day, before a huge crowd of 25,000, the streak came to an end. Tech went ahead 7 to 0 in the second quarter, and the score remained that way until the last two minutes of the game, when Stumpy Thompson scored again for the home team.

In a win over Mississippi A&M, E.W. Yerby, the editor of the *Greensboro Watchman*, attended and reported on the game. Not all of his attention was on the game, as he wrote,

> There was a big, fat, sandy-haired, blue-eyed man who sat immediately in front of us on the grand stand who took the game so seriously that great beads of sweat would break out on his face and neck when Alabama looked as if she would lose the game. He was not happy at all—and when we rose up and cheered an especially fine play by a Mississippi boy, that serious, earnest, troubled gentleman turned around and looked us over with a strong stare as much as to say, "If you ain't for the home team, what business have you here?"

Georgia defeated Alabama in newly dedicated Legion Field in Birmingham in late November before 25,000 people. 1927 ended with a 5-4-1 record, the worst record in Wade's eight-year tenure in Tuscaloosa.

* * *

An idea by Champ Pickens led to an all-star game between the Southern Conference seniors and the Pacific Coast seniors. The game was held in late December in Los Angeles. Wallace Wade, Dan McGugin, and William Alexander of Georgia Tech were chosen to coach the Southern squad. Fred Pickhard, James Bowdoin, and Tolbert "Red" Brown represented Alabama in the starting lineup. The Southern team won 8 to 0, in yet another game that proved football in the south could compete with anyone anywhere.

* * *

One of Wade's players signed a pro contract after the season, but it was in baseball. Emile Barnes, out of Grove Hill, Alabama, signed with the Birmingham Barons. Barnes was a good football player during his days at the Capstone, but he was better at baseball. Wade coached baseball at Alabama from 1924 to 1927, winning a conference championship in 1924 with a record of 17 wins and six losses, including two wins against future football rival North Carolina. Wade's baseball record was 21 and 6 in 1925, with one of the losses to the major league team Cleveland Indians. In the four years Wade coached baseball at Alabama, his record was 61 wins and 32 losses with two ties. Wallace Wade could also coach baseball, and this game remained dear to his heart for the remainder of his life, second only to his beloved football.

* * *

Over 1,000 people attended a season-ending banquet for the football team in Birmingham, which was held at the Municipal Auditorium. Earle Smith of Haleyville, Alabama, was selected as captain for 1928, and Dumpy Hagler from Blue Springs, Alabama, was chosen as alternate captain. Wade was asked after his speech something to the effect of "What's wrong with Alabama," considering the record of 1927. True to form, Coach Wade answered his questioner with few words but very directly, replying, "Nothing's the matter with Alabama. If you think there is, just watch us."

CHAPTER TWELVE

1928 AND 1929

It was a busy offseason between the end of 1927 and the start of football in 1928. Wade was not a bit happy to have finished 5-4-1 in 1927, and he put in long hours with his team on the field and by himself in his office. Along with preparing for the upcoming season, Wade held three very successful and well-attended coaching schools, or what are today commonly called clinics. One of these was in Lakeland, Florida.

During the summer of 1928, ex-Alabama baseball players continued to star in the major leagues. Emile Barnes had just finished his football career at Alabama in 1927 and had spent 1928 in the American League, being touted as one of the fastest outfielders around. He flirted with a .400 batting average for part of the season. Andy Cohen played second base for the New York Giants, filling the vacancy created by the trade of the great Rogers Hornsby to Boston.

Denny, in his annual report of the university, talked of how money made by the football team would be put to use, writing that

> the net proceeds of the two California trips made by our football teams are being invested in the first unit of an athletic stadium. This unit will seat twelve thousand people. Obviously, this valuable addition to the resources of the university, made without soliciting a single dollar from the alumni and friends of the university, puts us under many obligations to the athletic authorities, to whom we express our gratitude and appreciation.

The Rose Bowl teams of 1926 and 1927 enabled Alabama to have the funds to build Denny Stadium, what is now Bryant-Denny Stadium.

Wallace Wade was also busy as director of athletics. In the 1928 freshman student handbook, Wade stressed the importance of physical activity in a college student's life:

> For those who care to devote considerable time to athletics and wish to benefit by the training and experience of playing in intercollegiate games, freshman teams are organized in football, baseball, basketball,

track, tennis, and golf. The athletic department furnishes equipment for players on these teams and competent coaches are in charge. For others, intramural contests in football, baseball, basketball, and track are organized.

All students are urged to engage in some form of athletics, for it is a well recognized fact that physical training is essential to a well balanced college course. Every freshman should remember that athletes are made, not born. If you are willing to go by the training rules and have any stick-ability in your makeup, there is no reason why you cannot play in any of the sports. The athletic field, dressing rooms, and other equipment are open to any student. The coaches will be glad to advise anyone in regard to the best physical work for that individual.

Wade also instituted a four-year course in physical education at Alabama, one of the first southern universities to do so. This course enabled students to prepare for work as an athletic coach or director or as a teacher of physical education. Wade also gave guidance to a former Alabama student, J. Graham Bickley, in writing a book called *A Handbook on Athletics*. The book covered football, baseball, basketball, and track and was mainly designed to assist high school coaches and players.

* * *

Alabama rebounded somewhat from 1927 and finished 6 and 3 in 1928. The Tennessee Volunteers came to Tuscaloosa and beat the Tide 15 to 13 on Homecoming Day. Monk Campbell ripped off a 30-yard run to the Volunteer 12 as time expired.

In November, Alabama took a long road trip to play Wisconsin in Madison, where they lost 15 to 0. Wisconsin, under Glenn Thistlethwaite, would only lose one game in 1928, to Minnesota.

On December 8 in Birmingham, Wade defeated his good friend and former assistant at Alabama, Russ Cohen. Cohen was in his first year as coach at LSU, where he finished 6-2-1.

* * *

Jess Neely, who had played for Wade at Vanderbilt, replaced Cohen on Alabama's staff. Neely would stay on the Tide staff through 1930, when he became head coach at Clemson. From 1931 through 1939 at Clemson, Neely won 43 games with 35 losses and seven ties. He was 0 and 3 against his old mentor, Wade, when his Clemson teams played Wade's powerhouse Duke teams. After going 9 and 1 in 1939 and beating Boston College in the Cotton

Bowl, Neely was hired at Rice. Boston College was coached by Frank Leahy, the future coaching great at Notre Dame. Neely's replacement at Clemson was Frank Howard, who played for Wade at Alabama. Howard coached at Clemson from 1940 to 1969, so two of Wade's former players ran the Clemson program for 39 consecutive years.

Neely guided Rice to six bowl games while compiling a 144-124-10 record over 27 seasons. After retiring at Rice, he returned to Vanderbilt, where he was athletic director until 1970. He was inducted into the College Football Hall of Fame in 1971 and died in 1985 at the age of 83.

In many respects, Neely was like Wade, at least in his directness and his ability to win football games. When a writer ran up to him excitedly after Rice beat Texas in 1946 and asked, "What made the difference out there today, Coach?" Neely calmly replied, "Five points." The score was 18 to 13. In 1947 Rice beat Tennessee 8 to 0 in the Orange Bowl. A reporter asked him why he had played so conservatively. "If you had wanted a circus, you could have gone to one. We came here to win a football game."

* * *

There was good news on the Alabama campus in late 1928 when President George Denny announced that he would remain as university president, turning down a job offer to resume his old position as president of Washington and Lee. Denny was so instrumental in the building of athletics at Alabama that Bryant-Denny Stadium bears his name. Faculty and students met the news with joy at retaining their beloved leader.

Alabama defeated Auburn on New Year's Day 1929, 6 to 0. But to the chagrin of most football fans in Alabama, it was not Wallace Wade's eleven against the Tigers but an alumni game. Fans of both schools had hopes that the game would be an overture for the resumption of the football rivalry, but the two teams would not meet on the gridiron until 1948. A local editor called for the schools to come together:

> Clearly, the people of the state deserve the congenial intercourse in every line of activity by these two leading institutions of higher learning. Would it not be decidedly to the advantage of both schools and to the genuine pleasure of the state's public for Auburn and Alabama to meet on the athletic field in the friendly rivalry of sports?

Many former players participated in the game, played in the Cramton Bowl in Montgomery. Herschel Caldwell, who in 1929 was coaching the Sidney Lanier High School team, played well. Pooley Hubert played, as did Alabama's first All-America, William "Bully" Van de Graaf. Jimmy Johnston, who had scored the only touchdown for Alabama in the 1927 Rose Bowl, scored the only touchdown against Auburn.

O.C. Cottle, an Alabama graduate of 1924, penned *The Battle of Cramton Bowl*. A few stanzas follow:

> And Bully's thrust and Hubert's might,
> And Johnston's final plunge
> Took rising Tide o'er Tiger goal
> In one great general lunge.
>
> The Tigers rose to dazzling heights
> Like Auburn's men of old,
> The spirit of old Pasadena
> Couldn't stop their passes bold.
>
> The Tide was tired and on retreat
> When the final drums did beat
> And stopped the march of an Auburn team
> That never knew defeat.
>
> The mighty crowd that saw the fray
> In silence left the stands,
> No partisan shout did rend the air,
> Old foes had shaken hands.

* * *

On September 28, 1929, Denny Stadium first opened its doors. On that day Alabama beat Mississippi College 55 to 0. It was officially dedicated in front of a sell-out crowd of over 12,000 the following Saturday, October 5, in a win over Mississippi. Governor of Alabama Bibb Graves was on hand for the festivities, as was the governor of Mississippi, Theo Bilbo. The man who first brought football to Tuscaloosa, William Little, was also there. At this time, 1929, Denny Stadium consisted of only a large grand stand on the west side of the field running parallel to what is now Wallace Wade Avenue. The grand stand was 45 rows high and covered the length of the field from goal line to goal line. The new Denny Stadium was modeled after the Yale Bowl.

Alabama had played its home games on the quad up to 1914, and then played at Denny Field behind Little Hall two blocks east of what is now Bryant-Denny Stadium. The Tide compiled a 43-2 record at Denny Field from 1915 to 1928. The only losses were to Florida in 1921 and to Tennessee in 1928; the Tennessee loss was Wallace Wade's only loss on Denny Field from

1923 to 1928. The monies earned from the 1926 and 1927 Rose Bowls were used to pay for the construction of Denny Stadium. The stadium cost approximately $150,000.

A reporter who attended the dedication game wrote that

> the press box was full of newspaper people, and both WAPI and WBRC from Birmingham conducted broadcasting of the dedication exercises and the game itself. A separate stairway leads to the newspaper men's quarters, which are enclosed in glass that can be raised in warm weather. Four telegraph wires are permanently installed in the box, and a telephone system between the box and the playing field also is in use. The stadium seats 12,171. A complete system of underground tile is laid under the turtleback field, making a comparatively dry field even in the event of hard rains. After the game came a concert on the Denny Chimes and at 7 there was the annual smoker extended visiting "A" club men in the gymnasium, followed by the "A" club dance. Classes were not dismissed, and college work went on as usual, giving any visitors who desired to see the university machinery in action an opportunity to do so.

Denny, in part, expressed his thanks in a speech, saying,

> Eighteen years ago, in my first public utterance in Alabama, I expressed the hope that I might become a real part of the student life of the university, all the way from the scholarly enthusiasm of the classroom to the victorious shoutings of the athletic field. Personally, I should prefer to give to this great structure a more appropriate name. Had it been left to me, I should have named it in honor of our alumni who fell overseas, or in honor of the great coach and the great athletes whose skill and prowess made possible its erection. On behalf of the University of Alabama, I accept this great gift of the Athletic Association.

Ironically, on the same day, October 5, 1929, that Denny Stadium was dedicated, Duke University played its first football game in their new home, then called Duke Stadium. Duke Stadium now is called Wallace Wade Stadium. So on the same day, a stadium that Wade's teams paid for, Denny Stadium, and a stadium that was to be named for Wade, were opened.

* * *

As the 1929 season continued, Wade remained true to his nickname as the "Bear." Yes, Wallace Wade was Alabama's first bear, earning this name from players for his tough practices, unbending, rigid discipline, and high expectations of his teams. During practice, Wade would run a play over until it was done with perfect execution, no matter how long it took. He stressed simplicity of attack, but done with exacting precision.

Off the field, Wade was demanding as well, expecting his players to perform in the classroom and elsewhere, and reminding them constantly that they were representatives of the University of Alabama. Fred Sington, who became a great All-America player in 1930, said that the team referred to Wade as the Bear:

> Not to his face, though. He was rough and tough, and that's why we called him Bear. He had a big Chrysler and he used to cruise up and down University Boulevard. If I saw him coming, and there were any coeds around, I would cross the street. He didn't like to see his players with girls.

John Henry Suther, who played for Wade from 1927 to 1930 and was later sheriff of Tuscaloosa County, recalled an incident related to girls. Coach Henry Crisp caught Troy Barker holding hands with a girl on the way to class one day. At practice that afternoon, no doubt acknowledging Wade's stance, and perhaps with Wade's full consent, Crisp took hold of Barker's hand and walked with him hand in hand around the field, much to the delight of the other players.

Despite the iron hand with which Wade ruled, his players had nothing but respect for him. Sington recalled,

> Oh, we respected him greatly. We had a reunion observing 25 years since he had been back to Alabama. A lot of his old players were there and were smoking. When he walked in the room, they all threw down their cigarettes and stomped them out. They didn't want him to see them smoking.

A former Duke player under Wade related a similar incident in Durham, North Carolina, years after Wade was retired from coaching. This player was at a gas station, and upon seeing Coach Wade drive up, his immediate instinct was to get rid of his cigarette as quickly as he could.

Another event that Sington remembered relates that although Wade once coached baseball at Alabama, football was his passion. Sington had just thrown a no-hitter against Mississippi State.

> After the game, the old man called me in. I thought I had done pretty good and he wanted to congratulate me. But he said, "Son, I want you to know football is first," said Sington. Sington also recalled, "In

the spring of '28, we had just gone through spring training for six weeks, six days a week. At the end we were all relieved it was over. But he gathered us around and said we hadn't done too good and he thought we ought to practice another two weeks. He said, "Let's vote on it." It was the only election I've ever seen that was won one to nothing. We practiced another two weeks.

Hoyt Winslett once remembered that Wade had used some unusual psychology on him shortly before he became an All-American player at Alabama. Calling Winslett aside one day during a practice, Wade said, "Hoyt, I believe if you want to make a letter at Alabama you'd better go out for track."

A biting wit could also be unleashed by Wade. Once during a game, a defensive back was having a hard time covering receivers. Coming over to Wade on the sideline, he said, "Coach, they're sending two receivers my way every time. How do I know which one to cover?" Wade looked at him with an icy stare and told him, "Why, cover the one who they're going to throw the damn ball to." Frank Howard recalled during a game once, that Wade used a little sarcasm on him.

Coach Wade was a sarcastic old devil. I was supposed to go out for a pass on this one play, but I didn't get there. They threw the ball right where I was supposed to be. Coach Wade hollered, "Howard, where were you on that play?" "Coach," I tried to explain, "I didn't get out because the tackle held me in." He said, "Well, I'll be doggoned. Next time, ask the tackle to please not hold you."

Wade earned his reputation as a tough taskmaster who was unwilling to compromise his convictions. Later, in his retirement, he said that he pretty much ignored talk about how tough he was.

I don't pay much attention to that talk. The boys like to say I was an old (bleep) that worked them too hard. They do that to make their lady friends think they had it tough and really went through a lot of hardships. A lot of what they say about me is true, but that's the way it is in life. People want other people to think they've been through hard times. I was in the Army, before I ever started coaching, in World War I. I realize you must have discipline. You can't accomplish a thing unless you face up to what you're undertaking. You have to control yourself to the extent that you're willing to go through with it. I don't question that I was tough as a coach, but I was doing it for the good of my players.

Another incident clearly shows how tough Wade could be. In the middle of one game, a player told Wade he felt too sick to continue playing. "Sick, sick!" replied Wade. "Boy, get sick on Christmas Day, get sick on the Fourth of July, get sick any time, but don't you dare get sick in the middle of a football game."

* * *

After opening 1929 3 and 0, Alabama went to Knoxville and was beaten 6 to 0. Another key loss was to Vanderbilt and Dan McGugin. Alabama went on the road to beat Georgia Tech but dropped their last game of the season to Georgia in Birmingham, to finish the season 6 and 3.

The match-up with Tennessee had started in 1928, and the rivalry between Wade and General Robert Neyland would continue through 1950, when Wade retired from coaching. From 1926, Neyland's first year at Tennessee, to October 14, 1933, Neyland won 63 games with only three losses. Two of the losses came to Wade, one while Wade was at Alabama and one when Wade was at Duke. The loss to Alabama in 1930 stopped a 33-game unbeaten streak for the Volunteers. The loss to Duke, under Wade in 1933, stopped a 28-game unbeaten streak for Tennessee. On the other hand, Neyland certainly had big victories against Wade too. In 1931, Wade's first year at Duke, the Volunteers beat Duke 25 to 2 which, along with a loss to Syracuse in 1923, 23 to 0, were the two biggest defeats in Wade's career, in terms of point differential.

Robert Neyland was simply a great coach. In 21 seasons spread over 26 years, taking time out for the army in 1935 and 1941 to 1945, his record was 173 victories, 31 defeats, and 12 ties. Neyland Stadium in Knoxville now bears his name. Neyland and Wade both preached the importance of a sound kicking game and a containing defense while employing a fairly basic offense with a few plays, but those few plays were run with uncanny accuracy, timing, and precision. Their military background no doubt contributed to this football philosophy, with Neyland rising to general and Wade to lieutenant colonel in their soldering careers.

Neyland was quite the stud athlete at Army, starring on the football team, compiling a 35-5 record as a pitcher for the baseball team, and winning the heavyweight boxing championship three years in a row. After serving in World War I, he served as an aide to Douglas MacArthur, then superintendent at West Point. He became head coach at Tennessee in 1926. Neyland was hired to a large degree to beat Vanderbilt, who Tennessee had not beaten since 1916. The Vols beat Vanderbilt in 1928 and then beat them on a regular basis thereafter.

By 1938, Neyland was one of the best-known coaches in all of football. He and Herman Hickman attended the Pittsburgh at Duke game in Durham for scouting purposes and to share a few moments with his coaching rival and good friend, Wallace Wade. After the game, Neyland and Hickman set out on foot to a local restaurant. They were offered a ride and accepted. Neyland said, "This is Herman Hickman and I'm General Neyland." "That's fine," said the driver, not for a minute believing he had just picked up the famous football coach. "This is General Robert E. Lee and I'm Jesus Christ," he replied.

During World War II, Neyland won a Distinguished Service Medal among other honors for his service in the China-India-Burma theater. Neyland always maintained that a football coach should run his team much like a group of army men. Wade believed this also, many times saying that "football is a lot like war." Both Wade and Neyland were chosen in 1942, before going overseas for service in World War II, to coach army teams against professional teams in a series of exhibition games. As another testament to their coaching greatness, they both defeated teams from the pro ranks while serving this part of their duty, with both chafing to be called into actual combat, which they eventually were. Neyland's favorite quotation was:

> Yesterday is already a dream and tomorrow is only a vision, but today, well-lived, makes every yesterday a dream of happiness and every tomorrow a vision of hope. Look well, therefore, to this day. Such is the salutation of the dawn.

Neyland would send many former players into impressive coaching careers, such as Bobby Dodd at Georgia Tech, where the slogan "In Dodd We Trust" became well known; Dodd also coached against Wade while Wade was at Duke.

After Wade left for Duke, the rivalry picked up there between Neyland and him. At Alabama, under the leadership of Frank Thomas, the Volunteers and Crimson Tide game developed into perhaps the south's most bitter rivalry, with both schools competing for national honors on a regular basis.

As Alabama grew as a university and as a nationally recognized power on the football field in the 1920s, countless young men and women selected Tuscaloosa to be their home for their college years. Many a young football recruit would go away to play and attend classes, with best wishes and goodbyes from family and friends. The following letter personifies this breaking away time like few can, expressed with conviction and true love by a former football player in college to his son, about to enter the same school in the 1920s.

> It seems but a year and a day since I tucked the ball under my arm and sped down the gridiron, sustained by the yells of my partisans. Life has been good to me, and every age has its gifts for the man who is willing to work for them and use them temperately.

I can still appreciate a pair of sparkling blue eyes, and I am not oblivious to the turn of a pretty shoulder; although I trust that my interest is now impersonal and merely artistic. Some fathers say to sons upon the first home leaving—"Beware of wine and women!" I do not. If your home life has not taught you the virtues of a temperate, clean life, as I hope, then no words of mine can do it, and you must learn, as too many others have, from a bitter intimacy with its antithesis. As to women, I never avoided them; I sought them out, from the time when a red-cheeked youngster I trudged to school beside a red-cheeked lassie. I have no advice to offer you on this great subject; its ethics are not taught by letter.

You will probably play cards in college, most men do—I did. The gambling instinct in man is primordial. Kept under due bounds, if not useful, it is at least comparatively harmless. I should be glad if you never gambled, but I do not ask it. I ask nothing of you in the way of a declared position on religion. I ask but this; that you will give earnest, serious consideration to the fact that we exist on this planet for a shockingly brief fraction of Eternity; that it behooves every man to diligently seek an answer to the great question—Why am I here? And then, as best he can, to live up to the ideals enjoined by his answer. And if this carries you far, and if it leads you to embrace any of the great creeds of Christendom, this will be to your mother an unspeakable joy, and perhaps not less so to me.

Last of all, while you are in college, be of it and support its every healthful activity. I ask no academic honor your natural inclination may not lead you to strive for; no physical supremacy your animal spirits may not instinctively reach out and grasp. You will, I presume, make the fraternity I made, and, I hope, the societies; you will probably then learn that your father was not always a dignified bearded man in pince-nez and frock coat, and that on his side of the barrier he cut not a few capers which, seen in the clear light of his summer, gain little grace.

Finally, if you make any of the teams, never quit. That is all the secret of success. Never quit! If you can't win the scholarship, fight it out to the end of the examination. If you can't win your race, at least finish—somewhere. If your boat can't win, at least keep pulling on your oar, even if your eyes glaze and the taste of blood comes into your throat with every heave. If you cannot make your five yards in football, keep bucking the line—never let up. Never quit! If you forget all else I have said, remember these two words, through all your life, and come success or failure, I shall proudly think of you as my own dear son. And so, from the old home life, farewell and Godspeed!

Your Affectionate Father

Years later, in 1980, at the age of 88, Wallace Wade wrote a letter to his grand-daughter, Nancy Wade, then a student at East Carolina University. Among other topics, Coach Wade advised Nancy,

> In college one should acquire mental training and discipline. Only worthwhile courses should be taken. Snap courses are no good. One should study English, mathematics, science, and such courses that will develop your mind and knowledge. I am certain you will do well, if you apply yourself.

Nancy was the daughter of Coach Wade's only son, Wallace Wade, Jr., who was born in 1918. Young Wallace is pictured with his father's teams throughout Wade's tenure, usually sitting on the front row in many team pictures. A daughter, Frances, was born in 1921.

* * *

The year 1929 also saw the release of the *Carnegie Report*. The Carnegie Foundation for the Advancement of Learning was the major agency in the reform of higher education, and many in the agency believed that football debased the university experience. From 1926 to 1929, Carnegie men visited many colleges and universities, seeking answers to athletic practices. Few colleges received a clean bill of health. Of the 130 that were visited, only 28 were found not to subsidize athletes. Subsidization involved loans, employment, tuition allowances, and athletic scholarships. Purists of the game regarded these "payments" as violation of true amateur standards. Other findings were the lack of good medical care given to athletes, in many cases athletic trainers did not possess even basic medical knowledge. The report charged that some coaches "chose deliberately to sacrifice the actual or potential welfare of a player or players to the putative exigencies of victory."

The *Carnegie Report* also claimed that the prevalence of recruiting and subsidizing in college athletics led to "shopping around" by high school athletes, a process of auctioning athletic skill to the highest bidder. The report also found that participation in sports, such as football, which required long practice hours, impaired academic performances.

As for salary, the report found that the average salary for head football coaches in universities around the country was $6,107 in 1929, while professors at the same schools had an average salary of $5,158. (Author's note: Wallace Wade was making $8,000 at Alabama.)

Not just finding fault, the *Carnegie Report* offered solutions:

> What ought to be done? The paid coach, the gate receipts, the special training tables, the costly sweaters, and extensive journeys in special Pullman cars, the recruiting from the high school, the demoralizing publicity showered on the players, the devotion of an undue proportion of time to training, the devices for putting a desirable athlete, but a weak scholar, across the hurdles of the examination—these ought to stop and the inter-college and intramural sports be brought back to a stage in which they can be enjoyed by large numbers of students and where they do not involve an expenditure of time and money wholly at variance with any ideal of honest study.

The *Carnegie Report* basically publicized practices that today are an accepted part of the game, such as athletic scholarships and aggressive recruiting. Though it failed to alter athletic policies for the most part, it was at the time the most comprehensive effort to present a complete picture of college athletics.

CHAPTER THIRTEEN

1930—Nine Games:
Alabama-247, Opponents-13

America had suffered depressions before. But none hit so hard as the one of the 1930s. Banks failed, jobs were hard to find, people lost their homes, savings accounts were wiped out, and breadlines appeared with hundreds of ragged and hungry people waiting for food.

The Great Depression certainly battered Alabama also. Many people in the state had been poor before 1930, and they were used to hard times. As one said, "Hard times don't worry me, I was broke when it first started out." People in the middle and upper classes noticed the most drastic changes.

More bad news rocked the state of Alabama when Wallace Wade announced his resignation, becoming effective after the 1930 season. Wade was leaving to become head coach at Duke in 1931. Duke University, located in Durham, North Carolina, had enticed Wade with what was in 1930 one of the highest salaries of any coach in the country: $12,500 a year plus a percentage of gate receipts.

Denny paid tribute to Wade, saying,

> Duke University is fortunate to obtain a coach of Wallace Wade's ability. It is with deep regret that I learn Coach Wade is going to leave us after the 1930 season. He has made Alabama not only a great coach but a great leader of young men.

Wade's resignation was a complete surprise to most Alabama fans, students, alumni, and football fans nationwide, especially in the south. There is no doubt that the caliber of play of Wade's teams had dropped in 1927, 1928, and 1929, when the combined record was 17-10-1. The 1929 team was 6 and 3. There was some unrest expressed by people associated with the program. For sure Coach Wade heard some of this, and there is also no doubt that it did not please him, especially after winning two national titles and having a record of 51-13-3 after the completion of the 1929 season. Wade could take criticism, and he was tremendously confident in his ability to get Alabama back in contention for national titles. But he was human also, and after tasting victory on a national scale, Alabama fans were not satisfied with 6 and 3 seasons, and they voiced their opinions.

There is no question that Coach Wade's job was never in jeopardy, as President Denny knew what kind of a coach he had, as evidenced by the offer of a new five year contract extension in 1930. Salary may have played a part, but Wade's salary of $8,000 at Alabama put him near the top of the scale. Another factor was that Wade had truly enjoyed his experience at Vanderbilt, a private institution like Duke, and Wade felt that it might be a good situation to build another program, much like he had done at Alabama.

Was there a rift between Wade and his boss, Denny? The two men respected each other, but were not the best of personal friends. Denny knew Wade could coach football like few men ever had, and Wade knew that Denny was a good leader and administrator who had built the university into a nationally respected institution. At the same time, Wade knew that football and athletics were the parts of university life that he was suited for, and he wanted pretty much to have total control of his programs. Denny enjoyed attending practices and staying right on top of things in all university matters, including athletics, which as president was his prerogative and, some would say, his job.

Later in life, Wade was asked about his relationship with Denny. He replied that "President Denny built the University of Alabama up from almost nothing and he deserves credit for that. We both had jobs to do at Alabama, and I feel the university benefited from my football teams and his leadership. It was just time for me to move on."

One important sign of respect Denny showed to Wade was that he accepted Wade's choice of successor. Wade told Denny that

> there is a young backfield coach at the University of Georgia who should become one of the greatest coaches in the country. He played football under Rockne at Notre Dame. Rockne called him one of the smartest players he ever coached. He is Frank Thomas, and I don't believe you could pick a better man.

Denny told Wade to go ahead and make the first contact with Thomas. This happened in the spring and summer of 1930, and with the certainty that Wade would honor the last year of his contract and coach through the 1930 season. Wade was a man who throughout his life tried his utmost to do what was right, and he would never have considered breaking his contract with Alabama.

Calling Thomas, Wade set up a meeting between the two of them at a track meet in Birmingham. Thomas agreed, not having any idea that Wade had resigned. He agreed because he knew Wade from his assistant coaching job at Georgia, where they had played Alabama, and he agreed because the name Wallace Wade had nationwide respect, perhaps second to none other than the great Rockne.

Meeting underneath the west stands of Legion Field as rain was pouring down, Wade got right to the point, as was his custom. "Well, I've done it, Frank," said Wade. "I've resigned to become head coach at Duke University, and I have recommended you to succeed me at Alabama." Thomas was stunned. Wade continued to tell Thomas what a good situation Alabama would be for him, but Thomas did not need much convincing.

"You'll hear from Alabama within the next few days," Wade said before departing. Sure enough, Thomas was called to meet with Denny in Birmingham on July 15. Borden Burr, an influential Alabama alumnus, and Ed Camp, an Atlanta newspaperman, also attended this meeting in which Thomas was officially offered the job.

After the contract was signed, Denny told Thomas, in his own unique way, that winning football games at Alabama was very important.

> Mr. Thomas, now that you have accepted our proposition, I will give you the benefit of my views, based on many years of observation. It is my conviction that material is 90 per cent, coaching ability 10 per cent. I desire further to say that you will be provided with the 90 per cent and that you will be held to strict accounting for delivering the remaining 10 per cent.

Upon leaving the meeting, Thomas commented to Camp, "Those were the hardest and coldest words I ever heard. Do you reckon his figures are right?"

"I think the proportion was considerably off," said Camp, "but there is no doubt the good doctor means what he said."

Frank Thomas would carry on the great tradition at Alabama started by Wallace Wade. Thomas and Wade would always remain good friends, with Thomas being most appreciative of the fact that Wade had gotten him the job. Wade was content knowing he was leaving the program in the good hands of a good man. In later years, after Thomas developed health problems that would force him to retire from coaching, Wade convinced him to seek medical care at Duke Medical Center in Durham, North Carolina where Wade was coaching. Thomas later on wrote a nice letter of support for Wade to be inducted into the College Football Hall of Fame.

* * *

Not everyone was as shocked as most seemed to be over Wade resigning. Jeff Coleman, who served Alabama admirably as athletic business manager while Wade was there, and later as director of alumni affairs, knew that Wade had been somewhat riled by the criticism of his 1927 to 1929 teams. Hoyt Winslett also said that he knew Wade was a little unhappy leading into the 1930 season.

Lawrence Perry, a well-known newspaperman of the time, wrote the following shortly after hearing about the resignation:

> When he goes he will leave a soundly organized football system at Tuscaloosa. Material has been gravitating toward Alabama for so long as to make the trend a fixed habit and Wade's successor will not be worried by lack of cannon fodder. Approximately 4,000 students are now enrolled at the institution and they hail from most of the states of the union, and part of that is because of the national acclaim the football team under Wade has garnered.

Wade also recommended that Hank Crisp succeed him as athletic director, and this was accepted also. Wade said that "Crisp is a great man for the job, the best man anywhere, and I do not think the university could have made a better choice had it searched the entire nation."

Wade hired two former players, Herschel Caldwell and Dumpy Hagler, to immediately go to Duke and serve as assistants under the coach at Duke, James DeHart. In this way, Caldwell and Hagler could start to implement the Wade system of football, and when Wade himself arrived in 1931, football matters would be much further along. To his staff at Alabama was added Paul Burnum, who had been the coach at Tuscaloosa High School, and they had developed a close friendship. The Black Bears had established themselves as a national power in the high school ranks, winning 70 games against only two losses and two ties in the years leading up to 1930. The Black Bears had defeated teams from around the country, including Senn High of Chicago; Lakeland, Florida; McKinley Tech of Washington, DC; and University City High from St. Louis. One of the players was John Henry Suther, a star player at Tuscaloosa High and at the University of Alabama. Former Wade player Al Clemens replaced Burnum at Tuscaloosa High. Wade had signed players from Burnum's teams to play for him for years and Burnum had attended Wade's football coaching schools, so they had a good relationship.

Also added to the Tide staff for 1930 was Orville Hewitt, better known as "Tiny," although Orville was anything but tiny. A local reporter described him in this way: "When Tiny was at the height of his football career his weight was around 200 pounds, but since leaving school he has gained and now is quite rotund. He is a jolly fellow and has a pleasing personality." Tiny had made several All-American teams playing at Pittsburgh before going to West Point and becoming a second lieutenant.

Wade had positioned the Alabama program to be good in football for years to come. Many of his former athletes had graduated and gone on to become high school coaches in Alabama, such as Herschel Caldwell at Sidney Lanier, Leo O'Neil at Lawrence County, Melvin Vines at Haleyville, and Al Clemens at Tuscaloosa High. This aided recruiting greatly. Wade held his coaching schools in Tuscaloosa every summer and these were well attended. His coaching schools at Alabama had been among the first in the country. He also was invited to speak at other schools as a guest lecturer on coaching football. Wade had initiated year-round training at Vanderbilt and continued this at Alabama, which kept his athletes in shape throughout the year. He was innovative in the area of football equipment, being among the first to experiment with lower cut shoes and lighter pads to add speed and quickness. His newspaper columns proved popular, and his writing on subjects including southern football, intramurals, the value of the kicking game, defensive strategies, and even baseball and basketball gave Alabama much publicity. These articles appeared in newspapers around the south and had some coverage in other parts of America.

Of course, the best players were coming to Alabama in this time due in part to the bad years that Auburn was having. Auburn had five different head coaches during Wade's eight-year tenure at Alabama. Boozer Pitts was 7-14-6 from 1923 to 1924, and 1927, Dave Morey was 10-7-1 from 1925 to 1926, George Bohler was 1-8 in 1928, John Floyd was 2-7 in 1929, and Chet Wynne was 3-7 in 1930. This amounted to a record of 23 wins with 43 losses and seven ties while Wade was going 61-13-3 during the same eight-year period at Alabama.

* * *

As the University of Alabama made plans to celebrate its 100th anniversary in 1931, Wallace Wade and the Crimson Tide football team readied for the 1930 season. Wade was absolutely determined to have a successful season, and he called his players together on the first day of practice and said, "Boys, I'm going to win the damn championship this year. Now those of you who want to be part of it, let's get going. If there is anybody here that is not 100% committed, leave now." No one left.

The backfield for 1930 equaled any in the country, with Johnny Cain, John Henry Suther, and Monk Campbell; with Fred Sington, Frank Howard, Charles Clement and Carney Laslie at tackle and guard spots, the line looked to be exceptional. For sure, this was going to be a team to be reckoned with.

Zipp Newman thought the Tide would be good, writing that, "The Crimson Tide will be a most feared opponent. A team dreaded more than the plague. And why? Because Wade will have another bone crushing line and a squad that will outfight its weight in wildcats." Wade downplayed expectations to the press, while building his team's confidence when meeting with them. "We have despaired of uncovering a triple threat, even a great passer. Given a Pooley Hubert or Bobby Dodd, I would rate Alabama's chances with Tennessee, Georgia, and Vanderbilt," said Wade before the season.

There is absolutely no question that Wade, possessed of fierce pride and determination, wanted to go out with a bang. He had built Alabama into a power, and he wanted to be sure he left the program at the top. Preseason practices took on a higher intensity than any seen in his previous years, and Wade's practices had always been characterized by hard-nosed, intense effort. But Wade drove his players even harder than before, and the results of this preparation would take the college football world in 1930 by storm.

Alabama opened the year with an easy 43 to 0 win over Howard in Tuscaloosa. In this game, Hugh Miller drop kicked a field goal from 40 yards out for three points.

* * *

In 1943, Navy Lieutenant Hugh Miller credited Coach Wade with saving his life during World War II. Miller, then 33 years old, said that the "will to win" he learned during his playing days at Alabama helped him survive a 43-day stay against the Japanese on Arundel Island in the Solomons. From Tuscaloosa, Miller served as a gunnery officer on the destroyer Strong, which was sunk in Kula Gulf on July 4, 1943. Despite serious injuries from underwater explosions, he saved the lives of two men who were trapped against the side of the sinking ship, then joined 16 other men on a life raft.

They drifted for four days and when they landed on Arundel Island, only four were still alive. "There were Japs all around," Miller recalled. "I was losing so much blood I didn't think I had a chance to get through. I ordered the other three to take the equipment we had saved and go on. They did so reluctantly." Alone and bleeding badly, Miller laid on the ground and waited for death to come.

"I was doing a lot of thinking," said Miller, "and I remembered what Coach Wade used to tell us—that if you believed you could win, nothing could stop you. I asked myself what the hell I was lying there for and began to feel better."

Soon the Japanese found his tracks on the beach, and sent out patrols looking to capture him. Miller found some dead Japanese soldiers that had earlier been killed by an American P-T boat, and stripped them of what equipment he could use. His old quarterback days at Alabama came into use one day when he was cornered by a five-man patrol. He threw a grenade right on target and killed all five. He also had gotten a bayonet and ran to the men to see if any were still alive, but none were.

Miller remembered,

> I got so I knew the jungle better than the Japs. I've hunted throughout Alabama, Mississippi, and Louisiana and know how to live in the wilds. My football training, however, saved me from sure death, but I don't know how much good it would have done me if I hadn't played under Coach Wade. I think he is the greatest coach in the game.

Miller continued to elude capture on the island until August 16, when he was rescued.

Earlier in 1943, before the Miller incident, Lieutenant Colonel Wallace Wade, then commanding officer of the 272nd Field Artillery Battalion, was recuperating from a broken leg suffered in training at Camp Butner, North Carolina. A reporter in Augusta, Georgia, had asked him, while Wade was getting treatment at Oliver General Hospital, about whether football would continue to be played during World War II. Wade told him:

> I know of nothing that is a better preparation for a young man who is going into the Army than football. The greatest benefit that football gives to a young man is that it teaches him to be a competitor, to never give up, to get back up after you're knocked down. Success in both football and war depends upon morale, loyalty, and sound fundamentals.

In January of 1957, Wallace Wade was asked to appear on the television program "This Is Your Life." The show was about the life of Hugh Miller, who had requested that his old coach be there. On the program, Miller again credited Wade for his survival due mainly to Wade's "never give up" philosophy of life. A man of 65 years and one whose greatest loves in life were football and the military, Wade embraced Miller and modestly said that Miller had "a fighting spirit" in him from the time he came to Alabama to play football, and that was the reason for his surviving those horrid days eluding the Japanese in 1943 on that dense, jungle island at the height of World War II.

* * *

Alabama stayed home on Denny Field for its next game and blasted Ole Miss 64 to 0. It was during the Mississippi game that Alabama picked up the elephant as its mascot. Wade had held his regulars out to start the game, then sent in his rather large first team. One of the spectators shouted, "Here come the

Monk Campbell. Courtesy of W.S. Hoole Special Collections Library, University of Alabama.

horses," and another fan exclaimed, "Those aren't horses, they're elephants!" An Atlanta sportswriter heard this and the new elephant mascot was born.

On October 11, Alabama beat Sewanee 25 to 0 in Birmingham to run its record to 3 and 0. Powerful Tennessee came to Tuscaloosa on October 18 for what may have been Alabama's biggest test of the year. An overflow crowd of 18,000 fans jammed Denny Stadium on Homecoming Day. General Neyland's Volunteers had not lost a game since November 13 of 1926, a stretch of 33 games without a loss. Tennessee, like Alabama, 3 and 0 coming into this game, had outscored its three opponents 99 to 0. After this game against Alabama, which Tennessee lost, the Volunteers would not lose again until 1933, and it would be to Wallace Wade and his Duke Blue Devils.

Wade used a psychological ploy against Tennessee by starting his second string team, the same tactic he used in most games in 1930. Wade had a strong belief that, at the very least, his second team could hold the opponent score-less, then, when he sent in his first team, it would be demoralizing to whomever they were playing. Against Tennessee, he kept his first team off the field until late in the first quarter, when the Volunteers began a sustained drive. When they reached Alabama's 28-yard line, the regulars came in, and behind the inspired play of Fred Sington, Monk Campbell, and Charles Clement on defense, they kept Tennessee out of the end zone. From their own ten-yard line, where Tennessee had run out of downs, Alabama ran the ball straight down the field on eleven straight plays, with Johnny Cain bursting off tackle for 14 yards to end the scoring drive. In the second quarter, Alabama gained possession on the Volunteer 40-yard line. John Henry Suther, the Tuscaloosa High product, ran for nine yards and then sprinted the remaining 31 for a 12 to 0 lead at the half.

In the third quarter, with the home crowd sensing an upset win for the Tide, Alabama recovered a fumbled punt and had the ball on Tennessee's 12-yard line. Monk Campbell scored and it was 18 to 0, Alabama. The huge Homecoming Day crowd was in pandemonium. In the last quarter, Bobby Dodd of the Volunteers led them on a scoring drive to make it 18 to 6, but the Tide held on for its most important win probably since the 1926 Rose Bowl.

The next week Alabama beat Vanderbilt 12 to 7 in Birmingham. This was to be the last time Wade met his old mentor, Dan McGugin, on the field. McGugin had beat Wade in 1927 and 1929; Wade beat him in 1926 and 1930. In the 12 to 7 victory, Suther and Campbell scored touchdowns for a 12 to 0 lead, then Alabama held on behind good defensive play from Cain and Sington. Cain also put on a fine punting display.

McGugin praised the performance of Alabama and the coaching acumen of Wade after the loss. He stated that

> in her victory over Vanderbilt, Alabama showed a perfection in running offense seldom equaled in American football. Included in this are power, timing, effective blocking, deception, sharp handling of the ball, superb line play, truly great backs, and team speed. Alabama moves to the point of attack with cohesion and precision—a combination of eleven men, striking as one. Along with Alabama's great offensive and defensive ability, it uses the kicking game with brilliance and skill. Then Alabama has certainty of judgment and a certain cool, clear intelligence. If any coach feels the Alabama team is not a thinking team, plan for the game and feel the shock. Alabama has won from Tennessee and Vanderbilt without the aid of a pass, and with this weapon doubtless developed but not needed. It would be a shame to pick stars on such a team because stars are usually those who avail themselves of opportunities furnished by faithful teammates. Sington, Cain, Suther, and Campbell are among the great ones.

Blinkey Horn of the *Tennessean* newspaper, also summed up the game rather well, writing "The main facts, stripped of their trimmings, about this battle with Alabama are simply these: Vandy was beaten by a great team which played great football. The Wademen were surging forward with ferocity."

Vanderbilt was, as usual, one of the top teams in the south in 1930, posting an 8 and 2 record, with a win at Minnesota, and shutting out Auburn 27 to 0. So with the key wins over Tennessee and Vanderbilt, the Tide was 5 and 0. The seven points Vanderbilt scored would be the last points registered against Wade's defense the rest of the year. Wade stuck with his favored 6-2-2-1 alignment for most of that season: six linemen played up front, then behind them were what are today called linebackers, and then three played the defensive backfield, with one of those back deep.

November 1 found Alabama in Lexington before 22,000 fans. The Tide beat the Wildcats 19 to 0. The pass was revealed in this game as Suther caught a 44-yard touchdown pass from Jimmy Moore. Alabama served as the opponent for Florida on November 8 as the Gators dedicated their new stadium. J.B. "Ears" Whitworth kicked two points after touchdowns in this game and played well at his tackle position.

After posting a record of 22-27-2 from 1950 to 1954 as head coach at Oklahoma State, Whitworth would go on to become Alabama's head football coach at the start of the 1955 season, and his tenure did not turn out well. (That may qualify as one of the biggest understatements Alabama football fans will ever read.) Alabama went 0 and 10 in 1955, even with Bart Starr at quarterback. Whitworth had a record of 4-24-2 in his three years, and, even worse, Auburn scored 100 points to Alabama's 7 in its three victories over Whitworth's Tide.

After his 1957 team went 2-7-1 and lost to Auburn 40 to 0 in the last game, Whitworth was let go. On December 3, 1957, Alabama signed Paul "Bear" Bryant to a contract, and Alabama would start winning like they never had. Upon announcing that he was leaving Texas A&M to come to Tuscaloosa, Bryant explained his reasoning in two words: "Mama called." Well, Coach Bryant did not disappoint "Mama," as he won 232 games at Alabama from 1958 to 1982, against only 46 losses and nine ties, with six national championships and 13 Southeastern Conference titles.

The Tigers of LSU came to Montgomery to play a Tide team that was 7 and 0. It was no contest as Alabama won 33 to 0. A big dance was held in Coach Wade's honor after the game in Montgomery, at the Standard Club, where both teams attended. LSU was coached by Wade's former assistant at Alabama, Russ Cohen. Cohen would compile a record of 23-13-1 at LSU from 1928 to 1931, going 0 and 2 against Wade. Starting with Wade at Alabama in 1923, and being part of the national championship teams of 1926 and 1927, Cohen had been enthusiastically endorsed for a head coaching position by Wade. The two remained lifetime friends.

The last game of the regular season had Alabama in Birmingham against the Georgia Bulldogs. Georgia came into the game 6-1-1 with a big win earlier in the season over Yale at Yale. Georgia was coached by Harry Mehre. By the date of this game, November 27, Washington State had already been chosen to represent the West in the Rose Bowl, and the winner of the Alabama-Georgia game was the probable selection as the opponent. Two Washington State scouts sat in the stands and saw Alabama beat Georgia 13 to 0.

The game at Legion Field had not only the Rose Bowl on the line but also a Southern Conference championship and an undefeated record at stake in Alabama's case. Fans totaling 29,000 attended the game, and they saw Johnny Cain run for 118 yards and two touchdowns. J.B. Roberts, Jr., a local reporter, was at the game along with many newsmen. He wrote,

> William Wallace Wade bid a dramatic adieu to the University of Alabama as his football eleven, the men who have learned all of the football that they know from him, swept a determined and inspired Georgia team aside to gain a 13 to 0 verdict. The atmosphere around Legion Field seemed to breathe of an Alabama day, and the 29,000 gaping fans who wedged their way into every available space within the enclosure, had the feeling that the Tide was bound for glory. Just before the game began, and after Georgia had gained a distinct advantage by winning the toss and getting a stiff wind at their backs, Wallace Wade gathered his red-clad boys around him and with a quivering chin, spoke to them and asked them to give their very best. And the way Captain Clement, Freddie Sington, and the rest of Alabama's great crew slapped the departing leader on the back and shook his hand, made the issue practically certain to those who knew. Straight bucks and off tackle sweeps by Johnny Cain, Suther, and Campbell accounted for big yards. At halftime and at the end of the game, Coach Wade received the tribute of the witnessing thousands as mighty Wade, Wade, Wades resounded through Legion Field. Few men have ever been accorded the honor that was Mr. Wade's.

M.E. Nunn, also at the game, wrote,

> The South as a whole owes a debt of gratitude to Wade for bringing national recognition to this section of the country. In the departure of Coach Wade for Duke at the end of the present season, the University of Alabama has lost a great coach, a builder of character, a teacher of ideals, and a man who has commanded the respect of students, fans, and sportsmen. When the whistle sounded ending the game against

Georgia, the vast crowd rose and cheered long and loud for the man who had done so much for Alabama and southern football.

Interestingly, as Coach Wade was about to leave for Duke University, an advertisement appeared in the *Alabama Crimson-White* student newspaper. From whom? The Duke University School of Medicine was recruiting new students. Certainly, Duke was about to get one good man in Wallace Wade.

But before leaving Alabama, there was another matter to attend. The Rose Bowl invited Alabama to oppose Washington State on New Year's Day, 1931.

* * *

The Crimson Tide just totally dominated its opposition in 1930, outscoring its nine regular season opponents 247 to 13. It had beaten very good teams in Tennessee, Vanderbilt, and Georgia, that finished a combined 24-5-1. Florida was respectable at 6-3-1 and LSU was 6-4. Only one game remained from another national title and a perfect record. It was all building up to what just might have been the greatest swan song in the history of college football.

Great players were on the 1930 team. Fred Sington made the All-America teams for the year at his tackle position. Sington attended Phillips High School in Birmingham where he starred in football, baseball, basketball, and track. Ernest Tucker was his high school coach at Phillips. Sington played at Alabama at six feet, two inches tall and weighed 230 pounds, which was mammoth in his time. Not only excelling in football and baseball at Alabama, Sington won virtually every academic honor at the university, including serving as senior president of the student body and was Phi Beta Kappa.

During the win over Tennessee in 1930, Sington showed his courage and football smarts. He recalled,

> Bobby Dodd, the future Georgia Tech coach, was giving us some trouble. So we got in the huddle with Coach Wade. You didn't speak up much to Coach Wade, he ran it. But I did that day. 'Coach,' I said, if you change me from right tackle to left'—Dodd was retreating to his right and when I was right tackle he got further and further away—'I believe I can slow him down some.' Coach Wade told me to go ahead.

The next day *The Tuscaloosa News* reported that "Sington broke through the Tennessee offensive front repeatedly." Sington also recalled how the players feared Wade:

> You never went to see Coach Wade. It was like they tell you in the Navy: don't volunteer. Finally, you'd get up the courage to see the old

man, and here you'd be, 6'2" or 6'3" and 230, walking into his office with a trembling heart. You'd get up courage to speak and you'd say, 'Coach Wade, I'd like to do so and so.' He'd always say, 'How's that?!!' Most of the time, you wouldn't even repeat it.

Recalling another example of Wade's toughness after going with him to Duke, Sington said,

> I'll never forget the first practice after we went to Duke. A boy from Philadelphia held his hand up. We expected him to ask about some play he didn't understand. He said, 'Coach, I just wondered. They're having a dance Friday night before the game. Will it be all right if we go?' I nearly fell out of my chair. If we had been in a room full of gasoline and someone had struck a match, I couldn't have been more apprehensive. But Coach Wade realized he was in a new world. All he said was, 'No.'

Sington became so well known during the 1930 season that the song "Football Freddy," released that year by Rudy Vallee, celebrated his football success. In part, it went like this:

> The women folks galore,
> They know how he can score,
> Especially when the lights are low
> Football Freddy, rugged and tan.
> Football Freddy, my collegiate man
> When he huddles, he's dynamite,
> How he cuddles on a Saturday night!
> He's got style, he's got class
> Oh, how they fall for his forward pass!
> X, Y, Z! B, V, D! He doesn't miss a sign,
> Ha, cha, cha! Sis, boom, bah!
> Oh, how he runs for a sweet ma-ma!

Grantland Rice, the famed sportswriter, heaped praise on Sington. "Tackles such as Sington rarely come along." Knute Rockne called him the greatest lineman in the country. Wade always said that Sington was one of the best players he ever coached. In fact, they thought so much of each other that Sington joined Wade at Duke as an assistant coach from 1931 to 1933.

Sington also played professional baseball during the summers while at Duke. His career in baseball spanned ten years and he played for the Washington Senators and Brooklyn Dodgers. While with Chattanooga in the minor leagues, he led the Southern Association in batting with a .384 average, earning league MVP honors.

After his playing days as well as his time serving in World War II were over, Sington opened up a chain of sporting goods stores in Alabama. He also officiated Southeastern Conference football games and served as president of the University of Alabama Alumni Association twice. In this role, he played a large role in bringing Bear Bryant to Alabama in 1957. He recalled what happened:

> Alabama was playing Tulane in Mobile in 1957 and Dr. Rose [President of Alabama, Frank Rose] sent word he wanted to see me. He said he wanted me to go to Houston with him after the game. Jeff Coleman took my wife, Nancy, home so Dr. Rose, Ernest Williams, a trustee, and I could fly to Houston that night.
>
> We got a suite on the top floor of the Shamrock, and Bryant came up and we talked. Coach Bryant was concerned about two things. He asked about Hank Crisp, who was serving as athletic director at Alabama at the time. Coach Hank had recruited Bryant out of Arkansas. Bryant wanted to be sure Coach Hank would be taken care of if there was a coaching change. I admired him for that.
>
> The other thing he was concerned about was his control over the football program. He asked Dr. Rose about it, and Dr. Rose told him, "You'll run the show." As I remember, Texas A&M was having a good season and Bryant wanted to keep it quiet, but there was an agreement that night. He agreed to come back.

Helping to bring Bear Bryant back to Alabama would, by itself, ensure that Fred Sington would be remembered forever by Crimson Tide football fans, but he accomplished so much more. He loved the state of Alabama and he loved the University of Alabama, and he contributed years of service to both. He was chosen as Birmingham's Man of the Year in 1970, and worked tirelessly to bring the Hall of Fame Bowl to Birmingham. In 1991 the press box at Legion Field was named in his honor. Sington was inducted into the College Football Hall of Fame in 1955, the same year his old coach, Wallace Wade, was inducted. The state of Alabama still presents the Fred Sington Trophy to the state's top male and female athlete.

In later years, Sington said, "Everything I do, I try to do with the University of Alabama in the back of my mind, and anything I can do to bring honor to it or my city, I will." What honor he brought to the university, Birmingham, and the state of Alabama.

In an interview I had with Fred Sington, Jr., who played for Bryant at Alabama in 1958 and 1959, Sington, Jr. commented on Wade. "Coach Wade

Johnny Cain. Courtesy of Anita Caldwell.

commanded respect, I could tell that from the 50th reunion of his 1930 team. His players thought so much of him. Coach Bryant told us once that before Wade there was no tradition at Alabama, that Coach Wade had developed the foundation for all the teams that followed."

* * *

Johnny Cain, another member of the 1930 team, had prepped at Sidney Lanier High School in Montgomery under Herschel Caldwell, who had played for Wade and then followed Wade to Duke. Cain also played for Frank Thomas in 1931 and 1932. In his three years on the varsity at Alabama, the Tide was 27 and 3. He is now enshrined in the College Football Hall of Fame. In a letter promoting him for the Hall, Zipp Newman of the *Birmingham News* wrote,

> From all the great backs I have seen play since 1913, I rate Johnny Cain the greatest all around back I ever saw. He is one of the South's all-time long and accurate punters—a coffin-corner specialist. He was a fine deceptive left-handed passer. He ran with a hip-swinging

motion—terrific in a broken field. He was a fine power runner. I never saw a more deadly tackler.

Cain is listed as the punter on Alabama's All-Centennial Team, selected in 1992. Fred Sington is on that team also.

After graduating from Alabama in 1933, he coached under Frank Thomas for two years before becoming head coach at his old high school of Sidney Lanier. From 1937 to 1941 he was head coach at Southwest Louisiana, then went to Ole Miss in 1947 to be an assistant after serving in World War II. He coached at Mississippi until 1972, coaching among others, Archie Manning. While at Ole Miss, the Rebels won a national championship and six SEC titles.

Cain, who gained the nickname of "Hurry" early in his career, was well thought of by his players. Warner Alford, an offensive guard at Old Miss, said the following about Coach Cain. "Cain had an ability to relate to his players; he always made you want to do a little more than you might have thought possible. But, you ended up doing it."

* * *

Another player from the 1930 team is in the College Football Hall of Fame, but due to his coaching days more so than his playing days. Frank Howard was born in Barlow Bend, Alabama, on a large farm. Later in life, Howard was jokingly called "The Baron of Barlow Bend." He graduated from Murphy High School in Mobile, which he said was "three wagon greasings from Barlow Bend."

While playing for Wade at Alabama, Howard developed into a good player. But Howard was a character off the field and on. He remembered,

> In my senior year, I had a date lined up with this pretty little ol' girl. It was my first date with her. I was in the bathroom shaving and getting all pretty when Coach Wade walked in. He didn't like for you to go with girls. "Howard," he said, "what are you doing tonight?" "Nothing, Coach. Not a thing," I replied. "Well, I want you to come around and baby sit with my two children," Coach Wade said. "Be there at 7:30. Mrs. Wade and I are going to the picture show." So, I had to call that gal and tell her I couldn't make it. Coach paid me a whole 25 cents to baby sit. And, you know, I never did get a date with that gal again.

In 1931, Coach Wade asked Jess Neely, a former player under Wade at Vanderbilt and an assistant coach under Wade at Alabama in 1930, to consider hiring Howard at Clemson. Neely was starting his first year as head coach of football in Death Valley. Neely hired Howard as his line coach for $2,200. Howard recalled that in addition to being the line coach in football and the head track coach, I also managed the ticket sales, recruited players, and had charge of the equipment room. In my spare time, I cut the grass, lined the tennis courts, and operated the canteen while the regular man was out to lunch.

After Neely left to become head coach at Rice in 1940, Howard was nominated at a Clemson Athletic Council meeting to take Neely's place. Howard, standing in the back of the room, said, "I second the nomination." He got the job and won 165 games at Clemson from 1940 to 1969, while also serving as athletic director.

Frank Howard and Bear Bryant were lifetime friends, and genuinely enjoyed each other's company. Howard recalled one incident involving the two of them and Hayden Fry, the Iowa coach:

A bunch of us from around the country got invited every year to a coaches' golf outing. One year the event was in Arkansas where a river ran right alongside the golf course. The organizers, knowing I didn't play golf, arranged for me to go fishing down the river. Now that I liked. On my way to meet the fishing guide, I ran into Coach Fry. He said it sounded like fun and came along.

When we got to the river, we found we were going to drift the river in a canoe, not a boat. After we got under way, the guide told Coach Fry to pick a lure out of the tackle box and tie it on the end of his line. I guess Hayden figured, "the bigger the better!" He picked out a big ol' spinner lure and cast it out with all his might.

You'll never believe this, but the thing sailed a mile high, went up in a tree alongside the bank, and hooked a squirrel! The squirrel tumbled out of the tree, splashed into the river, and Coach Fry stood up in the canoe to reel him in. Between him standing and me dying of laughter, the canoe tipped over. We're lucky we didn't all drown.

Soaking wet, we managed to make it to the river bank. When we climbed up, we found ourselves on the edge of one of the fairways of the golf course. And who is coming down in the next foursome but the Bear. "Frank, what in the world happened to you?" Coach Bryant asked. "Well, Bear, I'll tell you," I answered. "Everybody's always told me that you could walk on water, so I thought I'd try it myself."

* * *

CHAPTER FOURTEEN

1931 ROSE BOWL

Washington State was coached by Orin Ercel "Babe" Hollingberry, who compiled a 93-53-14 record over 17 years at WSU. Washington State came into the Rose Bowl 9 and 0, with big wins over California, Southern Cal, and Washington. They had two linemen who struck terror into opponents. Mel Hein, a 6'3", 225 pound center, was an All-American on the 1930 team and is still considered by some to be the finest center in college football history. Hein is now a member of both the College and Pro Football Hall of Fame. Turk Edwards, a member of the 1930 team also, is listed as an offensive tackle on WSU's All-Time Team, chosen in 1995.

Wade, in speaking about the game, said, "Washington State has one of the best defenses I have ever seen. I expect Washington State has a better team than any we have beaten, but we are going to do our best to win. We've done pretty well so far, but we have been very fortunate in getting the breaks. Fine spirits, strong defense, and good blocking probably are our strongest points." Wade was never one to brag about his team, or downgrade an opponent.

Accompanying the team on their trip was Frank Thomas, at the invitation of Wade. Wade liked Thomas, and wanted to assist him in any way possible, so he figured it would be a chance for Thomas to get to know the players he would be inheriting for the 1931 season. Also on the train headed west were President Denny, Governor Bibb Graves of Alabama, and Dan McGugin, who was a guest of Wade. Coach Wade's wife, Frances, his daughter, Sis (Frances), and his son, Wallace, Jr., were also making the trip.

Graves spoke to the team:

> We have been hampered industrially by an unfair picture the world seems to have of Alabama as a state of undersized, weak people living in swamp lands full of malaria and tuberculosis. None who have seen Wade's Tide in action, or who read of the account of the game, will continue to embrace the idea.

Upholding the pride of the south was again a motivating factor for the Alabama team, just like it had been in 1926 and 1927.

On the trip to Pasadena for the 1931 Rose Bowl. Coach Wade is in the middle. Courtesy of W.S. Hoole Special Collections Library, University of Alabama.

Pooley Hubert was among 100 or so well-wishers who greeted the team during a stop in Meridian, Mississippi. The train made a special stop in Picayune, Mississippi, so that Frank Howard's mother could ride to New Orleans with her son. The team stopped in San Antonio and Tucson, Arizona, to practice and "limber up."

Wade always was known for his neat appearance, and he expected his teams to dress well, too. Zipp Newman, with the team reporting for the *Birmingham News*, sent in this report while on the trip to California: "The Crimsons not only play good football, but dress smartly. They are wearing the latest creations in two-tone sweaters, last minute styles in plus-fours, and what the collegians use for headwear."

Arriving in Pasadena on December 23 after a five-day journey, the team was met by movie star Johnny Mack Brown. WSU Coach Babe Hollingberry, upon seeing the Tide players, commented, "Gosh, they're big."

True to form, Wade had his team on the field practicing at 9:30 a.m. on Christmas Day. Newman called the practice "one of the most strenuous workouts an Alabama team has ever gone through on California soil." Wade was all business, cutting down on sightseeing and not even allowing his players to watch the Rose Bowl parade. Wade's reasoning was, "We can celebrate after we win the game." Fred Sington did recall, however, that Coach Wade did re-

Preparing for the 1931 Rose Bowl. Courtesy of the W.S. Hoole Special Collections Library, University of Alabama.

lent somewhat and announced to the team that they would go on an outing. "We did go on a little trip—out to an orange grove," Sington said. "We picked two oranges each and came back. That was his big outing."

* * *

In the locker room before the game, there is a deathly silence. Coach Wade walks around kneeling down beside some players and talking very quietly to them, giving last minute instructions and encouragement. Then Wade tells his team to gather together. All eyes fixate on their great coach as he discusses first half strategy. He pauses, and again, utter silence, so much so that the dropping of a pin would have sounded like thunder. Wade told them:

> You don't have to win this game, but you have got to fight, run hard with the ball, tackle and block harder than Washington State. We are going to fight, Alabama has a reputation for fighting, blocking, tackling, and playing clean football to uphold. Are you going to fight?

A resounding "Yes!" shook the foundations of the Rose Bowl. The question was if Washington State was ready for what was coming.

* * *

Walking with the team to the field for the Rose Bowl was an unexpected player. Bruce Bell was an Alabama student who had tried unsuccessfully to make the football team. But on the day of the game, he showed up in Pasadena at the team's hotel. Wade tells the story:

> Bruce was a chap who was out for our team, but I hardly knew him. We were standing in front of the hotel waiting to catch the bus for the stadium, when he walked up to me and said, "Coach, can you get me a ticket to the game?" Well, I knew the boy lived out in California somewhere and he had dead-beated his way out there, but I told him I couldn't possibly find him a ticket at that point, just before the game.
>
> Well that boy turned away from me and started walking. Something in the way he walked got me to thinking. I said, "Now here is a boy who has come all the way out here—he lives out here—to see his team in the Rose Bowl and he's not gonna get to watch the game." Now all that went through my mind, so I called him back.
>
> I said, "Bell, we've got some extra uniforms with us. Just go over there and get on the bus and go to the stadium with us." That tickled him to death. That was better than him getting a half-dozen tickets. So he did that and sat on the bench during the game. We never heard a thing out of him.
>
> Finally, we had put everybody on the squad in the game except him. And we had a lot of players out there. Anyway, I called Bell up and said, "Do you know how to line up in formation?" He said, "Yes, sir," so I told him to go in and not to get offsides.
>
> He went in and stayed two or three plays. In other words, the only football he was ever in was the Rose Bowl. Now, can you beat that?

* * *

A drizzling rain was falling as Alabama and Washington State started the game in front of 70,000 fans. Wade, as usual, started his second team, and right from the start, it was obvious Alabama had come to play. Early in the first quarter, Bill Bonkin of WSU was flattened receiving a punt. Late in the first quarter, with the score 0 to 0, Wade sent in his "Red Elephants," as they were now being called. The ground seemed to shake as the huge bodies of Fred Sington and company trotted on the field. After starting the game with 13 straight running plays, Wade had WSU concentrating on the run. Jimmy Moore pulled out from his end position, circled into the backfield and took a handoff from Johnny Cain. While this was going on, John "Flash" Suther ran downfield, where Moore hit him with a perfectly thrown ball at WSU's 22-yard line, and Suther scored.

Shortly afterward, Jess Eberdt intercepted a pass by WSU's star halfback Tuffy Ellingsen. After Monk Campbell plunged into the line for three yards, Alabama tried the same play that had resulted in the touchdown. Moore took the handoff from Cain again, but this time his target was end Ben Smith, who out-jumped two defenders and came down with the ball at the one-yard line of the Cougars. Campbell scored from there and it was 14 to 0. Campbell ran 43 yards for another score and it was 21 to 0 at the half.

In the third quarter "Ears" Whitworth, the future head coach of Alabama, kicked a field goal to run the score to 24 to 0. WSU was completely bottled up by the Tide defense, and future pros Mel Hein and Turk Edwards, of the Cougars, were controlled at the line of scrimmage. As the game ended, the Alabama players carried their coach, Wallace Wade, off the field. The first great era of Alabama football had ended. The Crimson Tide were again national champions.

Wade had told his team that the time to celebrate would be after a win. So after the game, he told them,

> I am proud of you for the fine fighting ability you showed me out there on the field. Tonight I want you to make me prouder still. I want you to remember that you represent a great university and a great section of the country. In breaking training, remember that you are southern gentlemen. Be true to your training. Have a good time, but stay in bounds.

* * *

Following the game, Braven Dyer of the *Los Angeles Times* wrote:

> Alabama's mighty men of muscle, combining brains with brawn, hold the unique distinction of scoring the most decisive football triumph ever recorded by an invading team at Pasadena. It was entirely fitting that this spectacular achievement should come on the first day of the year of the University of Alabama's Centennial celebration.
>
> Speed and deception. Such were the keynotes of Alabama's success. I have never seen such big men exhibit such speed in a football game. It was deception that approached perfection because of the efficiency of execution. To Wallace Wade then goes the major share of credit for the great victory, for he conceived the plays, trained the players, and

had his men in the right mental and physical condition to perform at their best.

Alabama will be welcome at the colorful Tournament of Roses classic any time the Crimson Tide can muster another great team. But it won't seem like old times with Wallace Wade gone. Wade belonged to Alabama and Alabama belonged to Wade.

Coach Hollingberry of Washington State heaped praise on Alabama, especially the play of Fred Sington. Even Turk Edwards had a hard time with Sington, who exhibited a rare combination of size and speed. Hollingberry said, "Sington is the most powerful man that I have ever seen. We did not think that a man could be so large and still so fast. He is as great as Jack Cannon of Notre Dame was last year."

Frank Thomas, about to assume the post of head coach of the Crimson Tide, was also most impressed with the effort: "Just as the score would indicate, Alabama completely dominated the game. Not in a game this season did the Wade machine click as it did here. The Washington State rush line that had been heralded as one of the greatest ever developed on the coast, met its match in the hard charging Alabama forwards."

Along with the success on the field of Wade's teams, the football teams also brought in much needed money. Denny Stadium had already been built from football money, but the 1930 team brought in net receipts of $93,298 in the regular season, with the largest sum of that being $26,047 in the Georgia game, and $51,005 from the Rose Bowl against Washington State. The total net receipts for the season were $144,303.

Wilma Ellis wrote a poem called *We Heard You, Alabama* shortly after the Rose Bowl. Several stanzas follow:

Oh, we heard you, Alabama,
Some two thousand miles away,
When you made those glorious touchdowns
In the Rose Bowl New Year's Day.

Yes, we heard you Alabama,
Hear the cheers, the music gay,
And we shrieked with joy incarnate
As you made each telling play.

Crimson Tide of Alabama,
Crowned kings of football fame,
We salute you dauntless winners
Of the year's most glorious game.

* * *

Wallace Wade was soon on his way to Duke University, while Frank Thomas took over at Alabama. Before departing, Wade told the student body that

> it is impossible for me to feel other than that I am going away and leaving a big part of myself, inasmuch as I have put into this university the best eight years of my life. It has been a great privilege to me to associate for a period with the fine young people of this university. I am certain that a finer lot of people cannot be found anywhere. I have especially enjoyed the contacts which I have had with the Alabama athletes. I cannot feel that I am leaving them, for their memories will stay with me. There is only one worthwhile record that a coach has. This is the privilege of intimate association with the finest class of people in America. I should like to acknowledge the help that the cooperative spirit of the faculty has been toward athletics. During my stay here the attitude of the Alabama faculty toward athletics had been as near ideal as it is possible for it to be. Few people have ever had the good fortune to work with as loyal a group of associates as I have had among the coaches at Alabama. I cannot express the appreciation that I owe to Crisp, Cohen, Neely, Propst, Haygood, Hewitt, Burnum, and Coleman. I congratulate Alabama on the prospect that is in view for fine leadership by Coaches Crisp and Thomas. When I wish Alabama well I am only expressing a selfish desire, for I like to feel that I am a small part of Alabama.

* * *

Frank Thomas was just the man to take over for Wallace Wade. As Allen Barra, author of *The Last Coach: A Life of Paul "Bear" Bryant* told me, "Wallace Wade built the Alabama football program, Frank Thomas built on the success of Wade, and Bear Bryant resuscitated the program, brought it back to life, and carried it to its greatest success."

Thomas played for Knute Rockne at Notre Dame from 1920 to 1922 and roomed with George Gipp, the Fighting Irish star who was immortalized when Rockne asked his team once to "Win one for the Gipper," and this was put into the movie *Knute Rockne, All-American*. Rockne had once predicted that Thomas would achieve coaching greatness. "It's amazing the amount of football sense that Thomas has. He can't help becoming a great coach some day." He definitely proved Rockne correct.

Wallace Wade hands the ball off to Frank Thomas.
Courtesy of Duke Sports Information Department.

Thomas won 34 games, lost 11, and tied two as a head coach at Chattanooga and was coaching at Georgia as an assistant when Wade called him. In 1931, his first season in Tuscaloosa, the Tide went 9 and 1, losing only to Tennessee. But Thomas gained the respect of General Neyland and beat Neyland in 1933. Neyland once said this about Thomas, "That little bastard is the smartest damn coach I ever coached against." For his coaching career at Alabama, which spanned 1931 to 1946, he earned a record of 115-24-7 and won two national titles and four SEC titles. His winning percentage is third-best all-time at Alabama, with Bryant first and Wade second.

In 1945, Alabama, still coached by Thomas, played Duke in the Sugar Bowl, losing in an exciting game 29 to 26. The two close friends, Thomas and Wade, did not coach against each other however, as Wade was then serving in World War II and his assistant Eddie Cameron was coaching the Blue Devils in Wade's absence.

By 1946, a heart condition and high blood pressure greatly affected Thomas' health. He got so sick he had to conduct some practices from a specially constructed trailer. He visited Duke Hospital to consult with medical specialists at

Wade's urging as Wade was at Duke. Thomas retired after the 1946 season at the age of 48. He died in Druid City Hospital in Tuscaloosa in 1954.

* * *

Bear Bryant arrived on campus at Alabama in the fall of 1931. Bryant had fallen in love with the program of Wallace Wade's, even leaving the game in Dallas on New Year's Day 1931 to listen to Alabama beat Washington State. As he said, "I was in Dallas at an all-star game an Arkansas coach was in, but I caught a street car back to the hotel so I could listen to the Rose Bowl on the radio. The Arkansas people never knew that."

At this time, Alabama football had quite a few players from Arkansas. Many had been sent to Tuscaloosa by Jimmy Harlen, a Pine Bluff businessman who developed a strong affection for Alabama. But it is doubtful if Bryant would have decided to attend Alabama had it not been for the winning tradition established by Wallace Wade. Listening to the 1926 Rose Bowl involving Alabama's dramatic win over Washington just captivated the twelve-year-old Bryant, from Moro Bottom, Arkansas.

Wade's departure for Duke disappointed Bryant, but he arrived through the recruiting of Hank Crisp. Bryant, for the rest of his life, admired Coach Crisp. He said,

> I practiced with the team as a redshirt freshman. Johnny Cain and I roomed together. We stayed in the gym. All the hell-raisers stayed in the dorm, but I always stayed in the gym. We all had jobs and Cain had a hard one. He had to get me to class every day at Tuscaloosa High. Basically, I was a lazy fat-butt who could barely read and write. [Bryant had enrolled at Tuscaloosa High School in math and other classes to complete requirements for admission to Alabama.] I was in awe of those great players. I was scared, and embarrassed, and broke. Ears Whitworth helped me a lot, but the guy who really saved me was John Tucker. He was older and more experienced than me. When he talked, I listened.

Bryant and Wade became close after Bryant entered the coaching ranks. They called each other quite regularly while Wade was retired and living in Durham, North Carolina, and Bryant was coaching at Alabama from 1958 to 1982. "I expect I knew Coach Wade better than his players ever did because they were all so scared of him," Bryant said. "The first time I really got to talk to him much was when I was at North Carolina Pre-Flight [in the Navy], and he was at Duke." (Bryant coached the Pre-Flight team in 1944 to a 13 to 6 win over Duke, but the head coach of Duke was Eddie Cameron; although Bryant ev-

**Bear Bryant and Wallace Wade. Courtesy of Duke
Sports Information Department.**

idently had a chance to talk to Wade. Bryant obviously turned the program at
the N.C. Pre-Flight around because the previous year, 1943, Duke clobbered
Pre-Flight 42 to 0, again under Cameron.) Bryant added:

> Then, later, when I was coaching at Kentucky in 1949, Coach Wade
> and I were on a train ride together to San Francisco. We were going
> to a convention and there were two trains. We got snowbound a few
> miles from Grand Island, Nebraska, and were stuck for three days.
> One train was about two miles ahead of us and it was without food
> and drink. But our train was loaded. We had the best eating and car-
> rying-on you can imagine.

Wade made special visits back to Alabama after he retired from coaching. He came to see games, be inducted into the Alabama Sports Hall of Fame, and visit Bryant. During one practice, a highway patrolman had been sent by Bryant to pick up Wade and bring him to the field. The car brought Wade close to where Bryant was conducting practice, and Bryant immediately signaled for his players to gather around the elderly man. "Boys, this man here is the reason you and I are at the University of Alabama."

On another occasion, September 9, 1982, at Legion Field, Duke was playing Alabama. Wade had long been retired, but was invited to the game. Bryant was on the field about fifteen minutes before the kickoff, when he was told Wade was in the press box. Frank Dascenzo, long-time sports writer for the *Durham Herald-Sun*, described what happened:

> Bryant, guarded by two Alabama state troopers, came around the Legion Field fences to the press box elevator. When the doors opened behind press row, Bryant stood and greeted Wade. Understand now, this is highly unusual for a head coach to be in the press box moments before his team is to begin a game. In normal situations, Bryant would have been in the Alabama locker room delivering last minute instructions. Bryant wore his black and white checkered houndstooth hat, a sky blue short sleeve shirt and red necktie. Wade had his white cowboy hat on, no tie, but wore a white long sleeve shirt, buttoned at the neck. It was 92 degrees at kickoff. And no wind. The two Southern gentlemen shook hands and began conversing. By this time, the famed Alabama Million Dollar Band had taken the field, and the two teams, through with warm-ups, headed back to their dressing rooms.
>
> When the two men shook hands, a tremor shook the press box. One night in Birmingham the Bear was commanded by the presence of one Wallace Wade. Grown men stood up to get a look and if one person said "excuse me" so did 12 others, all trying to elbow their way to get a glimpse of Wade and Bryant together. The scene had power. It had history. It had winners and it had a heavy overtone, not just for the two schools but for college football. One night in Birmingham, two men commanded an audience that, if stares were of monetary value, everyone would have gone home a millionaire.
>
> Bryant stayed, and stayed. The captains came on the field for the coin toss and less than three minutes remained on the scoreboard clock. Bryant and Wade were eyeball to eyeball, laughing. Wade chuckled, then Bryant, Wade pointed, then Bryant pointed.

Miraculously, the Bear made it down to the sidelines in time to see the kickoff. Duke played an excellent first half and trailed only 14-12. It is assumed Bryant had a few choice words at half-time because the final score was 35-12.

I've often wondered if they'd have held up the start of the game that night if Bryant had remained upstairs talking with Wade. I guess they would have.

* * *

In 1980 Wade came back to Tuscaloosa for a 50th reunion of the 1930 team. He was a man then 88 years of age, but still as sharp as could be. Bear Bryant was close to retirement himself. The first Alabama Bear, Wallace Wade, and Bear Bryant, the most successful coach in the country, found time to talk alone, the two men most responsible for Alabama being at the top of the college football world. It's not known exactly what the two talked about—probably it included the 1930 team, Bryant's 1980 team and prospects for the future, how Wade was enjoying retirement, that train trip they took together and ended up stranded in the middle of Nebraska, Hank Crisp, Johnny Mack Brown, how much longer Bryant would coach, and changes in the game over the years, the good and bad. One thing is for sure, coaching greatness sat side by side as Coach Wade and Coach Bryant talked that day in Alabama in 1980.

Wallace Wade's impact on the Alabama football program will forever be felt. He simply established the tradition of outstanding football in Tuscaloosa. His record speaks for itself. He won over 80% of his games, won the first four conference championships in the history of Alabama football, won its first three national titles. He won what many football historians call the most important game in the history of southern football: the 1926 Rose Bowl. All-Americans played for him, such as Pooley Hubert, Fred Sington, and Johnny Cain. A movie star played for him—Johnny Mack Brown. These players and others generated enormous publicity for the University of Alabama, and there is no doubt that the growing enrollment of students during the 1920s was due in large part to the national acclaim of Wade's teams. Denny Stadium, what is now Bryant-Denny Stadium, was started with funds from the 1926 and 1927 Rose Bowl. Alabama's mascot, the elephant, was started with the 1930 game.

Wade was an innovative coach. He was one of the first football coaches to have his own radio show, WAPI in Birmingham. The 1927 Rose Bowl was the first national broadcast of a football game on radio. Year-round conditioning was not practiced in the south before Wade started it at Vanderbilt and con-

A bust of Coach Wade at the University of Alabama. Photo by the author.

tinued it at Alabama. His coaching schools were among the first to appear, and his network of high school coaches who had played for him was among the most extensive recruiting tools of any school in the country. His use of low cut shoes, especially on the Dothan Antelope, Johnny Mack Brown, to increase speed, was a strange look in an era of high top shoes. Wade even got a shoe salesman to experiment with different types of athletic shoes, in one instance placing football cleats on baseball shoes. Lighter padding that still offered ample protection was introduced by Wade. In practices, Wade used a metronome, being such a stickler for precise timing. He was sought after for his defensive genius and his kicking game knowledge.

Wade picked his successor, Frank Thomas, who went on to coaching greatness at Alabama. Probably most notable of all, is that the fame of his great teams reached over state lines to capture the imagination of a young country boy growing up in Arkansas. As Allen Barra wrote in *The Last Coach*, "Bryant, who would become as awe-inspiring as any coach to ever step onto a college field, never got over his awe of Wallace Wade." Bear Bryant never got to play for Alabama's first bear, Wallace Wade, but Wade was certainly a huge factor in Bryant coming to Tuscaloosa.

Wallace Wade Avenue next to Bryant-Denny Stadium. Photo by the author.

A former player of Wade's at Alabama, J.B. Whitworth, became head coach at Alabama. Several of his assistant coaches had lasting impact on the program, such as Hank Crisp, Paul Burnum, and Carney Laslie.

Sure, Wade left Alabama. Maybe he did feel a little unappreciated after having less than stellar years between 1927 to 1929. He still produced good teams in 1927, 1928, and 1929, but directly because of Wade, Alabama fans wanted championships every year. Wade's early success worked against him in this respect. So he decided to leave; more money beckoned, the chance to have total control over his program, and the opportunity to start anew all factored into his decision. But he honored his contract, gave Alabama a parting gift of yet another national title, and never uttered a negative word about the university he had grown to love. In fact, in many interviews in years to come after leaving Tuscaloosa, he had only praise for Alabama. He chose for Alabama the best coach in the country available to continue what he had started, Frank Thomas.

Bear Bryant will always be the coach against whom others are measured at Alabama, and rightfully so. His coaching greatness was captured when Bum Phillips said of Bryant, "He can take his'n and beat your'n and then take your'n and beat his'n." Coach Bryant is an icon; his success and personality captured the imagination of Crimson Tide football fans everywhere. Grown men don hounds-tooth hats just to show their support for the great coach, young boys dream of playing for him, even today, 23 years after his death.

William Wallace Wade, the first Bear to stalk the Alabama sidelines, will forever be remembered as the "godfather of Alabama football." He started the greatness that shook the college football world. He will never, and should never, be forgotten. As Henry Wadsworth Longfellow tells us:

> Lives of great men all remind us
> We can make our lives sublime,
> And, departing, leave behind us,
> Footprints on the sands of time.

CHAPTER FIFTEEN

A BLUE DEVIL

Wallace Wade arrived at Duke University in the spring of 1931. The entire campus and Duke community was abuzz with excitement at the arrival of the great Alabama coach. Two of his assistant coaches, Herschel Caldwell and Dumpy Hagler, had arrived already, serving as assistants to James DeHart in 1930. Both Caldwell and Hagler had played at Alabama under Wade, and had been sent ahead to Duke to start installing the Wade system of football, while Coach Wade honored the final year of his contract in 1930 at Alabama. Duke finished 8-1-2 in 1930 in DeHart's last year, so Wade had material to work with as he started his career.

Other coaches, upon learning that Duke had an opening, applied for the position, but Duke wanted Wade and only Wade. Duke did not have a storied history of football up to 1931, but the newly endowed university by tobacco magnate James B. Duke had promise of better days ahead. President William Few, in a letter in 1929, foresaw an improvement in football shortly after the new Duke Stadium had been dedicated October 5 of 1929. He had written: "There have been many pleasant echoes of the stadium dedication despite the fact that our football situation needs further development. This will doubtless come along without undue delay." Well, that "further development" came along in 1931 with the arrival of Wallace Wade. In his time at Duke, Wade won 110 games against 36 losses and 7 ties, with two Rose Bowl appearances and 6 Southern Conference championships. Duke basketball, under the legendary Mike Krzyzewski, is now the dominant sport on the Duke campus, but in the 1930s and 1940s, football was king. In fact, from 1932 to 1941, Duke had the best record in the entire nation, winning 80, losing only 16, and tying one.

* * *

Football in 1888 was brutal. There was little padding used, many players participated without helmets, injuries were frequent, and medical care was very haphazard. As one reporter of the era wrote, "The very brutality of the sport tends to so animalize the players as to make fighting come naturally." Many believed that college football also took attention away from academics. *The Wesleyan Christian Advocate,* an official publication of Georgia Methodism, called for the ban of football, as "the Apostle Paul teaches us that bodily exercise profiteth little," and that football encouraged "mere animal currents" and freed "the lower impulses of the physical man." Reverend C.L. Chilton disagreed somewhat with Apostle Paul in recognizing the need for exercise, saying, "Any young man can acquire that at home in the useful emoluments of cutting his mother's yard or driving his father's plow." Some religious leaders in Alabama encouraged others not to attend the University of Alabama or Auburn but to send their sons to Southern University "where the YMCA takes precedence over the football team, and where the legs and head are not developed at the expense of the soul."

On the other side of the argument were those who felt football could be an integral part of college life. Advocates of the strenuous life, popularized by Theodore Roosevelt, thought that football developed "manly traits" needed to compete in a competitive world.

John Franklin Crowell became president of Trinity College in 1887, which was then located in rural Randolph County, North Carolina. While a student at Yale, Crowell covered the football team for the student newspaper. Crowell liked the game, and thought that southern colleges, where the game was slow to materialize, "must possess themselves of its service if they wished to keep pace with the times." At Trinity (which changed its name to Duke in 1924) in 1888 Crowell became the first football coach.

On Thanksgiving Day that year, Trinity College played the University of North Carolina in front of about 500 fans, who were curious to see what this football business was all about. The game was played at the North Carolina State Fairgrounds in Raleigh. Trinity won the game 16 to 0. Crowell later wrote, "That single game probably did more than anything else to send into limbo the age-long habit of the condescending attitude with which certain friends of that venerable institution [UNC] were inclined to look upon the denominational colleges in general and Trinity in particular."

The rivalry between Duke and UNC eventually became one of the most heated in the nation, but even in this first game between the two, passion was evident. An incident in the game led one Trinity player to challenge a UNC player to a duel, and the two students went as far as selecting seconds and completing arrangements before it was called off.

Crowell would win 4 games while losing only to Wake Forest in his two years as coach in 1888 and 1889. Duke would play a few games a year until 1895, when the game was banned because it "was too dangerous physically and it distracts from academics." Crowell, who remained as president until 1894, fought for keeping football, saying that young people's rambunctiousness led "to the old-fashioned sort of deviltry like putting oxen in chapel, or a goose in the professor's desk," and could be controlled through participation in football.

Trinity beat UNC 6 to 4 in 1893, and apparently after the game there was much joy, and a reporter wrote that "the Trinity boys are holding a great rejoicing at the college tonight." One week later Trinity defeated the University of Tennessee 70 to 0 in a game that was stopped early because of a "mercy rule." This game, among other factors, prompted Tennessee to drop football during 1894 and 1895. A rivalry between these two schools would develop in the 1930s that was among the fiercest in the nation, with coaching giants Wallace Wade and Robert Neyland butting heads.

Trinity traveled to Lynchburg to play Virginia on November 11 of 1893, and was badly licked. Trailing 30 to 0 in the first half, Trinity refused to continue. Its deficit was due in part "to the incompetence and inefficiency of the umpire," according to some Trinity players. Some reports stated that the team apparently drowned its sorrows in a keg of beer on the train coming back to Durham, where Trinity moved in 1892. Some tawdry details of the revelry got back to the general Methodist community, of which Trinity was affiliated. This precipitated more calls for football to be banned.

Crowell resigned under pressure in 1894 and John Kilgo succeeded him as president. Kilgo adamantly opposed football saying it was "unfit to be played by young men at college, especially at a Christian College." One game was played in 1894 and then Trinity banned football from the campus. Kilgo said it "has grown to be such an evil that the best tastes of the public have rebelled against it ... under no condition will a match game with another college be allowed." There would not be another football game played at Trinity until 1920, despite many student protests. Trinity was not alone in banning football. Wake Forest, Furman, and Wofford, among others, did also.

In 1924, Howard Jones served as Duke coach, winning 4 and losing 5. Jones had been head coach at Syracuse, Yale, Ohio State, and Iowa before coming to Duke. He only stayed in Durham one year before accepting the head coaching job at Southern Cal in 1925, where he compiled a 131-36-13 record through 1940, winning two national championships. Coach Jones is now enshrined in the College Football Hall of Fame.

The year of 1924 was also when tobacco tycoon James B. Duke made Duke University the prime beneficiary of a $40,000,000 trust. James Duke, in giving the money, said he believed that "education, when conducted along sane and practical, as opposed to dogmatic and theoretical lines, is next to religion, the greatest civilizing influence."

Hanes Field 1926. This is where Duke played its home games
before the construction of Wallace Wade Stadium.
Courtesy of Duke University Archives.

President William Few, who succeeded Kilgo in 1910, was most instrumental in the growth of Trinity College into Duke University. After the announcement of the Duke Endowment of $40,000,000, Few received a warm
letter from the president of the University of North Carolina, Harry Chase.
Chase congratulated Few, writing:

> Two universities, located as ours are, growing up side by side, the
> one in response to private benefaction and the other under State con-
> trol, should supplement each other, and each, I believe, will be a
> stimulus to the other's development, I am genuinely glad for you, and
> I believe that Mr. Duke's gift in advancing your institution will ad-
> vance at the same time the whole level of thinking about higher ed-
> ucation in the State and in the South.

Few also received a letter from an alumnus, upset not so much that Trinity
changed its name to Duke, but the fact that Mr. Duke did not move the campus to Asheville. Few explained to the alumnus that Mr. Duke was opposed

to the idea of moving the campus. "When you go out to get $40,000,000 from a man, you will find that he has some ideas of his own."

James DeHart was hired to coach football at Duke in 1926. DeHart had been at Washington and Lee University the previous three years and had been the first four-letter athlete at Pittsburgh, captaining both the football and baseball teams. Serving through 1930, he would finish with a 24-23-2 record, including the 8-1-2 record in 1930 in which the only loss was to South Carolina. But before 1930, Dehart's record was 3-6 in 1926, 4-5 in 1927, 5-5 in 1928, and 4-6 in 1929. So Wade came into a program in 1931 with little tradition.

The 1929 season was highlighted by the opening of Duke Stadium, now named Wallace Wade Stadium. Pittsburgh was the opponent on October 5 for the first game in the stadium, and manhandled Duke 52 to 7. Pitt went on to finish 9-1 in 1929, losing only to Southern Cal and Howard Jones in the Rose Bowl. A local reporter wrote about the opening of the stadium:

> From everywhere the cars poured into Durham and the alumni and patrons of the game arrived early for the biggest event in the history of Duke football. Nearly everyone of the 25,000 spectators was in his seat by the time of the kick off. Governor Gardner and his party of official guests arrived in time for the exercises and were comfortably settled in the guest box when young Tony Duke, the son of Angier B. Duke and grandson of Benjamin N. Duke, trotted out with the team and put the ball in play. The students made whoopee over in their sections and the crowd was in great spirits.

O.B. Keeler of the *Atlanta Journal* was on hand also, and wrote,

> I am of the opinion that the new campus of Duke University at Durham, N.C., probably is the most beautiful thing of the kind in America. The new buildings, of a lovely native stone found only in one spot in the world—and that spot within fifteen miles of the campus—is of a curious, blending type, which, with the careful adaptation of the roofs, will give these buildings the appearance of having been there a couple of hundred years by the time the landscape has been gardened and the turf springs up. Some chap with a whimsical sense of humor said Duke had managed to build a very neat little stadium, with some loose change found in a pair of Mr. Duke's old pants.
>
> I'll say they managed a stadium. It isn't the biggest in the United States, by a whole lot, though 35,000 is a lot of seats. But the point is, so cleverly was the great horseshoe designed that when you sit in any one of those 35,000 seats, you are facing automatically and pre-

cisely toward the center of the field below. On either side is a com-
modious special box, one for the press, the other for special guests.
At the closed end is the box for the scouts.

Coach DeHart of Duke was not at all downcast by the 52-7 victory
by the great Pittsburgh outfit over his team. Jock Sutherland (Pitt
coach) has a wonderful machine this year, as I suspect a number of
crack teams in other sections will discover.

Not only did Keeler notice the beauty of the campus, but so did J.B. Rhine.
In his poem, *The University,* a stanza spoke to this grandeur: "How eloquent
these halls and towers of stone! What freighted symbols of man's power
shown! This sculpture of the cumulative past, Antiquity itself in granite
cast!"

* * *

In ways other than the hiring of Wallace Wade, 1930 was a momentous
year. Even though football had been played on the new West Campus in 1929,
it was 1930 when most of the 31 new stone buildings, comprising a vast
Gothic unit, were occupied for the first time. These new buildings were designed by Julian Abele, the first black graduate of the University of Pennsylvania's architectural school. Abele also designed Harvard's Widener Library
and the Philadelphia Museum of Art.

Work began on the Duke Chapel, which is now, along with Cameron Indoor Stadium, one of the landmarks of the entire campus. Duke Hospital,
currently one of the most renowned hospitals in the world, was also opened
in 1930. Degrees were conferred upon 336 graduates, the largest class in
Duke's history up to 1930.

After William Wannamaker, the dean of Duke University, and Wallace Wade
exchanged their initial letters (see Introduction), they continued to correspond
throughout much of 1930. Wade had agreed to come to Duke in 1931, but was
finishing his contract at Alabama. While he was certainly able to focus on his
job at Alabama, as his team won the national championship, Wade also was as-
siduous in making sure that football matters at Duke in 1930 were being looked
after.

Even in April of 1930, Wade expressed concern about the Duke schedule
and recruiting in a letter to Wannamaker from Tuscaloosa.

It might be well to play the North Carolina game on Saturday,
twelve days before Thanksgiving. I would suggest that you discontinue
the intersectional game for 1931. I am sending Mr. Jordan (Charles
Jordan) a letter which I received about some boys in Georgia who are

interested in going to Duke. I hope that you can make some kind of arrangement with someone who will follow up carefully the prospective material so that we will have strong freshman material this fall.

Wannamaker replied on May 15:

In speaking of the schedule for 1931, you suggested we 'discontinue the intersectional game.' Do you think we ought to discontinue playing the Navy? We shall in all probability not want to play Villanova after next year. But I have the feeling that the game with Navy is not a bad thing, though I am not at all insistent on that point. Mr. Jordan got the letter which you sent to him and has attended to it. He also had a letter from Caldwell. You will be interested to know that developments on the new campus (West) are going on in a most satisfactory way.

Ellis "Dumpy" Hagler and Caldwell were making plans to go to Duke during May of 1930. In a letter from May 15, Hagler writes to Wannamaker:

I am looking forward with much pleasure for the time to come for me to take up my duties in the Department of Physical Education at Duke University. You may rest assured that I will cooperate to the fullest extent possible with Mr. DeHart in carrying on the athletic work at Duke. Feel free to call on me if I can be of any service to the University before I arrive this fall.

Also on May 15, Wade continued to try to stock his material at Duke, writing to Wannamaker:

Today Mr. Shirling told me that he wanted his nephew, Allen Pogus of Greenville, Alabama, to go to Duke next year. He was interested in getting some financial assistance for him. I suggested that he write to you in regard to work, scholarship, and loan fund aid. I told him that on account of my position here that I could not discuss the matter with him. We have been trying to get Pogus to come to Alabama. He is an unusually fine athlete and student.

On May 21, Wade wrote again to Wannamaker:

In reply to your letter in regard to continuing the Navy game, I feel that you are in a better position than I am to know whether this game is worthwhile to Duke. I prefer to have you use your judgment in this matter as I realize that I am not familiar with the conditions. I doubt very much however, if it would be advisable for us to play both the

Navy and Kentucky. I also recommend that you do not schedule more than nine games. After I come to Duke and have become better acquainted with conditions I shall feel that I will be better able to make these decisions and accept the responsibility that goes with them. I am very anxious to have the privilege of making a trip to Durham this summer but am not certain yet whether I will able to do so.

I have a letter from Mr. Sterling Nicholson suggesting that I make application for membership at this time in the Hope Valley Country Club in order to take advantage of a fifty percent reduction in the regular initiation fee. I would like to have you write me whether you consider that this is the club that my family and I would prefer to join.

On the same day, May 21, Wannamaker had written Wade:

It has occurred to me that it would be a happy idea for Hagler and Caldwell to come here either about commencement time, June 1 through 3, or soon afterwards. There is great interest among our friends and alumni over your coming to Duke and I know that many men would be glad to meet your two men who are to start work in September. Furthermore, many alumni will want to talk with somebody who knows you about possible athletes who will want to work under your guidance. There are a good many very promising football players who have informed some of us here, that they want to come here shortly after commencement and to talk with somebody who can give them first hand knowledge of the situation. Mr. Lee showed me your letter to him in which you mentioned such a man as Feathers (Beattie Feathers went to Tennessee and became an All-American). It seems to me that if Caldwell or Hagler could go with someone from here to see this man, it would be good for him to do so. Write me frankly at once, please, what you think of this idea.

On May 24, Wannamaker responded to Wade about the country club membership.

The Hope Valley Country Club is really the only country club here. Its membership comprises the best people in Durham and the Club is altogether a good one. If you want to play golf or if Mrs. Wade would care to attend some of the pleasant functions at the Club, I advise you to take membership in it. Your membership would permit all members of your family to the privileges of the Club. When you finally decide the question of coming here for a visit this summer, let me know in order that I may be sure to be on hand.

June 3, 1930, Wannamaker to Wade:

> Caldwell arrived yesterday and we are taking care of him. I was pleased with him. All letters of the kind you have been sending from prospective students are being carefully and promptly answered.

June 9, 1930, Caldwell to Wannamaker:

> I have checked my expenses for my trip to Durham and the total including railroad fare, Pullman, and three meals on the train was $61.00. I enjoyed my visit up there very much. I will be looking forward to seeing you again in September. I assure you that you will hear from me when I hear of a good prospect.

On July 1, Wade showed his loyalty to the university that had employed him for eight years.

> Information has come to me that Fred Brown of Dothan, Alabama, is now employed in Durham by someone that is interested in having him enter Duke University this fall. Fred's family are very good friends of mine. Three of his brothers have played on the football team here under me. The most outstanding one was the famous Johnny Mack Brown who was one of our best football players. On account of the fact that Fred's brothers, who have come to the University of Alabama, have done very well here and are so well thought of, this influence will be a great deal of help to him. I feel that it would be better for Fred to come to the University of Alabama than for him to go to Duke University. I had a conference with him early in the spring in which I advised him of this. In consideration of these facts I am asking that you be kind enough to use whatever influence you can to send Fred away from Durham as soon as possible.

Again, this last letter shows the character of Coach Wade, who could have just accepted the fact that Fred wanted to follow him to Duke and play football for him. But Wade knew the family of Brown wanted him to stay home, and even though he certainly could have used a player of Brown's caliber and lineage, he truly thought that Brown would be better off at Alabama following in the footsteps of his brothers.

July 4, 1930, Wannamaker to Wade:

> It seems Brown has a friend who is a Duke student, and this friend is working in Durham this summer. Brown came here about June 10 alone. He has a job paying 35 cents an hour when the weather per-

mits working. I have never seen him and should not know him if I did see him. He has made absolutely no application for admission to Duke University. I will find out as soon as possible from his friend what Brown intends to do and will do myself what I can to help in this matter as I feel it is wise. I appreciate your point of view.

July 15, 1930, Wannamaker to Wade:

It has been suggested that we take as assistant coach for football Francis Tappan, the star end of Howard Jones' team. Tappan has finished his time as a player and is now a second year student of law in the University of Southern California. Our Dean Miller of the Law School, who comes from there, knows him quite well and assures me that he is an unusually fine youth and a good student of high standing. The father is a judge and would be quite willing, as is Tappan, for the boy to complete his law training here—two more years—under Dean Miller. He feels, however, that Francis should not make the transfer unless he could earn enough to justify his so doing—not far from $2000. Miller says Tappan was known as the brains of the team and that Jones relied greatly on him. He ought to be of help to us as end coach.

Now, I should be unwilling to consider the suggestion without your advice. Do you have yet worked out your scheme of things far enough to be able to say whether or not you would approve our bringing in Tappan? Naturally Tilson and Cameron are to be thought of; we do not yet know how they will fit into your plans. Cameron is, I feel sure, a man of ability, both as basketball and football coach, and Tilson has promise.

Wade's reply on July 23, 1930:

I think we should plan carefully our organization. The first men we should engage should be the important men such as first assistant, basketball coach, etc. I do not want to make a decision about Tilson and Cameron at this time. I also doubt if it would be wise to bring in a young man [Tappan] with little experience who would be there only one year with me, this might interfere some in our getting a man who would fit into our plans and would be with us permanently. My best judgment is that we should let the matter of engaging assistants go until after this season is over. Then we will have a free hand to do what seems best at that time.

Caldwell and Hagler are expecting to report September 1st. They can come earlier if you desire it. I hope you are enjoying this summer, it is dreadfully hot here.

On August 14, Wannamaker returns to the discussion of Fred Brown in a letter to Wade:

Last Saturday afternoon for the first time he came to my office to discuss the chances of his entering Duke University next month with financial assistance. The cause of his coming then was the receipt of a telegram from his home telling him a Dr. Frazier would send him money to defray his railroad expenses if he would go to the University of Alabama. He showed me the telegram and said further that Mr. Crisp had told him that he, Brown, would get there just what his brothers received and that he knew they got room, board, university fees and railroad expenses. I asked Brown where he wanted to go to school and he said he wanted to attend Duke, but that he needed money and could come here only if we gave him as good terms as Alabama gave him. I told him that without regard to help I felt that he ought to enter the University of Alabama and advised him to go there. But he said frankly he did not want to go there because he did not want to "travel" on his brothers' reputation, and asked if we could not do as well for him here. I told him that he could not be considered for help open to all needy students until he had applied in writing for admission and had on file an official certificate of his high school credits showing that he was entirely eligible for admission. I told him we had a number of Freshman scholarships for one year open to all Freshmen, which are awarded only by the Faculty Committee on Student Help, of which I am Chairman, and that if his papers should prove satisfactory he would be considered for one of them, that he would be helped to secure a job just as are all students needing and willing to work. I also explained our student loan fund to him. But he said he did not want to have to pay back the loan and that he supposed he would go to Alabama or elsewhere.

Brown seemed greatly disappointed at having (as he felt) to leave here and said he could not understand why we would not do what other places are doing for football players. He left Monday. He had heard that his father is ill.

I have told you this in order that you may clearly see that we have made no effort to hold Brown from going to the University of Alabama. He told me you had advised him to go there. But he really

seemed bitterly disappointed at not being able to come here. Personally speaking, I believe it was best for him to go to Alabama — it
seemed the natural thing and his coming here would have aroused ill-
feeling. I try always to be fair to the others concerned and have so
acted in this case. Brown has here a warm friend, young Mullins,
from Dothan, who is at work this summer here, and it was with
Mullins that Brown was living. He had a job as a waiter in the hospital dining room.

I am especially desirous that the people there attach no blame to
you in connection with the boy's coming to Durham this summer.

If they criticize us at all, they are in error. Both I and Mr. Jordan,
whom Brown talked with before seeing me, advised him, in our first
interview with him, to go to Alabama. And had we put up the money,
a thing we do not do, we could have had him here according to his
asseveration.

In another letter concerning the coaching staff, Wannamaker wrote to Wade
in late August of 1930:

In regard to the interview with the man recommended by Mr.
Zuppke [Illinois coach recommending Carl Voyles, an assistant to
Zuppke], use your own best judgment. I am glad you are keeping
our needs in mind as to the staff. The selection of men is, as you
know better than I, of the utmost importance, and we should take
every opportunity to know a man in and out before engaging him.
I have the feeling too, that you will want to observe Cameron and
Tilson carefully. Both are popular here among the students,
Cameron especially, being highly respected as a coach, chiefly of basketball, though the Freshman football teams coached by him have
been quite successful and his boys have almost without exception expressed great satisfaction with his handling of the men individually
and as groups.

August 25, 1930, Wade to Wannamaker:

Caldwell and Hagler expect to report for duty September 1st. I
shall appreciate it very much if you will guide them in their work with
a personal interest. They are both inexperienced boys who are anxious to do what is right and will appreciate any advice or assistance
which you may give them. I have particularly stressed to them the importance of their cooperation thoroughly with Coach DeHart as long
as he is at the head of the Athletic Department.

August 28, 1930, Wade to Wannamaker:

> I had Mr. Carl Voyles, freshman coach at the University of Illinois, down on Saturday for a conference. He impressed me very favorably and I believe that he would make a splendid addition to our staff. I hope that everything that can will be done during the next few weeks to bring a good lot of freshman material. Have we a chance to get Hackney [Elmore "Honey" Hackney] who lives in Durham and attends Georgia Military Academy? I heard that he was considering Florida.

August 28, 1930, Wannamaker to Wade:

> I am glad to know that you were pleased with Voyles. I also will be more than willing to lend Caldwell and Hagler any assistance in my power to aid them in finding their way successfully and happily here.

September 1, 1930, Wannamaker to Wade:

> Hackney, according to what some of our people have told us, is seriously thinking of coming to us. I met him for a few minutes in my office with one of his friends two days ago and was impressed with him. I think that it is largely a question of finance with him. I do not think he has any money and naturally there has been a great pull to get him at several other schools. His brothers went to the University of North Carolina. I send my best wishes for a great final year at Alabama.

September 14, 1930, Wade to Wannamaker:

> I talked to Major Neyland at the University of Tennessee by telephone. He told me that they would be glad to play Duke in 1931. There will be a meeting of coaches in Atlanta next Sunday to discuss rules, and he said that we could discuss the matter further at that time. I make the following suggestions for your consideration. 1) Tennessee would be a more desirable team to play in 1931 than Kentucky; 2) Find out tentatively if Villanova will be willing to call off the 1931 game; 3) See if South Carolina game can be arranged for a later date; 4) See if N.C. State game can be played earlier and UNC game played on Nov. 15th; 5) Try to arrange games with Virginia, Wake Forest, and Wofford; 6) If these arrangements can be made, I do not believe we would need the Navy game.

September 16, 1930, Wannamaker to Wade:

Unfortunately there is a clause in the Villanova contract which calls for a forfeit of $3,500 in case we should decline to play Villanova here in 1931. [Duke played and won 18 to 0.]

December 2, 1930, Wannamaker to Wade:

I am expecting you as early in January as you can come, but you need not put yourself to any inconvenience in order to get here during the first few days of January. We resume college work on January 3rd.

You spoke of my house located on Buchanan Boulevard at the west entrance to the College of Women. Although I have had many requests to rent the house, I have not acceded to them since I much prefer to sell the property. At present several parties are still urging me to let them have it. However, if I do not sell it by the middle of December or have made no definite arrangements to sell it by the end of the year, I will hold it for you. As I told you, I have quite a sum of money tied up in the house. The location is a very desirable one and property there is expensive. I could easily have sold it two years ago, but declined to do so since I did not know just when I was to move into the new home. A rental income of $125.00 a month would not net me more than six per cent of my investment in the property. If I do rent it, I intend to spend some money on making some changes in the upstairs bathroom and in the redecoration of two of the rooms on the second floor. I suggest, therefore, that at your earliest convenience you write frankly about the matter and I shall be more than glad to discuss the whole question further with you. The house is unquestionably located most conveniently for your family since the children could easily attend good schools nearby and you would be not far from your work either. Furthermore, Mrs. Wade would find the location convenient from her own standpoint since she would be easily able to get to engagements and likewise to form her social connections with university people and others in the city.

I am giving serious thought to the carrying out of the suggestions we made to one another as to the staff. I will write you again before long about that matter. I think highly of your suggestion as to Sington. I advise you to take up with him promptly the possibility of his coming here in the capacity you suggest and at the salary you name. He would find the opportunity to study law here unexcelled in any law school I know.

* * *

William P. Few served as president of Duke University from 1910 to 1940, and was a central figure in establishing Duke as a national university. Few wrote about his educational philosophy and Wallace Wade in this letter of 1931 to William Perkins, chief legal counsel to James B. Duke.

> Wallace Wade came here last week and is now in full charge of all our athletics and physical education. The more I see of him the more I am pleased with his personality and his program involving bodily development and character. I have all my life placed the moral and the physical above the intellectual in the education of boys. For I have believed that if we can make sure of a good character and a disciplined and fortified body for a boy, he will be apt to take advantage of his opportunities of whatever kind and go as far in life as his native endowment will permit. His intellectual immaturities, his lack of knowledge, and his vagaries of opinion will be cured as he develops, provided his education has put into him an unquenchable yearning to know what is true and do what is right. I hope that our expectation in Mr. Wade may be justified in the years to come.

Wade was hired in 1931 at $12,500 per year, which at the time made him one of the highest paid coaches in the country. As Clem Gryska, long-time assistant to Bear Bryant at Alabama, jokingly told me, "That's more than Coach Bryant paid me." For sure, it was more than most, if not all, of the Duke faculty. For comparison William Maughan was hired in 1930 as Assistant Professor of Forestry and Assistant Director of Duke Forest for $3,500. Howard Jensen, a Professor of Sociology, made $5,500 in 1931. Dr. Francis Carter was hired for $7,000 in 1931 as a Professor of Obstetrics. Top professional football players averaged between $3,000 and $6,000 per year in the 1930s. Even in 1946, Art Guepe was hired as the head football coach of Virginia at $8,000. Harold Bradley was hired to coach the Duke men's basketball team in 1950 at a salary of $5,500, of which $2,500 was for Bradley's job as an instructor of physical education and $3,000 as basketball coach. Just a tad less than Coach K makes in 2006 as basketball coach.

There is no question Coach K is worth every penny of his salary, and Coach Wade earned his keep also. One example is the effect of the national publicity the football team under Wade attracted. Many other factors, no doubt, increased enrollment at Duke in the 1930s, but for sure the football team played its part. Total enrollment in 1940 was 3,685, a 75 per cent increase over the 2,106 students in 1930.

CHAPTER SIXTEEN

1931—First Year at Duke

As Wallace Wade arrived at Duke in 1931, the campus was alive with activity. There was a Paderewski recital at Page Auditorium, with an overflow crowd listening to numbers by Beethoven and Chopin. Students frequented the Goody Shop on West Main Street of Durham, and the Dope Shop soda fountain on campus. Students worked hard, and looked for social activities to have a good time. As the *Duke Chronicle*, the campus newspaper, put it, "Drop the handkerchief and ring around the rosies have had their day. They no longer satisfy."

One activity that did seem to satisfy was dancing, with many dances taking place in the ballroom of the Union Building on the West Campus and Memorial Gymnasium on the women's East Campus. One alumnus was not pleased at all at such a spectacle occurring at Duke, writing to President Few his indignation that "such an abomination should ever have been tolerated in my alma mater." Nevertheless, students kept dancing during these depression years to such student orchestras as those led by Jelly Leftwich, Johnny Long, and Les Brown.

A relationship developed between Duke and its Durham neighbor, the North Carolina College for Negroes (now North Carolina Central University). The Duke Liberal Club invited a professor from NCCU to speak to them, and Dr. James Shepard, president of NCCU, spoke on the Duke campus. Through an exchange of letters, Shepard invited Few to speak at NCCU, and Few agreed, writing that "I have been much interested in the growth and progress of the North Carolina College for Negroes. I congratulate you on the work you have done and on the growth of the college."

* * *

Wade retained Eddie Cameron as an assistant coach, and hired Carl Voyles from Illinois and also hired Fred Sington, his All-American star from the 1930 Alabama team. With Herschel Caldwell and Dumpy Hagler already on the staff, four of the six coaches were from the University of Alabama, including Wade.

Cameron Indoor Stadium, the storied home basketball arena for the Duke basketball team, is named for Eddie Cameron. Cameron came to Duke in

Eddie Cameron and Wallace Wade. Courtesy
of Duke Sports Information Department.

1926 to coach the freshman football team, after an outstanding athletic career
at Washington and Lee University in Virginia, where he captained the football
and basketball teams. He became head basketball coach in 1929 and won 226
games through 1942. All the while he served as a key assistant to Wade in football. After Wade entered the service for World War II, Cameron served as head
football coach from 1942 to 1945, compiling a 25-11-1 record, including a
Blue Devil victory over Alabama in the 1945 Sugar Bowl. Against rival North
Carolina, Cameron was 4-0-1, and in 1943 beat UNC twice in the same season. Cameron became the permanent athletic director in 1946 and served
until 1972. As athletic director, Cameron became one of the nation's most influential sports administrators, playing a key role in the formation of the Atlantic Coast Conference.

Shortly after arriving at Duke in mid-January of 1931, Wade set about letting students, players, alumni, and fans know his expectations. One needs to
remember that only Knute Rockne of Notre Dame was better known around
the nation in 1931 than Wade. People were interested in what he thought,
wanted to hear this famous coach speak, and stood in lines for the chance to
meet him. Wade was never a dynamic speaker, possessing somewhat of a nasal
twang, but he had a way of getting his point across, mostly with the directness of his words. As someone once said, Wade was one of the rare people

**Wallace Wade and Wallace Wade Jr. in 1931. Courtesy
of Duke Sports Information Department.**

who did not have the capability of saying anything that he did not truly believe; he did not sugarcoat his words.

Meeting the student body, Wade stressed "that athletics will be secondary
to scholastic work," although he emphasized the importance of athletics.

> The aim of a college education is mental, moral, and physical devel-
> opment. We hope to organize and carry on athletics at Duke Univer-
> sity to assist in that development. Athletics should primarily help to
> make bigger men and better citizens to take their place in the world.
> I think that athletics should be made a part of the university cur-
> riculum, and that credits should be given to the participants on var-
> ious teams, just as they get when they have a course of mathematics,

Wallace Wade with Herschel Caldwell and Ellis Hagler.
Courtesy of Duke Sports Information Department.

or history, or any of the other subjects. It is our plan to develop intramural teams for all students.

Wade, as physical education director and athletic director, eventually developed an intramural program at Duke that was nationally recognized. He
hired Gerry Gerard from Illinois to come to Duke in 1931 to direct the intramural program. Gerard started soccer at Duke, along with becoming head
basketball coach in 1943. Gerard won 131 games with 78 losses, twice winning Southern Conference titles. Gerard definitely qualified as a good hire
for Wade.

On April 4, Wade addressed a Greensboro, North Carolina, gathering of
over 200 people. Wade asked the crowd for a moment of silence for Knute
Rockne, who had been killed in a plane crash just days before, on March 31.
On a flight from Kansas City to Los Angeles, where he was to complete a football instructional movie, the plane crashed in adverse weather in a wheat field
in Kansas. Rockne was only 43. Wade had met Rockne, and the two are gen-

erally considered to have been the two most successful college coaches in the 1920s era. Rockne's winning percentage of .881 is unmatched, having lost only 12 games while winning 105, with five ties. Years later, Wade would say of Rockne,

> Rock was a great coach, a good leader of men. He was a motivator, and boys would play hard and do anything for him. Rock was the reason I recommended Frank Thomas to Alabama. I knew he had been taught football from a great man.

After the tribute to Rockne, Wade spoke on the value of athletics. "Few athletes can be successful because of good fortune or natural skill. An athlete is good because he has the ambition to be good. Success comes only to the man who earns it." To the young boys who participated in athletics who were in the audience, and there were many, Wade talked about the importance of determination, a spirit of cooperation, unselfishness, and loyalty.

> Teach boys those qualities and you have taught them to succeed at anything. That is why we believe in college athletics. When a boy learns from the game of football to concentrate, to pay the price of success, to make a sacrifice, to be loyal, he has learned something that he can learn in few places. I am convinced that in athletics the fellow who fails does so because he does not make a determined effort. The failure comes back and says he did the best he could. The successful player comes back successful because of having done what it took to win.

Wade stayed busy during the summer speaking at coaching schools around the country. He spoke at Southwestern in Memphis, and also at Utah State. In an address at Bluefield College, he stressed tough love.

> I try to make my football practice as tough as I can get it, and I truly believe that I am doing my boys a favor by so doing. If they have the stick-to-itiveness to keep on sticking to it and going forward and mastering a task that is unpleasant in the learning, then they have accomplished something. But the boy who comes out of the well-to-do home, and who has been patted and pampered, hasn't the stuff it takes to stick through the tough spots, and I place all the blame on the parents. If you don't believe me, look at your son when he is forty years old. Place him up alongside the fellow who came from the poor home, who had to depend upon himself, and assume self-responsi-

bility, and the well-to-do boy will get a licking in business just as he did on the football field.

* * *

Kidd Brewer was selected to captain Wallace Wade's first team at Duke. Also on the team were Fred Crawford and Horace Hendrickson. Bill Murray had been an outstanding player on the 1930 team, but had graduated. Murray got to know Wade during the first months of 1931, however, and had been coached by Caldwell and Hagler in 1930. Upon retiring in 1950, just as he had done at Alabama, Wade picked his successor, and he chose Murray. Coach Murray would continue the tradition of strong football at Duke until retiring in 1965 with a record of 93-51-8, which included two Orange Bowl appearances and a Cotton Bowl win over Arkansas in 1960.

The Blue Devils went to Columbia to play South Carolina in Wade's first game as Duke mentor. The offense sputtered and turned the ball over three times as the Gamecocks won 7 to 0. The following Saturday, the Devils met VMI, winning 13 to 0. Brewer scored both of the touchdowns for Duke as Wade won in his first appearance at Duke Stadium. It was another poor offensive performance, as Duke was penalized a total of 135 yards. John Brownlee, a track star who held the Southern Conference record in the 220-yard low hurdles, ran for 98 yards. In between wins over Villanova and Wake Forest was a surprising 0 to 0 tie with Davidson.

Traveling to Tennessee for the first football contest between the schools, although not the first time Wade had met Volunteer coach Robert Neyland, the Devils lost by a 25 to 2 score. Beattie Feathers caught a 62-yard touchdown pass and Gene McEver, Tennessee's All-American who had faced Wade while Wade was at Alabama, ran well. Wade had gained so much respect for McEver since he had faced him first in 1928, that he visited the Volunteer dressing room after the game to congratulate McEver.

This 25 to 2 loss and a 23 to 0 loss to Syracuse in his first year at Alabama were the two worst defeats, in point difference, in Wade's career. Tennessee would finish 1931 9-0-1, the tie against Kentucky. The Vols would not lose another game until 1933, to Duke.

On November 21, Duke played the University of North Carolina to a 0-0 tie. Brewer had a touchdown nullified by a penalty. 20,000 fans attended the game in Duke Stadium and saw the defenses rule the day.

UNC's star quarterback, Johnny Branch, who had been suspended for the previous five games, was reinstated for the Duke game by Coach Chuck Collins. But neither team moved the ball effectively, with Duke gaining a total of 176 yards to UNC's 159.

Wallace Wade at Duke in the early 1930s.
Courtesy of Anita Caldwell.

The final game of 1931 was played at Washington and Lee, now coached by James DeHart, the Duke coach from 1926 to 1930. Duke won 6 to 0 on a kick-off return for a touchdown by Lowell Mason. Wade and DeHart had a good relationship, as DeHart had agreed to allow Caldwell and Hagler to help him in 1930, and Wade had decided to retain Eddie Cameron on his staff, which DeHart had wished for his former assistant. The two teams agreed to play again in 1932.

Duke finished 5-3-2, despite averaging just seven points a game, but only allowed four. But another game loomed for some of the Duke players. Four million people were unemployed in 1931, and bread and soup lines continued to grow. Post-season charity games were being held to raise money to combat the effects of the Great Depression. The Big Five schools of North Carolina decided to pitch in to raise money for the Governor's Council for Unemployment and Relief. Duke and North Carolina formed one team, called Dukolina, to play against Wakidson State, which was Wake Forest, Davidson, and N.C. State. Played at Duke Stadium on December 5, Dukolina, coached by Wade and Chuck Collins of UNC, won 14 to 0. Only 5,000 people attended, but every dollar was important during these hard times.

North Carolina, just like most of the rest of the country, was hit hard by the depression. Between 1930 and 1933, 194 banks closed in the state and many people lost their homes and businesses. Agriculture, the primary livelihood for so many in the state, was greatly affected. Cotton had sold for more than 30 cents a pound in 1923; by 1932 it had dropped to six cents. Tobacco farmers suffered as the price they received declined from 36 cents a pound in 1926 to just nine cents in 1932. Most farmers received less for their crops than it cost to produce them. Hunger affected thousands of North Carolinians, and once-honest, law-abiding men turned to stealing to feed themselves and their families. Orchards were raided and milk delivered before daybreak disappeared from front porches. Duke Hospital provided beds and care for the poor, and the Duke Endowment supported charity cases in other hospitals around the state.

* * *

Kidd Brewer, the captain of the 1931 team, became head coach of Appalachian State University in 1935. Brewer compiled a record of 30-4-3 in his four seasons in Boone, North Carolina. The stadium at Appalachian State is now named in honor of Brewer.

After serving as a naval lieutenant in the Pacific during World War II, Brewer became an assistant to North Carolina Senators Josiah Bailey and William Umstead in Washington, D.C. In 1956 Brewer ran for lieutenant governor of North Carolina, then he ran for governor in 1964. He became wealthy through land development and the insurance business, eventually selling the land that is now Crabtree Valley Mall in Raleigh.

CHAPTER SEVENTEEN

1932 — DUKE FOOTBALL STARTS TO RUMBLE

As Wallace Wade began his second year at Duke in 1932, Franklin Delano Roosevelt toured the country in his campaign for President. Amos n' Andy on radio was popular nationwide. Babe Didrikson made claim to being the greatest woman athlete ever, setting world records at the 1932 Olympics in Los Angeles in the 80-meter hurdles and the javelin. The Great Depression still had its vicious grip on the nation, as FDR was about to utter, "the only thing we have to fear is fear itself!"

In Durham, the home of Duke University, the economy was dominated by the tobacco market. Tobacco money built both Durham and Duke University. Riggsbee Avenue in Durham was once so loaded with tobacco warehouses that it was known as "Tobacco Row." Some college dances were even held in the warehouses, with huge fans blowing across 300 pound blocks of ice during Durham's hot season. Liggett and Myers and the American Tobacco Company employed huge numbers of people in the area.

Durham had been the site of the largest troop surrender of the Civil War on April 26, 1865. After completing his infamous trek from Atlanta to Savannah, General William T. Sherman journeyed into North Carolina in March with his sixty thousand troops. Sherman's "total war" policy included taking what his soldiers needed to live and destroying public buildings and factories. General Joseph E. Johnston failed to stop Sherman at the Battle of Bentonville.

Robert E. Lee had already surrendered to Grant at Appamattox by the time that Sherman and Johnston met on April 17 at the Bennett farm in Durham. On the 26th a final agreement was reached on a military surrender that ended the war in the Carolinas, Georgia, and Florida; it affected over 89,000 soldiers.

It seemed that Civil War memories and actual sites of importance followed Wallace Wade wherever he happened to be. He was born in Trenton, Tennessee, where the Battle of Trenton had occurred. Union forces had destroyed most of the University of Alabama in Tuscaloosa. In Durham, the largest troop surrender took place. This is perhaps poignant for two reasons. First, Wade was absolutely one of the most patriotic individuals one could ever meet. He served in World Wars I and II, eventually attaining the rank of Lieutenant Colonel and winning honor as Commander of the 272nd Field Artillery Battalion in WWII. It is my opinion that the military was Wade's true love, so to speak, even over football. He was a lifelong reader of military history.

Second, Wade brought more national recognition to the south for its brand of football than any other man. His teams at Alabama and Duke showed the nation that southern football was the equal of eastern, mid-western, and western teams. The 1926 Rose Bowl is considered the most important game in the history of southern football.

* * *

Playing a difficult schedule of ten games, Duke won seven and lost three in 1932, capturing the Big Five title by beating in-state rivals Davidson, Wake Forest, and North Carolina, while losing to North Carolina State. On October 8 Wade returned to the state of Alabama to play Auburn in Birmingham, losing 18 to 7. Auburn, under coach Chet Wynne, would finish the season unbeaten at 9-0-1, the tie coming against South Carolina. Lowell Mason, the 1932 captain for Duke, played well in a driving rain in the loss to Auburn.

After beating Maryland 34 to 0 and Wake Forest 9 to 0 to run its record to 4-1, Duke went to Knoxville to meet Tennessee. Fred Crawford scored on a 72-yard interception for Duke, and Lowell Mason scored also, before Breezy Wynn kicked a field goal in the fourth quarter to win the game for the Volunteers. Tennessee went on to finish unbeaten at 9-0-1 with Vanderbilt getting the tie. Duke lost to a good NC State team, coached by Clipper Smith, 6 to 0 in Raleigh. State finished 6-1-2, losing only to North Carolina.

On November 19, Duke went into Kenan Stadium in Chapel Hill and won 7 to 0. Nick Laney, the "Crooning Halfback" who sang with the campus orchestra, scored the only touchdown on a dive over the goal line from the two. Corky Cornelius booted the extra point, and the defense, led by Fred Crawford, Tom Rogers, Earle Wentz, Jack Dunlap, Lowell Mason, and Horace Hendrickson held UNC scoreless.

This win over arch-rival UNC in 1932 was Duke's first win in the series since 1893. Of course, from 1895 to 1919 Duke did not have a team, but Duke was 0 and 9 against UNC since 1893, with a tie in 1930. The Tarheels dominated Duke in the 1920s, winning eight straight from 1922 to 1929, the last four wins coming under Chuck Collins. This winning streak against Duke came despite the team having some down years itself; it was 4 and 5 in 1924 and 1926, and 4 and 6 in 1927.

A local reporter for the *Durham Morning Herald* filed this report on the game:

**Wallace Wade with Horace Hendrickson. Courtesy
of Duke Sports Information Department.**

Kicking from deep in Duke's territory, Laney booted a long, high spiral that struck the back of halfback McCaskill who was going down the field to block. Al Means, Duke tackle, fell on the ball on Carolina's 20-yard stripe. Coach Chuck Collins, Tar Heel mentor, displeased with the decision, went on the field to protest. Referee Hutchens inflicted a 15-yard penalty on Carolina, ruling the mentor had come on the field without permission and giving Duke a first down on Carolina's five. Captain Mason picked up three yards at center in two tries and then Laney dived over right tackle for the touchdown.

Carolina's offense never started functioning, due principally to the powerful rushes of Blue Devil ends who played a good part of the afternoon on Carolina's side of the line. The day was bad for foot-ball, recalling the famous battle of 'Lake Kenan' two years ago. Air attacks were out of the question and the teams stuck closely to their land attacks except when occasion demanded. Brilliant punting by Chuck Rossier, the big blond Dutchman from Pennsylvania, and Nick Laney, crooning halfback from Charlotte, figured prominently in Duke's triumph.

Following the game the presidents of the two student bodies gath-ered in the center of the gridiron, along with Captain Lowell Mason of the Blue Devils and Captain June Underwood of the Tar Heels. After an exchange of greetings between the student leaders, the hand-some football trophy donated by Carolina and Duke seniors three years ago, was turned over to Underwood who then presented it to Mason. The trophy will be at stake annually.

After the game, Coach Collins of UNC explained his trip on the field.

There was considerable question as to the officials' decision on the Duke punt. I thought it best to protest to the referee. The interpre-tation of the officials was that by placing one foot inside the field of play I was violating the rule against a coach coming on the field of play. This technicality has never been enforced this strict in any foot-ball game any place.

Despite this disagreement with the officiating, Collins was very gracious in his comments toward Duke. "Duke deserves all the credit for its well-earned vic-tory. The boys played heads-up football, showed fine spirit throughout the game, and exhibited excellent coaching and excellent sportsmanship."

Duke's three losses in 1932 come against teams that finished with a com-bined record of 24 wins, one loss, and four ties. This year marked the be-ginning of total domination of teams from the state of North Carolina and the Southern Conference that would continue for the next ten years. In the ten-season span from 1932 to 1941, Duke would compile the best won-loss record in the nation at 80-16-1. Against Southern Conference opponents in that span, Duke would go 48 and 6, with six conference championships. Against its closest three rivals, Duke was 26 and 4 playing UNC, NC State, and Wake Forest. Duke won 7 out of 10 games against UNC during these seasons.

An astounding statistic from this time was that the most points scored against Duke's vaunted defense in this ten-season span was the 20 Oregon State scored in the 1942 Rose Bowl. Of the 97 games Duke played in during this era, the defense shut out their opponents 50 times. The Wade system of football had been successfully transplanted from Alabama to Duke.

* * *

As athletic director and chair of the physical education department, Wade was successful in 1932. Duke's teams won Southern Conference championships in cross country, track, and golf. The first organized summer sports program of intramurals in the history of Duke was implemented by Wade in 1932. That year, 481 summer school students and faculty members took part in tennis, handball, swimming, ping pong, horseshoes, and other sports.

Beginning with the fall semester of 1932, physical education became a requirement for the bachelor of arts degree and the bachelor of science degree. The new requirements meant that graduates had to complete six semester hours of C work or better in physical education courses. Freshmen and sophomores were required to take physical education courses each semester. Courses offered were corrective gymnastics, tumbling and stunts, soccer, track, swimming, basketball, boxing, golf, tennis, and apparatus stunts. The program, announced Wade, would allow students to study in detail four different sports in the four semesters of their first two years, or if the students preferred, to continue in advanced courses of their favorite sport. This program was one of the first of its kind of any university in the south.

This type of physical training and sports participation was part of Wade's "man-building program," as he called it. Among staff members teaching these courses were W.W. "Cap" Card, Duke's first basketball coach and long-time gymnasium director, and Marshall Crichton, of the Hope Valley Country Club, who taught golf.

By the end of the fall semester of 1932, between the expanded intramural offerings and the new required courses in physical education, over 1,300 of the 1,436 undergraduate male students at Duke had participated in some sport or physical activity. 267 students took part in the intramural basketball tournament. Track was also a popular activity. By the end of the 1932–33 academic year, practically every undergraduate male student (the females had their own physical education program on East Campus), had taken part in some form of sports activity during the year. The greater share of the intramural entries were junior and senior students who had not been required to take physical education courses in their first two years, but who chose to get involved with the voluntary program of intramurals. Even students in the freshman and sophomore classes who were deemed "physically handicapped" were not exempt, but were assigned to the corrective gymnastics class to help overcome their "disabilities."

To encourage participation in intramurals, Wade awarded trophies and medals to tournament winning teams, and this was done before the entire student body at assemblies. Wade also initiated a Big Four Intramural Play Day to be hosted by Duke. Teams and individuals from Duke, UNC, NC State, and Wake Forest participated against each other in various sports.

Wade's philosophy of using physical training to aid the development of the intellect, while emphasizing academics over athletics, fit in well at Duke. The idea was to aid a student to become "the wholly awakened man," as Woodrow Wilson described the objectives of a liberal education. In 1965, the following was included in a "statement of rationale for the undergraduate curriculum" at Duke.

> A liberal education should help a man to know, to understand, to decide, and to express: to know the facts or how to find them, to understand those facts with insight and perspective, to decide only after understanding and conscious evaluation, and to express those decisions with ease and grace. These are not the sum of a liberal education, but they go far to assist the wholly awakened man in his unceasing quest to live with dignity and sensitivity in our complex world and to participate in the values and common purposes that infuse our civilization.

Wade believed strongly in this statement, but also felt the way to truly reach student's potential was to use physical activity as part of the curriculum.

CHAPTER EIGHTEEN

1933—Almost Perfect

Fred Crawford, a rising senior tackle on the 1933 team, stood six-foot-two inches tall, and weighed over 200 pounds. It was all muscle, save for the rock hard bone to which it was attached. He was fast, and on a football field he had a mean streak. His strength was widely known, especially by his opponents on the gridiron.

Born in Waynesville, North Carolina, he once picked up the front end of a car using one hand, then smiled toward his friends who witnessed the feat. According to Bob Quincy of the *Charlotte Observer*, Crawford had a handshake that had "the kind of grip that would have sent a cow to the moon had he been a milker." A reporter once asked Wade what he would do if Crawford weighed 225 pounds. Wade replied that he would not play him. The reporter, somewhat taken aback, asked Wade why not. "Because at that weight he would have killed somebody," was Wade's forthright reply.

Wade considered Crawford "the greatest lineman I have ever seen, and the quickest lineman ever across the line. He was as tough as iron and as true as steel, the most tremendous competitor I ever coached." Doc Newton, a coach at Davidson, once said, "If I had a choice of being locked up in a cage with Crawford or a bear, and I had a choice of which would catch me, I'd take the bear." Eddie Cameron, as assistant coach under Wade, said Crawford "was the fastest lineman I ever saw, especially at getting downfield on a punt. And he was a vicious tackler. He had a fine pair of hands and once he got you, you couldn't get away." Quincy also wrote about Crawford's uncanny blend of strength, size, and nasty football mentality. "He tackled with viciousness, but not meanness. Crawford without exception was the first man downfield on kickoffs and punts, smashing blockers like so many milk bottles, and often grabbing the ball carrier with one hand and shaking him like a doll." After watching Crawford play against his team, General Neyland of Tennessee said, "I never saw a greater exhibition of line play."

Crawford became the first player born in North Carolina to make the All-American team. In 1933 he received more votes than any player in the nation for the *Associated Press'* All-American team. The son of W.T. Crawford, a United States Representative, Fred is now in the College Football Hall of Fame.

Fred Crawford. Courtesy of Duke University Archives.

After graduation from Duke, Crawford played for the Chicago Bears along-side Bronko Nagurski. He also appeared in several movies, including one with Shirley Temple. He then spent 20 years working as a deputy commissioner with the Florida Motor Vehicle Division.

* * *

Duke established itself as a true national power in 1933. It easily defeated VMI and Wake Forest to open the season. Next was Tennessee, coming to Durham with a 28 game unbeaten streak, its last loss being in 1930 to Wade's last Alabama team. A crowd of 30,000 saw Duke win 10 to 2 over a team that had lost only two games since the 1926 season. In one of the great runs in college football history, Tennessee had recorded 63 wins, two losses, and five ties from 1926 to the Duke game of 1933. This win for Duke put it in the national spotlight, and prognosticators started to notice it as possible national title contenders.

Corky Cornelius, a halfback from Winston-Salem, scored all ten points for Duke. He kicked a 17-yard field goal in the second quarter, ran for a 15-yard touchdown in the fourth quarter, and then kicked the point after. Dick McAninch returned a punt back 61 yards to set up the touchdown. Horace Hendrickson, the Duke quarterback, did a superb job of leading the team; "perfect" was the word Wade used to describe Hendrickson's play.

Fred Crawford was heartily praised by Coach Neyland after the game. Beattie Feathers was held in check by the Duke defensive lineup. Feathers was a consensus All-American halfback in 1933. Bob Murphy of the *Knoxville Journal* described Feathers in the week before the Duke game: "Heavier than ever, Feathers this year has not one pound of excess flesh on his body. But he still maintains that great drive that startled 40,000 in Yankee Stadium in 1931 [in a win over New York University], and the same skill and daring that has raised him to southern football's dizziest heights."

Interestingly, Feathers and Hendrickson would both become head coaches in the future at North Carolina State. Feathers had a record of 37-38-3 from 1944 to 1951. He was succeeded by Hendrickson, who went 4-16 in 1952 and 1953. After serving as an assistant to Wade at Duke after graduating in 1934, Hendrickson became head coach at Elon College in 1937. From then through 1941, Horace compiled a record of 31-12-1, which remains the second-best winning percentage at Elon for any football coach with a minimum of five years. Hendrickson used many of the tactics he had learned under Wade, employing the single-wing offense with an unbalanced line, and his practices were very intense. In 1941, Elon finished 8-1, the lone loss to the Miami Hurricanes in Miami.

Hendrickson had great success also as head basketball coach at Elon, producing a five-year record of 95-20. As baseball coach for four years, he was 68-15. Hendrickson's combined record at Elon coaching football, basketball, and baseball was 194-47-1.

"The Horse," as Horace was often called, was considered "one of the greatest quarterbacks Duke University has ever produced, and a fine leader of men," according to Wade. An assistant football coach of Hendrickson's, Joe Brunansky, who also had played for Wade at Duke, became head baseball coach in 1942 at Elon.

* * *

Wild, joyous celebrations erupted in Durham and on the Duke campus after the Tennessee win. This was the first win in Duke's football history that really garnered national attention, as Tennessee was one of the dominant teams in the country. The buildup to the game had been unprecedented, with

Durham merchants putting up window displays of Duke players and coaches, and the Durham Chamber of Commerce and city officials decorating streets downtown with banners and flags. On the Duke campus, effigies of Tennessee football players could be seen hanging from the windows of many dormitories. An electrically illuminated sign of "Beat Tennessee" was displayed for the week preceding the game. One student composed a song entitled, "Who's Afraid of the Big Bad Wolf?" On the night before the game, most of the student body led a "pep parade," with the university band in tow, from the women's East Campus into downtown Durham. Hotels were swamped with reservations, as fan and alumni interest was high.

Six women students from Duke acted as "sponsors" of the teams. Three Duke students from the state of Tennessee sponsored the Volunteers, and three other students sponsored Duke. The young ladies sat along the sidelines in specially decorated boxes, and they wore either the colors of blue and white for Duke or orange and white for Tennessee.

* * *

Hosting Auburn on November 4, the Devils got revenge for their loss to the Tigers the year before, winning 13 to 7. After beating Maryland, Duke was 7 and 0 going into the North Carolina game. Fans totaling 32,000 packed Duke Stadium to see the rivalry game, the largest attendance to that time in the state for a sporting event. The excitement before the game was captured by the *Durham Morning Herald*:

> The Duke University Blue Devils, striving for their first national championship, met the University of North Carolina Tar Heels in a gridiron attraction that promised to attract the greatest crowd ever to see a game in North Carolina. Perfect weather prevailed.
>
> Carolina came on the field before game time and went through its warm-up exercises. Shortly afterwards, Captain Carl Schock led the Blue Devils onto the field, and they received a great ovation.
>
> Carolina's band, accompanied by Rameses III, marched on the field for a few warming up capers. He was accompanied by two Carolina students and, probably due to the fact that only yesterday he was the victim of kidnappers, attracted the attention of everyone in the stands.
>
> Coach Collins of Carolina was accompanied by the officials across the field to Duke's side of the stadium to exchange greetings with Coach Wade. Shortly before game time the Duke band marched on the field and took its place with the Carolina musicians. The Duke

mascot, a Blue Devil, shared the front position with Rameses. The Blue Devil, tired of waiting for the band, parked himself on Rameses's back and went for a ride.

As for the game itself, Horace Hendrikson scored two touchdowns in the first quarter to build a 14 to 0 lead. Wade was so confident in his defense that he played the second team for much of the rest of the game. Bob Cox intercepted a pass and returned it 25 yards for a touchdown in the last quarter, finishing a 21 to 0 victory. One local sportswriter, after witnessing the devastation Fred Crawford unleashed on the Tar Heels, wrote, "There never was another just like him and there probably never will be."

Freshmen on Duke's campus were especially happy after the win over UNC. It was tradition at Duke for freshmen to wear "dinky caps" to signify their status. Beta Omega Sigma, an honorary sophomore order, had announced that if Duke beat UNC, the freshmen could doff their caps for the rest of the year. This started another tradition, from 1933 on a Duke win over UNC in football would allow "doffing of the dinks." For most of the 1930s, freshmen at Duke could be seen bareheaded around campus after the annual battle with their rivals from Chapel Hill.

After beating NC State, Duke was 9 and 0 and on the verge of playing for a national championship. Army was also 9 and 0 going into its last game of the regular season, and Princeton was 8 and 0; these teams were the only undefeated teams left in the country.

Duke's last game was a trip to Atlanta to face a Georgia Tech team that was 4 and 5. The *Associated Press* reporter at the game summed up what happened in his opening lines:

> Duke's dreams of a perfect season and a possible Rose Bowl bid were dashed here today by a relentless and resolute Georgia Tech eleven that scored a second period touchdown and then stiffened to repulse every Duke threat in the closing quarters. The Engineers whipped the Blue Devils 6 to 0 and stamped a bitter climax to the record of the best team in Duke history.

Duke secured what was thought to be a tying touchdown, but Fred Crawford was ruled off-sides. This infraction pushed the ball back to the six-yard line, and Tech held Duke out of the end zone.

Wade attempted to motivate his team at half-time by reading players a telegram from the Rose Bowl Committee inviting them to the New Year's game if they won over Tech. But it didn't work. Columbia beat Stanford in the Rose Bowl 7 to 0.

This was without question one of Wade's most bitter defeats as a coach. Duke was a heavy favorite over a Georgia Tech team that was having a lackluster season. The Rose Bowl and an opportunity to play for a national title were on the line. Nevertheless, 1933 was a season that propelled Duke to national acclaim. Duke did win its first ever Southern Conference championship and Fred Crawford made all the All-American teams. Someone coined this poem about how hard it was, and is, to pick the All-American team.

> I know your tackles had the stuff,
> I know your guards were fine,
> I know your backs were fast and rough,
> No team could dent your line,
> I know your quarter was a dream,
> But hear me, distant brothers,
> I know you had a super team,
> But listen—there were others.
>
> I knew your kicker was a star,
> Your blockers were the best,
> Your passers pegged 'em true and far,
> Your spinners met the test,
> I know you should have won them all,
> But wait a minute, brothers,
> Far off I hear the wild winds call—
> But also—there were others.
>
> Believe me when I say that I
> Am for you all the way,
> Know your passers hid the sky,
> You held the foe at bay,
> I'd like to write up every name,
> That crowded space still smothers,
> But don't pain me—I'm not to blame—
> There are so many others.

* * *

One young man at Duke who probably did not attend all the football games in 1933 was Willis Adams. Willis needed to work through his college years, so he delivered milk. He would leave his parents' house in Clarksville, Virginia, each morning and load his delivery truck. On the 65-mile journey to Duke each day, he would deliver milk to his customers, and on the return trip home after classes, he would pick up the empty bottles.

CHAPTER NINETEEN

1934

As Coach Wade prepared for the start of his fourth year at Duke, other events around campus were taking place. Eleanor Roosevelt spoke in Duke Stadium before 8,000 people in June, emphasizing the role of public opinion as a means to world peace. Roosevelt also visited what is now North Carolina Central University in Durham. With World War II still seven years away for the United States, she said, "I feel very strongly that those among us who are old enough to remember the last war have a special obligation to tell of our own experiences." In May of 1934, the *Duke Chronicle*, the student newspaper, was declared the best college newspaper in the United States. The *Duke Chronicle* in 1935 went to a twice-weekly publishing schedule.

Jack Coombs and his Duke baseball team posted a fine record of 20 and 4. Dr. J.B. Rhine, associate professor of psychology at Duke, published a book entitled *Extra-Sensory Perception*. Bill Werber, a former Duke star in baseball and basketball, made headlines as the third baseman for the Boston Red Sox. Werber was among the league leaders in stolen bases, runs scored, and hits, while hitting well over .300 most of the year.

Grantland Rice, the most famous sportswriter in America, brought his Sportlight sound movie company to Duke to take pictures of the football and baseball teams. These movies were shown in theatres around the country. Coach Wade talked on camera about his "three don'ts of football": don't have punts blocked, don't have passes intercepted, and don't fumble. Wade was asked to speak at clinics, or coaching schools, around the country, in addition to running his own school at Duke during the summer of 1934. Harry Kipke, the Michigan coach, asked Wade to attend Michigan's spring football practice, and Wade accepted and shared his philosophy of football with the Wolverine coaches and players. Also, Wade spoke on the Duke campus to 420 high school boys about "Athletics and Character."

At his own summer school for coaches, Wade shared his knowledge with high school and college coaches. Wade believed strongly in the Dewey maxim, "one learns better by doing," and he emphasized actual demonstration on the field, while also making time for lectures by himself and his assistants. He did not talk much about detailed plays or fancy formations but emphasized plain, hard-hitting football based on a sound knowledge of fundamentals, which is the way he coached.

Wade made these important points in a lecture in 1934 at his coaches' school, which was packed with eager coaches wanting to know what made Wade, this man who had won so many conference and national championships by the age of 42, so successful.

> The fundamentals can be taught, but you can't teach a back to be as shifty as you'd like him to be or a lineman to be a tiger. Loose-jointed backs and man-eating linemen are born, rather than made.
>
> In the offensive stance and charge of linemen, the lineman should assume a comfortable stance with the feet spread about the width of the shoulders, one foot being slightly advanced, the weight resting equally on the balls of the feet. The heels should be directly over the toes, knees bent well and reasonably close to the ground. If the left foot is advanced, the right hand should be on the ground and the left forearm should be resting on the left thigh. The lineman should be careful not to have too much weight on his hand. The back should be straight and almost parallel to the ground. The hips should be slightly lower than the shoulders. In the charge, the linemen should drive hard from both feet, shooting the shoulders forward, the left knee dropping to within four to six inches of the ground. As the shoulders go forward the right foot (rear foot) should be brought forward for a short step.
>
> I don't believe in low-tackling, that is, too low. I want my tacklers to hit the opposing runner waist high, head always up with the eyes open. The arms should be locked around the knees of the runner, the shoulders at his waist, and the arms should be jerked with the feet driving hard. In this way, the runner falls backward and is deprived of those two or three yards he might have gained by falling forward.
>
> There are three things which will cause a team to be beaten: have a punt blocked, a pass intercepted, or a fumble recovered. A back cannot fumble and play for me. They need to learn the proper way to carry a ball, none of this carrying the ball in front of them in their hands. The proper place for it is one point under the pit of the arm with the hand over the other point.

An added touch to the intramural activities in 1934, which Coach Wade so strongly believed in, was an attractive blue and white handbook dedicated to "Sports For All and All For Sports." It contained intramural records of all sports on campus for the past two years and team honors and high scorers. Wade also added a personal note to students on the value of athletics, and got President Few and Dean Wannamaker to do the same.

* * *

There were plenty of returning players in 1934, such as the Dunlap brothers, Jack and E.B., Earle Wentz, Corky Cornelius, Gus Durner, and Jack Alexander. A sophomore made his varsity debut, one Clarence Parker, better known as Ace Parker. Parker would become, in time, what most consider the greatest football player ever for Duke. Parker is now in the College Football Hall of Fame and is one of three players from Duke in the Pro Football Hall of Fame. The other two are Sonny Jurgensen and George McAfee.

On October 20, Duke exacted some revenge for the devastating 1933 loss to Georgia Tech by beating them at home 20 to 0. On November 3, Duke traveled to Birmingham, site of so many Wade triumphs while at Alabama, and beat Auburn. Zipp Newman of the *Birmingham News* covered the game.

> Duke University staged a great fourth period rally to come from behind in the rain and slush in defeating Auburn at Legion Field, 13 to 6. The Blue Devils scored in four plays of the fourth period. Clarence Parker hit center for two yards and Cornelius got a yard on a lateral pass. Alexander made four yards on a spinner and on the fourth down, the Auburn secondary defense was caught off guard. Ace Parker took the ball from center and started moving backward. He located Corky Cornelius 15 yards down the field, and cut loose a pass right over the center of the line of scrimmage. The Corky one spun around and sold out for the goal line. Corky then put the Blue Devils out in front with a placement kick between the middle of the uprights.

> Later in the period the Blue Devils went to work for their second touchdown, getting it in two plays. Dick McAninch hit center for three yards, and then came the Wade spinner with Jack Alexander over his own left guard and running 38 yards for a touchdown. Jack Dunlap took out the secondary defense in Alexander's path, a very fine piece of blocking.

> Jack Dunlap, Ed West, and E.B. Dunlap were outstanding in the Duke line. Jack really knows what football is all about. He is hard to fool. Ace Parker was the outstanding back on the field. He overshadowed the field in running, punting, and handling the ball. Tab Parker, he is destined to become one of the great backs of the south. Jack Alexander was a pretty fair fullback. He led the yardage ticket with 80

in 15 tries with the ball, and that is fair yardage against a stubborn line with slippery footings.

Coach Wade showed a beautifully coached team, a team that was able to come from behind. And as long as his line continues to play the same article of line play as exhibited here, the Blue Devils will be in high cotton, or maybe it should be tobacco.

Jack Meagher was in his first year as head coach of Auburn. Meagher would compile a 48-37-10 record at Auburn through 1942, when he would be succeeded by an assistant to Wade at Duke in 1934, Carl Voyles. Voyles, who had been brought from Illinois to Duke by Wade, compiled a 15-22 record at Auburn from 1944 through 1947. He had much better success at William and Mary, where he became head coach in 1939 and won 29 games with only seven losses and three ties, including a Southern Conference championship in 1942.

Duke finished the season 7 and 2, beating NC State 32 to 0 in the last game. Wade's record in his first four years at Duke was 28-9-2 for a very good start, but better years were on the horizon.

* * *

The Duke freshman team finished unbeaten in 1934, winning its last game over the Tar Babies of North Carolina 21 to 18. Head coach Herschel Caldwell was assisted by Horace Hendrickson and Tom Rogers, outstanding players for the 1933 varsity team. Members of this team that would soon make a big impact on the varsity were Joe Brunansky and Elmore "Honey" Hackney. Caldwell also coached the freshman basketball team to a 13 and 3 record.

Also in 1934, Coach Frank Thomas led Alabama to a 10 and 0 record and a Rose Bowl win over Stanford on January 1, 1935. This win brought back to Tuscaloosa the school's fourth national title. Alabama beat such teams as Tennessee, Georgia, Georgia Tech, and Vanderbilt before being invited to the Rose Bowl. Stanford came into the Rose Bowl 9-0-1 under Coach C.E. Thornhill. Thomas was continuing the tradition Wallace Wade had started at Alabama, having compiled a 33-4-1 record since replacing Wade in 1931. His 34th win came over Stanford 29 to 13 in front of 85,000 fans.

The 1934 team featured the great Don Hutson, who was one of the best players to ever don a Crimson uniform, and went on to stardom with the Green Bay Packers. The success of Hutson and his teammate at Alabama, quarterback Dixie Howell, changed the way college teams looked at the forward pass.

Bear Bryant, who played with Hutson, best sums up Hutson's all-around athletic ability.

Once during an Alabama game, Hutson wore his tracksuit under his baseball flannels because a dual track meet was scheduled simultaneously on the track adjacent to the baseball diamond. Between innings, Don stripped off his baseball togs, got into the starting block, and ran the one hundred yard dash in 9.8 to win the race.

Howell, from Hartford, Alabama, was the MVP of the Rose Bowl against Stanford. Grantland Rice wrote: "Dixie Howell ... blasted the Rose Bowl dreams of Stanford today with one of the greatest all-around exhibitions football has ever known." Howell completed 9 of 12 passes for 160 yards, ran for 79 more, and punted six times for a 44-yard average.

The Rose Bowl game with Stanford was always a special memory for Bear Bryant, who played end on the team that year. In his autobiography, Bryant said,

> I remember every minute of the game. We had it won by the fourth quarter. It had all seemed like a dream come true to me—the thrill of being invited, of going, of getting to play in front of all those people—an ordinary football player among great players. All those things are rich in my memory.

Bryant truly showed what he was made of in 1935 against Mississippi State, breaking his leg in the first quarter, but coming back to play the second half. He started the game the next week against Tennessee. "It was just one little bone," Bryant explained.

CHAPTER TWENTY

1935

Duke won its second Southern Conference championship in 1935, and finished 8 and 2 with big wins over North Carolina and Tennessee. The Tennessee game was highlighted by great efforts from Ace Parker and Elmore "Honey" Hackney. On Duke's first score of an eventual 19 to 6 win, Parker had punted the ball 65 yards to back the Volunteers up to their 10-yard line. Tennessee fumbled on the first play after the punt, with Duke recovering. Parker ran over his right tackle for six yards, then Jule Ward ran for three. Jack Alexander then scored. Hackney ran the ball three straight times for gains of 19, 17, and 11 yards to score later in the game. Hackney added a seven-yard run to score Duke's final touchdown.

A 100-float parade was held the morning of the game with Tennessee as part of Homecoming. The mammoth parade was estimated to be three miles long, with special floats for "Miss Durham" and the Duke coeds who sponsored the game. Several female Duke students rode in the parade on horseback.

This annual game with Tennessee was becoming one of the great rivalries in the nation. Coach Neyland and Coach Wade had the utmost respect for each other, and they both often said, "If I've got to lose, I'd just as soon lose to Tennessee/Duke." In some years this game was so heavily anticipated that a play-by-play report of the game was staged over the Duke grid-graph in Page Auditorium on campus.

One Duke student, anticipating the encounters with Tennessee and UNC, and using Duke players Ace Parker, Ed West, Jack Alexander, and Jule Ward in his poem, wrote the following before the Tennessee game:

> The Volunteers and Tar Heels
> Are mighty men they say.
> Duke, licked by both in '34,
> Is out to make them pay.
>
> California [Rose Bowl] here we come,
> Is the theme song on the Hill,

> But they, I fear, have quite forgot
> That Duke's a bitter pill.
>
> Oh Ace is Ace, and west is west
> And never the Vols shall win.
> Alexander the Great will lead the team,
> As the Devils go on-Ward again.

UNC came into the Duke game undefeated and a favorite to get a Rose Bowl invitation if it won its last two games against Duke and Virginia. Duke came into the game 6 and 2. Fans numbering 46,880 turned out in Duke Stadium to watch, the largest ever to attend a college football game in the south up to that time. Fred Haney of the *Durham Morning Herald* wrote, "The University of North Carolina's Rose Bowl Special, already past seven serious obstacles, was completely wrecked here yesterday afternoon when a highly inspired Duke Blue Devil machine ran roughshod over their opponents to register a brilliant 25 to 0 victory." Jack Alexander intercepted a UNC pass and returned it 90 yards for one score. Robert House, Dean of Administration of UNC, confessed to a friend that his emotions had been "so terribly involved and my expectation of victory so complacently sure that the upset made me physically sick."

Most of the national newsreel organizations came to Durham for the game. NBC and CBS radio both aired the game nationwide. Ticket demand was extremely high. As the *Charlotte Observer* reported, "You'll have to pay $5.00 for a ticket. That's what the petty scalpers are asking. Some of the 50-yard line babies have gone for as high as $7.50." Ted Mann, sports publicist for Duke, was bombarded with ticket requests. In one telegram to John Oliver of the *Richmond News Leader*, Mann replied, "Sure, will take care of you. Will leave tickets in my office Saturday morning. Please advise if Hamilton plans to cover game. I sent the bald-headed scoundrel two press box tickets."

For the game, Duke used 140 ushers, along with 75 deputies, 30 Durham policemen, 35 state patrolmen, and 30 officers from the state internal revenue department. An extra parking field was used, and additional drinking booths were opened.

A few days after the UNC game, UNC's student paper, *The Daily Tar Heel*, charged that Duke had scouted the Tar Heels with a "slow-motion movie camera" at one of UNC's previous games and claimed the act to be unethical. In fact, there was no rule against the scouting, and many schools had started to do it with movies by this time. In a telegram sent to the *Associated Press* by Duke officials, it made plain that no violation occurred.

Coach Wallace Wade of Duke University today reported "the motion picture camera affair" to the Southern Conference and received the following telegram from Forest Fletcher, of Washington and Lee, president of the conference: "Inasmuch as there is no conference rule against the using of pictures in football, I can see no reason for an objection."

Woody Woodhouse of the *Durham Sun* simply thought it was sour grapes on the part of UNC head coach Carl Snavely, who had seen his Rose Bowl dream die with the defeat to Duke. Snavely even wrote a reply to Woodhouse's column, which also appeared in the *Durham Sun*. Snavely wrote to Woodhouse that

> some of your representations are so libelous and so distorted that, in fairness to myself and to friends of the university who have asked me to reply, I feel compelled to take exception to them. I want to make clear I was not in any sense responsible for the charges which appeared in *The Daily Tar Heel*. The moving picture incident unfortunately was given an importance which it never merited, and the assumption that I fell back upon it as an alibi is ridiculous, as I have said repeatedly and I say again that the motion pictures were NOT responsible for our defeat. As I told Coach Wade immediately after the game, Duke deserved to win because they played harder, faster, more alert, and better football.

In Woodhouse's reply, again in the *Durham Sun*, he wrote:

> We trust that the reading public took into consideration while perusing Mr. Snavely's epistle to the writer that it could have been just as easily tossed into any convenient waste basket as printed in this space. By way of suggestion, why not learn how to lose a football game gracefully. Lose the battle with that same grace and clean sportsmanship which characterized each triumph during your two-year reign at Chapel Hill.

Carl Snavely resigned after the 1935 season despite a two-year record at UNC of 15-2-1. It was speculated at the time that he left to go to Cornell because of the Graham Plan, an initiation led by Frank Porter Graham, the president of the University of North Carolina system, that would have de-emphasized the role of athletics in college life. Regardless of the reason, Snavely went to Cornell in 1936 and posted a 46-26-3 record through 1944. The 1939 team is considered to be Cornell's best team ever by some, going 8 and 0.

Coach Snavely, just as he had told Coach Wade that Duke deserved to win in 1935, showed his character in 1940. In a game against Dartmouth, Cornell's 18-game unbeaten streak was in jeopardy. Trailing 3 to 0 with seconds to play, Dartmouth batted away a last chance pass by Cornell into the end zone. Referee Red Friesell mistakenly ruled the pass had occurred on third down, and Cornell scored on a touchdown pass for an apparent win. Two days after the game, and the admission of the error by Friesell, Snavely and Cornell officials wired Dartmouth to concede defeat.

Snavely returned to UNC in 1945 and had some of the Tar Heel's greatest teams, going 25-5-2 from 1946 to 1948 with the great Charlie "Choo Choo" Justice. Snavely coached at UNC through 1952 and finished with an overall record during his two stops in Chapel Hill of 59-35-5. He also coached at Bucknell and Washington and Lee, and is now in the College Football Hall of Fame.

Wade and Snavely were bitter rivals, but still had much respect for the other. The movie-scouting episode was definitely overblown and was more of a dispute among the media than between the teams and coaches. There is no doubt, either, that the coming of Wallace Wade to Duke necessitated a renewed emphasis on football at UNC to keep up, along with other schools in the state of North Carolina.

* * *

Another interesting event took place well before the Duke-UNC game of 1935. Judge Walter Small excused Wade from jury duty in a murder case, just before Wade was to leave with the team for a game with Washington and Lee. Small, a University of North Carolina alumnus, admonished Wade,

> If you were about to play Carolina, the court might detain you, but as you are going out of state to play a great school that bears the names of two of the world's greatest generals, I will excuse you this time, but I will try to be here just before the Carolina-Duke game and select you as a juror in order to lend a helping hand to Carolina.

Sticking to his plans for increasing athletic opportunities at Duke for its students, Wade had formed a "B" team at Duke for the 1935 season. Several northern schools had been organizing B teams, but this was the first time a southern team had such a team. The B team beat Campbell College, but lost to Lenoir Rhyne, Elon, Oak Ridge, and the Navy B team.

Head Coach Herschel Caldwell led the freshman team to its second consecutive Little Five championship, beating the Tar Babies of UNC for the crown. This team outscored its five opponents 107 to 6. Boding well for the future of Duke football was the play of two Baby Devils, Eric Tipton and Dan Hill, two future All-Americans.

After the season, accolades and tributes continued to pour in for Wade. He was featured in *Liberty* magazine. Duke renewed his contract for another five years, raising his base salary to $15,000 per year. After five years at Duke, his record stood at 35-11-2 with two conference championships. As the *Roanoke Times* put it,

> Wade has done very well for Duke since transferring his allegiance from the University of Alabama to the Durham school. Incidentally, he hasn't done badly for himself either. With a $15,000 coach, moving picture equipment for scouting purposes, and exceptional facilities for athletes, Duke has a right to expect the Blue Devils to go places on the gridiron. As yet they haven't gone as far as the Pasadena Rose Bowl, it is true, but just give Mr. Wade time. He's been to the Rose Bowl before, at Alabama, and Duke alumni are confident that in time he'll go there again. Meantime, they have the 1935 Southern Conference title to compensate them. A $15,000 coaching job isn't to be despised and probably there isn't a coach in the south who wouldn't gladly exchange his contract for Wade's.

Frank Graham, president of the UNC system schools, launched in 1935 his plan to clean up college athletics. Graham wanted to ban recruiting of any kind, athletic scholarships and loans, and the giving of jobs to any athlete. Freshmen would be ineligible for athletic competition. The plan was defeated, due in large part to the opposition of Wallace Wade. Wade was widely quoted as being against such reforms because they would limit participation in football to the sons of families with means of their own to pay tuition and fees. Had the Graham Plan been enacted, football at Duke, a private university with higher fees than the state institutions, would have been greatly affected. Ted Mann, director of sports information at Duke at the time, said that many Duke football players of the 1930s earned their expenses by working in the university's dining halls.

CHAPTER TWENTY-ONE

1936 — Ace Parker, an All-American

Before the 1936 season began, Ted Mann, the Duke sports information director, wrote a personality sketch of Wade. By this time Wade and the Duke football program were claiming headlines around the nation, and it was Mann's job to keep fans informed as to what was going on in football at Duke. It all began with Wade.

> His greatest and strongest belief is in hard work. He has had to work hard all his life and he expects the same from all those who are around him. His attention to the details is probably the reason for his success. He is generally recognized as the nation's outstanding authority on the fundamentals of blocking and tackling.
>
> "The Bear," as those who are associated call him behind his back, of course, is a fairly good looking man, his facial features are well formed. His face is bronze from frequent exposure to the southern sun and he has freckles on his neck. His bones are big, even in his fingers, and he has 185 pounds of flesh on his slightly under six-foot frame. He is graceful, or "has poise." His voice, soft in speaking and with a typical Tennessee drawl of the nasal variety, sounds as if amplified on the football field, it is one of those "carrying" voices.
>
> His practices are not boring because every 15 minutes the student manager blows a whistle and something else is started. There is no time lost as he tells his assistants beforehand what is to be done that day. The drills are short and snappy. But he does not hesitate to have a play run over and over when it is wrong. He wants to get it correct right now. And he will let his team run a certain play for two months before using it in a game. He says it takes that long, or longer, to perfect a play.
>
> Wade has able assistants in coaching the varsity but he does most of the coaching himself. He will get down on the ground with any of

his players. In demonstrating a play for the coaches attending his summer coaching school one summer, he broke two ribs.

His system is the single-wing, an outgrowth of the Warner style of play. However, he says, the system to use is the one that best fits your players. His system is well-balanced, the team spending about 49 percent of the time on offense and about 51 percent on defense.

His hobby is golf. In off-season he lives on the links and does a little hunting. He plays no golf during the football season. He shoots in the high 70s and occasionally in the low 70s.

Two quotes of his show his toughness. "Giving your best is not good enough if it doesn't get the job done," and, "The road to failure is paved with players who did their best. The best player is the one who does what is necessary."

* * *

Wade spoke in New York City during the summer of 1936 at the New York Herald Tribune Coaching School. Harry Cross of the *New York Herald Tribune* reported on Wade's topic of defense.

That Wade is a sincere talker was attested by the fact that he held more than three hundred men under his oratorical spell without one of them sneaking out. "The job of the coach," he said, "is not primarily to win games, but also to do his share as a part of the educational system."
Wade said that his charges were drilled thoroughly in rushing passers and kickers. He said the coaching staff at Durham tried to put the players in the mental attitude that during the season, a certain number of touchdowns were expected from intercepted passes and a certain number from blocked kicks. The business of blocking punts and intercepting passes, Wade told his listeners, was a phase which required as much schooling and drilling as any other part of the game.

Wade also spoke at a clinic in Pittsburgh, and by 1936, his own coaching school in Durham was attracting coaches from around the nation. At Duke in July, Wade told the assembled coaches to stress fundamentals.

You coaches should drill your men in the fundamentals of the game and keep drilling them along this line. Once the fundamentals are perfected, then you can set about the task of straightening your problems of offense and defense. Regardless of the number of stars on your squad, you cannot have a successful team unless your boys know the fundamentals of the game.

There must be balance before your team can succeed. Perfect timing is needed between your line play and attack. If one is better than the other, then ragged football results, and defeat is inevitable.

One attendee to Duke's coaching school in 1936 was well satisfied, among others to be sure. He wrote,

I joined Coach Wade's school last week at Duke, where many coaches from 12 different states assembled to receive instructions from Wallace Wade, Eddie Cameron, Carl Voyles, Ellis Hagler, Herschel Caldwell, and Add Warren. Of all the schools that I have attended in bygone days and years, this proved the most interesting and profitable. I refer particularly to the emphasis placed upon those qualifications of body and mind and spirit that are required for success anywhere and everywhere in human affairs. Coach Wade devoted three-and-a-half hours each day to lectures and demonstrations in the grid course. Blocking, tackling, line defense and offense, punting and passing, backfield maneuvers, kick for the extra point, and numerous other features of the game were taught and demonstrated. Great emphasis was placed upon the spirit of the players.

* * *

President Few received an interesting letter denouncing the Blue Devil mascot name. Mrs. J.H. Robertson wrote Few,

I read about the great architectural grandeur and beauty of Duke University, the staunch Christian principles and high ideals for which it stands, and I wonder why the ones in authority allow the whole picture to be blurred by the fact that the ball teams bear the name of the *evil spirit*. We have a fine, beautiful industrious bird, the blue jay. Why not change the name from Blue Devils to Blue Jay? We do not want to work or play like the devil as he deceives, defrauds, and causes trouble.

* * *

Colgate came to Durham for a game that received much national publicity. CBS and NBC were on hand to broadcast the game to the nation over radio. Newsreel companies took shots for distribution to the movie houses throughout the country. Hearst Metronome News was one of the newsreel companies that featured highlights of games such as Duke and Colgate on movie screens before the regular movie. Grantland Rice attended behind

Duke's newly erected glass-front press row. Duke shut out Andy Kerr's team 6 to 0 in front of nearly 30,000 fans at Duke Stadium.

After beating South Carolina, Clemson, and Georgia Tech, Duke was 5 and 0 heading to Knoxville to take on Tennessee. Tennessee had just played Alabama to a 0-0 tie in Birmingham in their last game. By 1936, Wade and General Neyland were at the top of their profession. Going into their battle in 1936, both of their records were superlative. Wade's record stood at 102-24-5, while Neyland's was 77-9-6, with two of his losses coming against Wade. Morgan Blake wrote *The Clash of Giants* right before their 1935 encounter.

> The fur will fly in Knoxville
> And loud will be the crash,
> The gore will flow in Knoxville
> When Wade and Neyland clash.
> Oh, what a treat in Knoxville,
> Oh, fortunate the fans,
> Who see the mighty struggle
> Between these gridiron clans.
> The cry is 'On to Knoxville.'
> Where history will be made,
> To see the clash of giants,
> When Major Bob meets Wade.

In a game that saw the lead change hands four times, Tennessee won as Red Harp grabbed a punt in the closing minutes of play and raced 82 yards for a touchdown and a 15-13 Vol victory. Elmore "Honey" Hackney scored first as he returned a punt 47 yards to put Duke up 6 to 0. In the third quarter, Tennessee recorded a safety to make it 6-2, then scored a touchdown and converted the extra point to lead 9-6. Early in the fourth quarter, Ace Parker caught a touchdown pass from Hackney, then Parker converted the point after.

Duke led 13-9 until the Harp touchdown. O.B. Keeler of the *Atlanta Journal* wrote after the game:

> Tennessee has beaten Duke—beaten the Blue Devils 15 to 13. Beaten Duke along the route, as everyone has been saying, that leads to the Rose Bowl, beaten Duke in the maddest, wildest, most topsy-turvy football game ever played in Knoxville, or, so swear the wild-eyed customers, anywhere else, since Walter Camp started the pastime at dear old Yale.

By the North Carolina game on November 14, Duke had rebounded to beat Washington and Lee and Wake Forest to run its record to 7 and 1. The *Asso-*

ciated Press, which started ranking teams in 1936, had Duke 13th in the nation going into the UNC game. However, before the loss to Tennessee, Duke was number two in the country, behind only Minnesota. UNC was 6 and 1 coming into the Duke game, and had beaten Tennessee 14 to 6, losing only to Tulane.

On a cool, sunny day at Kenan Stadium in Chapel Hill, Duke again dominated play against the Tar Heels just as they had in 1935. Early in the second half, Ace Parker grabbed a kickoff five yards back of his own goal and dashed 105 yards, and it was reported that a spectator, a UNC alumnus, Alvis Patterson, collapsed shortly after Parker's sprint and died in an ambulance enroute to the hospital.

Wade, as he had done on many occasions throughout his career, started his second team, with the exception of Parker. After UNC drove to the Duke 20, Wade sent in his first team, and thus kept Carolina from scoring. Shortly before half-time, Duke drove to the UNC 15-yard line. Eric "The Red" Tipton, so called for his flaming hair, ran the ball four successive times straight up the middle, scoring on the fourth line buck. Parker converted to put Duke up 7 to 0. Art Ditt scored to knot the score at 7 early in the second half, right before Parker's exciting kickoff return put Duke up 14 to 7. Bob O'Mara and Tipton scored later to make the final score 27 to 7.

Duke closed its season with a 13-0 win over NC State to finish 9 and 1, also winning its third Southern Conference title in four years. Duke finished eleventh in the nation in the AP's final poll. After the season, Coach Wade received a telegram from the Cuban government. It read,

> Would Duke University consider playing first class southern or eastern opponent football game in Havana New Year's Day? Teams to be personally invited by President Miguel Mariano Gomez of Cuba. Purpose of contest to promote international good will and closer unity between Latin America and United States. Signed: Carlos Henriquez, Commissioner of Sports, Republic of Cuba.

The game did not happen, however, as the Southern Conference ruled against it. It was reported also that the Orange Bowl, which had started in 1935, considered Duke for its game, but it settled on Duquesne and Mississippi State.

Duke only allowed 28 points in its ten games of 1936. The Tennessee loss probably kept it from playing for a national title in the Rose Bowl. This was probably Wade's best team in his six seasons at Duke, even better than the 1933 9 and 1 team led by the great Fred Crawford.

Ace Parker was a consensus All-American in 1936. He simply did everything on a gridiron one man could do. He punted 61 times for a 42.2 average,

**Ace Parker, Coach Wade and Dan Hill. Courtesy
of Duke University Archives.**

passed for ten completions for 180 yards, caught nine passes for 149 yards, ran for 647 yards, scored eight touchdowns, and kicked four extra points. In an era of single-platoon football, he also played well on defense. Wade commented on the play of Parker, who he always called by his real name, Clarence,

> I have always thought John Cain of Alabama in 1930 and Beattie Feathers of Tennessee in 1933 were the two greatest all-around backs in Southern football history. I have revised my list to include Parker. When it comes to kicking, passing, running, defensive play, and blocking, I think Clarence is the best all-around back I have ever coached.

Parker, from Portsmouth, Virginia, was the first native Virginian to make All-American. At a banquet in Portsmouth, after the 1936 season, over 400 people attended to fete their hometown boy. A large number of people had to be turned away. Parker was presented with a matched set of golf clubs with a leather bag and accessories. Wade spoke at this banquet also, praising Parker for his football prowess.

Wade related the story of Parker's recruitment. Parker had almost decided to go to Virginia Tech when Wade sent assistant Eddie Cameron to Virginia. Cameron went to Parker's home and told him "Let's go for a ride." Well, the ride took young Parker all the way to Card Gymnasium on the Duke campus, specifically to the office of Wallace Wade. Wade didn't travel to recruit players, he made them come to him. His national stature afforded him this luxury. Parker came in with Cameron into Wade's office, and Wade, in later years, recalled,

> Clarence came in and sat down. I told him he was a fine football player, and he should come to Duke and get a good education and win a lot of football games. As he was about to leave, I'm not sure I had him just yet. So I told him, "Clarence, now I want you to understand one thing. Duke University will do a lot more for you than you will ever do for Duke. I'm not sure you're good enough to play for me, anyway." Well, I could tell at that point that he was thinking to himself that "I'll come to Duke and show the old SOB just what I can do." Well, he sure showed me."

Parker was first called "Ace" by *Norfolk Virginian-Pilot* sportswriter Bill Cox, after leading Duke to a win at VMI in 1934. Ace was also an outstanding baseball and basketball player at Duke. He was a key player for Eddie Cameron's 1936 team, as Duke compiled a 20-6 record. In high school in Portsmouth at Woodrow Wilson High, he won the state high-jump title, and was a member of the state high school championship golf team, among his many athletic pursuits.

After leaving Duke, Parker was drafted by the Brooklyn Dodgers of the NFL. He made the All-NFL team in 1938, 1939, and 1940, and was NFL MVP in 1940 when he passed for 817 yards and 10 touchdowns, ran for 306 yards and two scores, and intercepted six passes. He also played major league baseball with Connie Mack's Philadelphia Athletics, hitting a home run in his first big league at bat. When World War II came, Parker enlisted and served for four years, short circuiting one of the most amazing athletic stories of the era. In 1945, Parker returned to the NFL with the Boston Yanks, then finished his career with the New York Yankees of the new All-American Football Conference in 1946. He then came back to Duke in 1947 and served as an assistant football coach through 1965 and as head baseball coach from 1953 to 1966, winning 166 games and earning trips to the College World Series in 1953 and 1961. In 1949 through 1952 Parker managed the Durham Bulls minor league team, compiling a 303-266 record while twice being named Carolina League manager of the year.

Parker, who was enshrined in both the College and Pro Football Hall of Fame, and Wade always remained close. Parker would stop by for extended visits to Wade's farm, Wadehill Farm, in Durham, after Wade had retired. Wade recalled one time when Parker stopped by and said he only had about 30 minutes, as he had to meet someone on the Duke campus. "Well, we got to talking, and that 30 minutes turned into three and a half hours. Finally, when I let him go, Ace jumped in his car and took off down the driveway going 60 miles an hour, I'll bet, over to Duke," Wade laughed. One statement that puts into perspective Wade's feelings on Parker was when he said, "Parker should long remain the pride and inspiration of Duke people everywhere."

* * *

A young student who arrived on the Duke campus in 1936 would eventually become the "Voice of the Blue Devils" radio network. In his memoir, Add Penfield recalled that year:

> I got my first glimpse of the Gothic cathedral known as Duke Chapel, its illuminated towers rising into the darkening sky in a magnificence I could scarcely forget. That first trip into Durham also served to introduce me to the pungent smell of tobacco which permeated Durham streets from the Liggett and Myers factories hard by the business district. It was an order this Yankee needed to get used to. After a while, it became an accepted, even cherished, aroma of my home away from home.

Penfield remembered other events from his long association as Duke radio man and friend of Wallace Wade.

> In 1936 Colgate played Duke. Ted Husing of CBS came down to do the play-by-play. Husing was not at all impressed with the facility assigned him. If you believe it he was supposed to have accosted Coach Wade in his tiny quarters of Card Gym where Wade dressed for practice sessions in his traditional baseball pants and cap, among other things. In language that was supposed to have been Brooklyn-blunt, the famed sportscaster registered his complaints, elegant tones and all, in such a way as to test Mr. Wade's restraint.

When Husing had finished his reported tirade, Wade is said to have told him: "Mr. Husing, up there where you come from, a man is an SOB until he proves himself a gentleman. Down here, a man is a gentleman until he proves himself an SOB!" There is no record of Husing's response. But it might be noted that the broadcaster never, to my knowledge, returned to Duke Stadium after the Colgate game in 1936.

As he prepared for the invasion of Andy Kerr and the razzle-dazzle Red Raiders from the Chenango Valley of New York state, Coach Wade worked the troops, in the field behind the stadium's south goal, the open end of the horseshoe. There was a wooded area to the East of the practice field and this freshman of a few days standing sought one afternoon to catch a glimpse of the celebrated coach and his athletes. Almost stealthily I tiptoed through the woods.

I had to see this man, and I guess I did, from a considerable distance and through late summer foliage. What I remember most, however, is one booming voice, not Wade's, that rang out almost constantly during the few minutes I eluded detection. It was an angry, compelling voice that belabored sweating Duke linemen who were indeed popping leather.... "Work your feet, head up, tail down...." There might have been a cuss word or two interspersed.

I was to discover that voice belonged to Ellis P. Hagler, an assistant coach who had played for Wade at Alabama. Hagler was the line coach. He was never meant to be anything else.

After getting a job under Ted Mann, the director of sports publicity, I got to make my first road trip to Charlotte to do what little needed to be done on a Duke-Carolina freshman football game. I rode to and from the game with Freshman Coach Herschel Caldwell and his wife, Anita. Caldwell, like Hagler, had played for Wade at Alabama. He coached freshman football, basketball, and baseball, and had a summer job managing in the old Coastal Plains League. Many pleasant hours of camaraderie with Caldwell were to follow that first road trip to Charlotte. Anita Caldwell was a source of counsel and comfort to a struggling young Penfield couple in Durham just a few years after that.

CHAPTER TWENTY-TWO

1937

In the spring of 1937, Duke University made news on the baseball field. Ace Parker joined the Philadelphia Athletics major league team, joining former Duke baseball players "Chubby" Dean and Bill Werber. This marked the first time any university in the country had three former students on the same major league team. Werber was a former player for the Boston Red Sox and New York Yankees, and Dean was the brother of Dayton Dean, business manager of athletics at Duke.

Coming off a season in 1936 in which a writer for the Intercollegiate Football Annual picked Duke as the best team in the nation based on its 9 and 1 record and the amount of points it scored versus points allowed, Wallace Wade's fame continued to grow. In October 1937, Wade was featured on the cover of *Time Magazine*. The story was mainly about his coaching, but also had this to say about the man:

> Wallace Wade, now 45, lives as quietly as his profession allows in a university-owned campus cottage with his vivacious wife, his daughter, Frances Margaret, 17, and "Little Wallace," 19, a Duke freshman who is too slight for football. He hunts, golfs (in the 70s), cultivates a watermelon patch, talks occasionally of hiring another coach and retiring into his other post of athletic director.

In the *Chanticleer*, the Duke yearbook, Wade wrote to Duke students explaining his department of physical education and athletics. Wade devoted many hours to his other two jobs besides football coach: athletic director and physical education director. He turned Duke's intramural and physical education departments into nationally recognized entities of Duke's campus. Believing strongly that everyone should take part in sports and physical activity, he constantly sought ways to get more students involved in intramurals or sports of some type. In the *Chanticleer* of 1937 he wrote,

> Our physical education classes are required for all freshmen and sophomores. Intramural sports are more advanced competition than the

Wallace Wade. Courtesy of Anita Caldwell.

physical education classes. Our intercollegiate athletic program is, of course, our most highly developed field. There are three distinct classes of athletic activity. Athletics should act as a rallying point around which the morale of an institution is built. Athletics should teach us to be partisans without prejudice, or at least to be able to recognize that our partisanship has a tendency to make us prejudiced.

In March, Duke played Clemson in what is thought to be the first spring practice game between two teams from the Southern Conference. Jess Neely, Wade's former player at Vanderbilt and former assistant at Alabama, was the head coach at Clemson.

In an *Associated Press* story in 1937, the writer referred to Wade's moniker of "The Bear," his love of football, his being the first coach to adapt low-cut baseball shoes with cleats on them for his Alabama teams, his greatest coach-

ing win (Wade claimed it was with his prep team Fitzgerald and Clark in Tullahoma, Tennessee in 1920 over Bryson College), and his routine of changing
drills in practice every 15 minutes. The reporter also asked Wade what kind
of jobs his players had, to which Wade replied, "Most of the boys have jobs at
the university to help them through: waiting tables in the union, working on
the information desk, ushering at basketball and baseball games during the
off-season, and doing other little jobs about campus."

1937 was also a year in which Amelia Earhart was lost at sea, Joe Louis became the heavyweight champion, and Adolf Hitler reviewed 600,000 Nazi
troops at Nuremburg.

* * *

Duke was ranked as high as number eight in the nation after starting the
season 6-0-1, the tie against Tennessee. Duke had beaten Georgia Tech in the
fourth game of the season in one of the most exciting games of the year. Duke
led 7 to 0, then Tech scored a touchdown to make it 7 to 6, then Tech went
ahead 13 to 6, Duke scored to make it 14 to 13, then Tech scored to move
ahead 19 to 14. Late in the game, Dan Hill recovered a fumbled punt on the
Tech 12-yard line.

Tech then drew a five-yard penalty for delay of game, then Honey Hackney
ran to the 6. Eric Tipton dived over a Georgia Tech player for the winning
score. Fans numbering 26,000 witnessed the game at Grant Field in Atlanta.
Wade commented after the game that

> It was one of those close games which are always thrilling for coaches,
> players, and spectators. I think our boys won the game by their fight;
> they just would not give up. I said last week that I thought Hackney
> played against Tennessee the greatest game of his career, but his per-
> formance today was even greater.

At Duke Stadium on November 6, Duke scored ten touchdowns to beat
Wake Forest 67 to 0. Sophomore George McAfee scored twice, and Hackney
and Tipton scored on long touchdown runs. The Deacons crossed mid-field
only once, very late in the game. D.C. "Peahead" Walker first coached at Wake
Forest in 1937. Walker would go on to coach there through 1950, and compiled a record of 77-51-6, the best winning percentage of any Wake Forest
coach in history. In his ten match-ups with Wade, Walker won three and lost
seven. Wade won the first seven, then Wake Forest beat Duke three straight in
1948 through 1950. Wake Forest played in the first Gator Bowl in 1946, defeating South Carolina. Walker later in his career became head coach of the
Montreal Alouettes of the Canadian Football League.

Wallace Wade on the bench at Duke Stadium. Courtesy
of Duke Sports Information Department.

In their game with North Carolina, the Tar Heels defeated Duke 14 to 6 in
Durham before 45,000 fans. UNC, under Ray Wolf, finished 7-1-1 and 19th
in the nation in the final AP poll. Duke finished 7-2-1 and 20th in the final
poll, after losing to Pittsburgh 10 to 0. Pittsburgh finished 9-0-1 and won the
national championship under Jock Sutherland. The tie came against Fordham.
Sutherland, a native of Scotland, won 111 games at Pittsburgh from 1924 to
1938, while losing only 20 and tying 12. He later became coach of the Pittsburgh Steelers.
    Talking about the season of 1937, Wade said,

> My boys played as good football, in proportion to their ability, as any
> team I ever coached. We just didn't get any end or tackle play all sea-
> son, that's all. I'll except the Pitt game. We got good end and tackle
> play in that game, but our backs came up fast and did much of the
> damage then. One side of our line was pitiful against Carolina. And
> we got the poorest punting that afternoon than in any game since
> 1932. Carolina had a fine team, a beautiful running attack, and a very

good passing attack. We may have used the wrong kind of defense against Carolina but we thought we were right.

Duke used a seven-man line against the Tar Heels.

On the subject of sophomores (freshmen were ineligible for the varsity), Wade said, "This league has gotten to be too fast for sophomores, it seems to me. It's very rare that a sophomore can go in our league."

Even though Coach Wade seemed to say that his team had played to its potential, a 7-2-1 record was the worst since 1932. Duke had won 33 of 39 games since 1933 going into the 1937 season, so more was expected. More came in 1938.

CHAPTER TWENTY-THREE

1938: Unbeaten, Untied, Unscored Upon

Army sent a coach to observe Duke during spring practice of 1938, as the Blue Devils prepared for the upcoming season. Duke figured to be good, with Dan Hill at center, Bob Spangler at quarterback, Eric Tipton at halfback, George McAfee at running back, and Bob O'Mara at fullback returning. Just how good remained to be seen.

Duke's baseball coach, Jack Coombs, wrote a book, *Baseball: Individual Play and Team Strategy*, that came out in early 1938. Connie Mack, the great big league manager, said that "there is not a player in the major leagues, not even the glamorous star, who would not be the better for reading it." Wade also did some writing, penning a nationally distributed newspaper article on the kicking game.

> The first requisite of a well-rounded kicking game is a kicker who can get both distance and height, and who can also place his kick; he will also need to have competent protection in order to get off an effective punt. It is also very important to cover punts well. When the opponents are kicking a team needs to harass the opposing punter, trying either to block his punt or to hurry him sufficiently to prevent him from getting off an effective kick. A safety who can both catch and return punts is needed for a well-rounded kicking game, and the safety needs protection from his teammates.

Bad news arrived even before the first game. George McAfee, expected to be a key contributor, had to have surgery to remove a growth from the bottom of his left foot. An infection then set in and another operation was necessary. McAfee would miss the first five games.

Wade, in sensing the loss of McAfee from Duke's offensive plans, shifted even more focus than normal to his defense. One of the greatest defensive seasons any college team would ever have came about when Wade allocated more practice time to defense, and became even more personally involved with the defense than usual.

To start the season, Duke defeated Virginia Tech 18 to 0 in Greensboro, then routed Davidson 27 to 0. A long train ride to Buffalo to meet Colgate was next. Scoop Roberts wrote a poem before the game:

> On the train the Devils go.
> Shufflin' off to Buffalo,
> The cars go rumbling through the night,
> Bearing men who sure can fight.
>
> On the field the Raiders stand,
> Clad in Red and looking grand.
> But hold! The boys in blue come out,
> While 50,000 people shout.
>
> The men line up, the whistle blows,
> Which team will win? Nobody knows,
> But true Duke spirit is the law
> Be it win, or lose, or draw.

Duke won 7 to 0 over Colgate, with Tipton scoring a touchdown in the third quarter on a two-yard run after being set up by a Bob O'Mara 39-yard off-tackle jaunt. Late in the game, the spirit, or what Wade liked to call "fight," of the defense really showed itself as Colgate had a first and goal to go on the Duke one-yard line, but Duke held Colgate out of the end zone.

The next game with Georgia Tech at Duke Stadium was the renewal of a long rivalry between Wade and Bill Alexander. This would be the 13th meeting between the head coaches, having started while Wade was at Alabama. Wade's record against Georgia Tech going into the 1938 game was 7-4-1, all the games against Alexander. But Alexander had registered some memorable, and painful, losses to Wade, such as a 33 to 13 licking in 1928, a year that saw Tech finish 10 and 0 and win the Rose Bowl over California. Also, the 6 to 0 win over Wade's Duke team in 1933 that was 9 and 0 and the favorite for the Rose Bowl, was one of Wade's most disappointing losses in his career. Alexander had a record of 134-95-15 at Georgia Tech from 1920 to 1944.

Tech had just battled Notre Dame in their previous game, losing 14 to 6 to a Fighting Irish team that finished 8 and 1. On several occasions, Wade had Duke punt on third down against Tech, choosing to play field position and hoping for a mistake on Tech's part, so that Duke could take advantage of it. The half ended in a scoreless tie. On the opening kick-off of the second half,

**Eric Tipton, Wallace Wade and Dan Hill. Courtesy
of Duke Sports Information Department.**

Bob O'Mara returned it to the Tech 29-yard line. Wes McAfee, George's brother, picked up 3 yards over his left tackle, then McAfee passed for 15 yards to Jim Marion for a first down. McAfee then scored and the 6 to 0 lead held up as Duke recorded its 4th straight shutout.

After this game, Duke was ranked 9th in the nation by AP. Bill Cox of the *Norfolk Virginian Pilot*, the man who had given Clarence Parker the nickname Ace, called the Duke team the "Seven Iron Dukes." The name was soon changed to "Iron Dukes." The Iron Dukes, by the end of the season, were the most proclaimed team in the country.

On October 22, Duke traveled to Winston-Salem to dedicate Bowman Gray Stadium in a game against Wake Forest. Bob Spangler woke up the day of the game with a temperature of 102, and Eric Tipton had some nagging injuries. Game observers generally agreed it was the worst performance by Duke of the season, but it managed to win 7 to 0.

North Carolina came into the Duke game in Chapel Hill 4 and 1, having beaten New York University 7 to 0 at Yankee Stadium earlier in the season. Duke got good news when it learned that George McAfee would be available for the UNC game. He made his presence felt in the 2nd period when he made a spectacular pass reception of 32 yards from Eric Tipton to the Tar Heel 13-

yard line. From there, Bob O'Mara gained a yard, then Tipton carried for eight. Eric "The Red" then ran for one to the Heel's three-yard line, ran again in a straight ahead line plunge for no gain, then took it into the end zone. Tony "True Toe" Ruffa converted the extra point and it was 7 to 0.

In the third quarter with the score still 7 to 0, Tipton intercepted a George Stirnweiss pass and returned it to the Tar Heel 35-yard line. Duke drove it into UNC's end zone again to make it 14 to 0, and its unbeaten and un-scored-upon streak continued. UNC had been intercepted five times, which accounted for the win for the most part.

Bob Spangler somehow managed to play. Willard "Easy" Eaves, Dan Hill, Tipton, O'Mara, both McAfee brothers, Willard "Bolo" Perdue, Frank Ribar, Allen Johnson, and Fred Yorke, among others, were cited by Coach Wade for their play.

The *Duke Chronicle*, the student newspaper, had a little fun reporting the game. A headline read: "Chapel Hill Streets Flooded by Tamed Tar Heel's Tears: Aspirin Heads Menu at UNC Eating Places This Week."

In its coverage, Al Burst and Scoop Roberts reported that

> Duke snatched a moral victory even before the game started. Paul Peters, versatile Devil mascot, broke up a Carolina farce depicting the downfall of the "Dooks" when he grabbed a red rag from "Tarzan," a porky Tar Heel booster and made for safer territory. Tarzan was irked to no end by the abrupt manner in which his clowning was halted and proceeded to pour out diverse incantations at the Duke band. We were quite fascinated by the Carolina cheerleaders. Throughout the first half, they were seven whirling dervishes, and yet when the fourth quarter ended, the lads in white stood out like seven solitary tombstones. Ah, 'twas a pitiful sight! After the game, when Carolina students were milling around the goal posts preparing to stop an expected onslaught upon them by Duke men, one wit in the stands remarked, "You can have the posts, we've got the game."

A good Syracuse team was next. The Orange had defeated Maryland, Cornell, and Colgate and was looking to beat Duke in Syracuse. But Duke dominated play, outplaying Syracuse in every phase of the game, as it won 21 to 0. Duke throttled the offensive attack of Syracuse's Marty Glickman, an Olympian speedster, and Wilmeth Sidat-Singh, its quarterback. In fact, Syracuse never penetrated beyond Duke's 40-yard line. This win moved Duke up to number four in the AP poll, with North Carolina State next on the schedule.

The game with Syracuse was notable because of Wilmeth Sidat-Singh, a black player for the Syracuse team. Since the beginning of college football, southern and northern teams had agreed to what was called a "Gentlemen's Agreement," in which no black player would be permitted to compete when the teams met. It did not matter where the game was to be played, be it Birmingham or Boston. The northern teams would simply hold their black players out of the game. In one example, New York University held out Dave Myers, a black star at NYU, when Georgia visited in 1929. But northern schools looked at the profits that were made on these intersectional contests and knew the only way to play these games was to acquiesce to the southern Jim Crow mandate.

Much credit goes to the University of North Carolina's Frank Porter Graham, who urged the UNC football team to allow Ed Williams, a black player for New York University, to play in its game in 1936, which it did. Thomas Dixon, author of *The Clansman* and *The Leopard's Spots*, the novels that inspired D.W. Griffith's film *Birth of a Nation*, delivered an address at UNC days before the game, and more than likely, this further encouraged Graham to push for Williams to play. Williams played, and as Roy Wilkins reported,

> So far the University of North Carolina is still standing and none of the young men representing it on the gridiron appears to be any worse off for having spent an afternoon competing against a Negro player. It is a fairly safe prediction that no white North Carolinian's daughter will marry a Negro as a result of Saturday's play, much to the chagrin of the peddlers of the bugaboo of social equality.

Wilmeth Sidat-Singh was one of the north's most celebrated players and Wallace Wade saw no reason not to play Syracuse with the black player competing. Wade had played alongside Fritz Pollard, a black teammate at Brown, and had grown to both like and respect Pollard. As Wade once said in an interview as to what his reaction was to the appearance of Pollard on the Brown team, "It didn't bother me. I was more concerned with whether he could help the team, what his skills as a player were." Wade had helped to raise money for Pollard while at Brown, and later in his coaching career, got Pollard tickets to a game.

Besides this, there is no question that Wallace Wade had a competitive desire matched by few, and he wanted to play his opponents at their best. He also knew that voters in the polls might vote against his teams if they insisted on other teams dropping some of their best players from games.

In 1937, Maryland had insisted that Sidat-Singh be held out of its game with Syracuse, even though the game was played in Baltimore. By the way, Sidat-Singh was definitely a black athlete, not Hindu, as some thought. In 1938, however, Maryland agreed to play Sidat-Singh and Syracuse in Syracuse.

By 1938, Wade was a dominating presence on the Duke campus. He was in a strong position to alter southern athletic practices, and he knew Duke's president, William Few, and dean, William Wannamaker, agreed with him. Wade wired Syracuse officials that even though "a previous contract states he will not be allowed to participate against Duke," Duke would not object to Sindat-Singh playing.

When word got out that Wade would face Syracuse with a black player, it raised alarm among players, fans, and alumni. The alumni were especially "up in arms" as Ted Mann, Duke's Sports Information Director, put it. A letter was sent to President Few simply demanding, "Don't play against that nigger. Patron." Another letter to Few was just as direct, "I notice in the afternoon paper that Wallace Wade has released Syracuse University from a contract that prohibits Syracuse from playing Negroes in its coming football game with Duke. If this be true, I regard it with disgust. Football is a sport, and if Wallace Wade looks upon it as a sport for his teams to play games with Negroes, he ought to be fired."

It took a man of Wade's stature, courage, and foresight to stand up to the criticism. He knew he had Few's and Wannamaker's solid backing, and he knew it was the right thing to do. After the game, *The Crisis*, the magazine of the National Association for the Advancement of Colored People (NAACP) put a picture of Sidat-Singh on the cover and lauded Duke for its enlightened stand. Wade had insisted to his players that Sidat-Singh was to be treated exactly like any other player, and not singled out for any rough treatment. He had seen what opposing teams had done to Pollard at Brown back in 1915 and 1916 and wanted no part of it. The Duke players carried out Wade's demands, as no incidents occurred outside of the normal crisp tackling and blocking that the Iron Dukes were becoming noted for.

As Patrick Miller, a noted scholar on racial practices in college athletics, wrote,

> Such intersectional contests as the games between UNC and NYU, Duke and Syracuse were remembered—across the racial divide— and thus served to alter prevailing practices in sports, marking breaches in the color line that would be widened in the years that followed. What is more, they would find their place on "Honor Rolls" compiled by black journals desiring to find allies in the cause of racial justice. The contests between UNC and NYU in 1936, and between Duke and Syracuse two years later, scored points against Jim Crow, both on the athletic field and beyond it.

* * *

Duke won its fourth Southern Conference title under Wade when the Blue Devils beat NC State 7 to 0. Just before halftime, Eric Tipton broke off a 12-

yard run to the Wolfpack 34. Tipton then passed to Jap Davis for 16 more yards. Two bucks into the line netted 15 yards by Tipton, then he ran the remaining three for a touchdown, with Ruffa converting. Duke's defense, using its usual 6-2-2-1 alignment, recorded its eighth shutout in a row.

Earlier in the week, Coach Herschel Caldwell's freshman team, the Blue Imps, beat UNC's Tar Babies. This finished another unbeaten season for Caldwell, who had many such teams during his career that did not lose a game during the season. The future looked good for the varsity team, as freshmen Steve Lach, Tommy Prothro, and Winston Siegfried filled starring roles.

Duke's last encounter of the regular season was against the Panthers of Pittsburgh. Jock Sutherland's Pitt team had won the national championship the year before, and came into the Duke game 8 and 1, having lost only to Fordham, and was ranked number four in the nation. Pittsburgh just simply rarely lost during the 1930s, compiling a record of 55-7-6 since 1931, going into the battle with Duke. Running back Marshall Goldberg was an All-American for Pitt in 1937 and 1938.

Duke entered the game 8 and 0 and ranked number three, behind only Notre Dame and Texas Christian. The Iron Dukes were having a season few teams ever experienced, by not only winning their games, but by dominating their opponents.

With the possibility of an unbeaten season at hand, the Duke campus was alive with excitement. Preparations for the annual Victory Ball in the Woman's College gym got underway. Portraits of the football team adorned the walls of the gym as Dutch McMillin and his Duke Ambassadors readied to provide musical entertainment. One person who had already agreed to be a chaperone to help keep matters under control was the most feared man on campus, yet one of the most respected, and definitely the most famous ... Wade.

Days before the game, William Dodd spoke at Page Auditorium on campus about the rise of Hitler and warned of his Nazi regime. America was still three years away from entering World War II, but Dodd had a keen sense of what was coming, as he had recently resigned as American Ambassador to Germany.

A network of 39 radio stations was engaged to carry the game to much of the nation. A short-wave hookup even sent the game to parts of Europe.

As many as 52,000 fans jammed Duke Stadium in snowy weather as the teams met in late November. Goldberg of Pitt ripped off big gains in the first half into Duke's side of the field, but the Blue Devil defense would stiffen.

The half ended scoreless. In the third quarter, Bolo Perdue blocked Pitt punter Chickerneo's kick and fell on it for a touchdown, as the largest crowd ever to watch a football game in the south went wild. Tony "True

Toe" Ruffa converted the point after, the Duke defense did its job, and Duke won 7 to 0.

Eric Tipton had perhaps the most remarkable game punting ever witnessed in college football that snowy day in late November of 1938. Coach Wade never looked at punting as a negative, in that his team was not giving the ball up but using the punt to play field position football. In the Pitt game, the frozen field and slick conditions made long, sustained drives next to impossible, so Duke turned to Tipton. Eric "The Red" punted 20 times in the game for a 41.3-yard average, but the amazing statistic for the game was that 15 of his punts were downed inside Pitt's 20-yard line. To be more specific, two were put inside Pitt's five-yard line, five between the 5 and 10-yard lines, five between the 10 and 15, and three between the 15 and 20. Every time Pitt gained possession, they were staring at a minimum of 80 yards of snow-covered field, with more snow falling in their eyes, and 52,000 screaming fans in their ears. Not only that, but the Pitt offense was looking across the line of scrimmage at the most feared defensive unit in the country. Dan Hill, Eric Tipton, Bob O'Mara, Bolo Perdue, Frank Ribar, Fred Yorke, Allen Johnson, Bob Haas, Bill Bailey, Bob Spangler, and Willard Eaves all looked back with steely eyes, taut muscles, and flexed knees ready to spring forward. There would be no scoring upon this outfit this day.

This would be the last meeting between Jock Sutherland and Wallace Wade on a football field, as Sutherland left the Pittsburgh Panthers to become coach of the NFL's Pittsburgh Steelers. While coaching the Steelers, Sutherland underwent four operations for a brain tumor, but the tumor spread and he died. Grantland Rice, as he had so many times before in his great writing career, came up with appropriate words to commemorate Sutherland:

> There's a fog over Scotland, and a mist on Pittsburgh's field; no valiant hand to flash the sword, or hold the guiding shield. There's a big braw fellow missing from the golden land of fame, for Jock Sutherland has left us—and the game is not the same.

* * *

Dan Hill grew up in Asheville, North Carolina, before deciding to come to Duke and play for Wallace Wade. Duke went 25-4-1 in his three varsity seasons as he became the top center in the nation. After his playing days, he became an assistant athletic director at Duke, where he served 15 years in that capacity. Hill was a lieutenant commander and gunnery officer in World War II, earning numerous battle stars. Later in life he became a vice president of Consolidated Cork Corporation in Brooklyn. Now enshrined in the College

A snowy scene in front of Duke Chapel before the Duke-Pittsburgh game of 1938. Courtesy of Duke University Archives.

Football Hall of Fame, Dan "Tiger" Hill, or "Demon Dan, the All-American Man," as he too was known, was one of Duke's greatest players ever on the best team in Duke history.

Eric Tipton hailed from Petersburg, Virginia, before coming south to play for the Blue Devils. He went on to play seven seasons of major league baseball with the Philadelphia Athletics and Cincinnati Reds. Tipton always maintained that baseball was a more intellectual game than football, saying,

> If a ball is hit to the outfield and a man is on first, the fielder has four or five alternatives as to where he will throw it. He really has to think, and he can't wait until the ball is in his hands to do it. With most positions in football, a player has an assignment on a particular play and that's all he has to think about. In baseball, you're on your own most of the time. You're up there at the plate and nobody can help you. But in football, a good line can make a mediocre back look good. Or, on defense, a good linebacker can make a mediocre tackle look pretty good. They compliment each other.

After coaching at William & Mary, Tipton became head coach of the light-weight football team and varsity baseball coach at Army, where he stayed from 1957 to 1977. His record in baseball was 234-201-5, but it is his football record that stands out. He compiled a winning percentage of 88%, winning 104 games with only 14 losses and one tie, with 13 league titles.

Bob Spangler, also a member of the 1938 team, later became head football coach at Atlantic Christian College, now Barton College, in North Carolina.

CHAPTER TWENTY-FOUR

1939 ROSE BOWL

Duke knew it would go to a bowl game, the question was where. By 1939, the Orange Bowl and Sugar Bowl were four years old. The Cotton Bowl began in 1937; so, unlike in the past, teams having great seasons had options other than the Rose Bowl. The most prestigious remained the Rose Bowl in Pasadena, California, the bowl that Wallace Wade had been to four times already, as a player and coach. The year 1939 marked Wade's fifth trip to the Rose Bowl, when Duke was chosen to face the University of Southern California.

Word spread quickly around the Duke campus and Durham that the Blue Devils would be California-bound. It would be the first bowl in Duke's history. It was reported that almost the entire student body, after hearing the news, crowded around Wade's then on-campus home to have the news verified. Wade came outside to let them know it was true, asked them to celebrate in a way that would make Duke proud, and thanked them for their support. After the little impromptu speech, demonstrations of wild enthusiasm followed throughout the campus, even into the downtown streets of Durham that carried on well into the night.

Wade even received a letter of support from Duke's most keen rival, the University of North Carolina. Dated November 30, the letter read:

> There is no compromise in the feeling between Duke and Carolina when they meet on the playing field, but let me tell you, we "Tar Heels" are behind Duke at the Rose Bowl 100%. Coach Wade, we know you have a great team and we all want that team to win all the glory it deserves. So, remember Duke University, give 'em hell, and Carolina is with you all the way.
>
> Sincerely,
> Your Best Enemies and
> Staunchest Friends—
> The Students at UNC

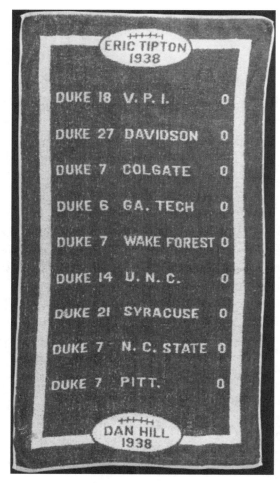

Unbeaten, untied, unscored upon. Courtesy of Duke University Archives.

William Harvey Godfrey wrote the following poem about the Rose Bowl matchup:

> Deep in the southland in a good-sized town,
> Is a football team of great renown;
> Duke's Blue Devils it is known to all,
> And so powerful and mighty it has yet to fall.
>
> To top off a season of the greatest success,
> Duke rated along with the best;

A huge crowd gives the Blue Devils a big send-off at Union Station in Durham. Courtesy of Duke University Archives.

> And even received the bid to play,
> In the Tournament of Roses on New Year's Day.
>
> This she accepted and will soon depart,
> To conquer the Trojans and earn the name,
> Of the greatest eleven in the football game.

An anonymous reader mailed a pair of silk panties to "Eunice" Tipton and "Agnes" Hill, in care of Ted Mann, the director of sports publicity at Duke. Suspecting someone connected with USC, some Duke fans decided to take the panties to the Rose Bowl and place them on Southern California's goal posts after the game to replace the pants Duke whipped off the Trojans.

Hundreds gathered at Union Station in downtown Durham to see the Blue Devils off to Pasadena. There were small Duke Blue Devils pinned to lapels, and blue and white stickers on luggage, and red roses could be seen everywhere. Three special cars comprising the "Duke and Duchess Special" were attached to the regular Norfolk and Western train. (One fan, Raymond Cox of Greer, South Carolina, hitchhiked all the way from Greer to Pasadena).

**The Blue Devil Special. Courtesy of Duke Sports
Information Department.**

One local reporter described the crowd that wished the football team good luck as "men in their finest clothes, and such an array of beautiful ladies and orchids and fur coats has seldom been seen in Durham. Miss Lyon wore a modest outfit of gray, with Alpine hat and shoulder corsage of an orchid surrounded by sprigs of lilies of the valley."

Jake Wade of the *Charlotte Observer* was one of the reporters who accompanied Duke westward.

> The "Blue Devil Special," the big iron horse, is divided into three parts. The first part consists of the athletes, quartered in two cars with a personal club car in which to lounge, to study for their examinations, and to discuss football and the facts of life, as young men do.
>
> "Easy" Eaves and George McAfee promenade up and down. Eric Tipton, who failed to shave this morning, reiterates to you that baseball is his first love, that he does not intend to play professional football. "Dinky" Darnell is engrossed in a slender book called *First Year Chemistry* and Wesley McAfee is writing a letter. "Sonny" Bragg is nursing his hand fracture, looking nevertheless cheerful.
>
> But I must tell you about the second part of the "Blue Devil Special." This consists of the press, presided over by Mr. Ted Mann, the

**Aboard the Blue Devil Special. Courtesy of Duke
University Archives.**

Duke publicity man. The third part is made up of 75 team followers
in several cars. Riding here is Stonewall J. Durham, who scored
Duke's first touchdown in football, that in a game in 1888.

Pausing briefly in Apex, Hamlet, and Monroe, the Duke players accepted
well wishes from other North Carolinians. Thousands of fans met the team as
it stopped in Memphis, not far from Trenton, Tennessee, the small town where
Wade grew up. Many old acquaintances showed up, some seeing their old
classmate or friend, who had become one of the most celebrated coaches in
the nation.

Duke stopped to practice in Stuttgart, Arkansas. Over 3,000 locals welcomed the Duke train, and many of these followed the team to the practice
field and stayed to watch the players run their drills and plays. Fans and curious people lined the field to watch the famous Iron Dukes, who had gone an
entire season without allowing a single point to be scored against them.

Jake Wade picks the trip up in Arkansas.

The iron horse reared through the darkness across Arkansas and on
into the plains of Texas. Later Coach Wade came into the press car. He
needed no invitation to sit down. So the moments rolled into hours
as the newspaper men draped themselves on cushions and suit cases
and listened to the great football coach give his highly respected opin-

**The Blue Devils practice in Stuttgart. Courtesy of
Duke Sports Information Department.**

ions of the state of football. He talked about professional football, and
with candor. "I'm afraid," he said, "that it is not far from professional
wrestling. It is so commercial they are always playing to the crowds."

After stopping for another practice in Lubbock, Texas, the team stopped in
Arizona for a sightseeing tour of the Grand Canyon. Wade continues his trip
narration as the train rolls into Pasadena on Christmas Eve.

> Nice town, this Pasadena. Beautiful green grass and trees, lovely
> homes. The juice of the native oranges at breakfast this morning was
> elegant. The headquarters Huntington Hotel, bristling with swank,
> is a dream. We are located in the imperial suite, equipped with such
> luxuries as chaise lounges and spacious dressing rooms, and over-
> looking a shrubbery-draped patio, green and crystal swimming pool,
> magnificent lawns.
>
> Newspapers on the stands here today were cordial enough. All ex-
> press a cherry welcome. With unanimity, however, they manifested the
> feeling that the big powerful legions of Troy would emerge triumphant.
>
> The Trojans are fast. This was obvious in the drill we witnessed.
> Mickey Anderson is a streak of lightning and Grenville Lansdell trav-
> els like an arrow. The big line, paced by All-American Harry Smith,
> is quick and mobile. Ollie Day, Anderson, and Lansdell all can whip

Nelson Eddy, Coach Wade, Jeannette Macdonald and Howard Jones.
Courtesy of Duke University Archives.

that ball. In fact they did little except pass. The formation was single
wingback, sometimes with a backfield shift, sometimes not. The re-
verses and cutbacks were scintillating. Nice looking attack. The Trojans were having a gay time as they worked. In fact, it looked more
like play than work. This is all very different from the ways and means
of Duke. Coach Wade is working his lads hard and strenuously. He
says it is the only way he can get them ready. The Dukes will engage
in considerable contact operations.

While Duke practiced hard, there was also time allowed to have some fun,
such as visiting several movie studios. Ann Morriss and Cecilia Parker, two
beautiful actresses, planted a kiss on each side of Eric Tipton's cheeks as bulbs
flashed. The players met Jeannette MacDonald as she was filming *Broadway
Serenade*. Cowboy Nelson Eddy, in his ten-gallon hat, greeted the team.

As the game neared, just as he had done in three Rose Bowl trips with Alabama, Wade told his team to focus totally on the game with the Trojans. In
fact, the team did not see the Rose Bowl parade; instead, a team meeting was
held in the Huntington. But Jake Wade (no kin to Wallace) was at the parade
and impressed with the festivities.

In five divisions, perfectly balanced and proportioned, the caravan
moved over all the principal thoroughfares of Pasadena. The big thrill

Rose Bowl 1939. Playing football with movie stars in Pasadena.
Courtesy of Duke University Archives.

for the thousands of fans was the grand marshal, a little lady by the name of Shirley Temple. In white ermine she graced the throne of a magnificent rose-white float. Much smaller even than she appears in the pictures, she turned on her finest smile, waved constantly. Everyone went just a little ga-ga.

With tongue-in-cheek, some Duke students had prepared quite a float. It was 40 feet long and 15 feet high, featuring a Trojan War Horse, its neck draped with a rope. At certain intervals, a young lady would tug at the rope and the horse would go down to its knees.

* * *

Before the game, Wade gathered his team around him in the locker room. His players both respected Coach Wade, and feared his wrath. When he turned on that rather low southern drawl, one could literally hear pins drop. The players were already primed to play their best; the preparations for USC had been thorough and tough. Only a few words of last minute motivation were needed. Coach Wade liked to measure the "look in the eye," as he called it, of

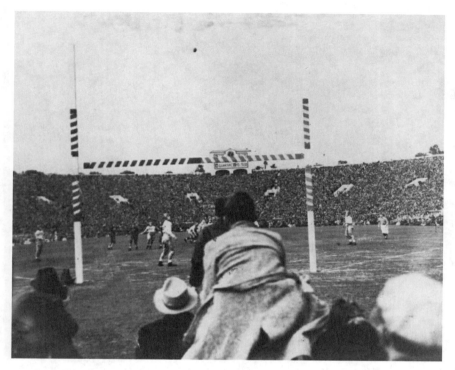

Rose Bowl 1939, 4th quarter. Duke kicks a field goal to go up 3 to 0.
Courtesy of Duke University Archives.

his players before games. He said his teams very rarely lost when they had both
the "look in the eye and the fire in the belly," and he sensed before the USC
game they had it, and he knew for sure his team would need it against a USC
program that was playing in its fifth Rose Bowl game. He had sent Eddie
Cameron and Carl Voyles to scout the USC-Notre Dame game on December
3 after learning that the Trojans would be their opponent. Both Cameron and
Voyles had brought back glowing reports of USC's 13 to 0 dismantling of the
Fighting Irish.

* * *

Bill Stern's NBC radio broadcast went into homes around the nation and
abroad. The stadium was packed with 91,000 fans. Duke and USC played a
scoreless first half, then the third quarter came and went with no team split-
ting the uprights or crossing the goal. The end of the third quarter marked 39
straight quarters in which Duke did not allow a point.

**1939 Rose Bowl action. Courtesy of Duke
Sports Information Department.**

Early in the fourth period, after a 21-yard punt return by George McAfee, who was still not one hundred percent, and a Tipton to McAfee pass, Duke had a first down at the USC 25. Roger Robinson ran for 5 to the 20, then Tipton got one more yard to the 19, making it third down and four. Bob O'Mara ran up center for three, making it fourth and one. Tony Ruffa came in and kicked the field goal to put Duke in front 3 to 0.

USC got the ball and was forced to punt, then Duke went on offense and made a first down, but was forced to punt. USC pushed the ball to Duke's 48, then punted. Bob Spangler, back for Duke, fumbled on Duke's ten-yard line, setting up an excellent opportunity for the Trojans. But the Iron Dukes made their most heroic stand of the day. On the first play from the ten, Spangler, upset at his turnover, smashed through and forced Grenville Lansdell for a four-yard loss. USC then ran a play for a four-yard gain to get back to the ten. A pass was attempted but knocked down, making it fourth down. A delay of game penalty followed, setting USC back to the 15-yard line. Phil Gaspar of USC then missed a field goal attempt.

Duke failed to advance the ball however on offense, and USC got the ball back with two minutes to go and the ball on the USC 39.

This is when Coach Howard Jones, who had been head coach at Duke for one year in 1924, sent in reserve quarterback Doyle Nave. Nave proceeded to complete three straight passes to Al Krueger to move the ball to Duke's 18.

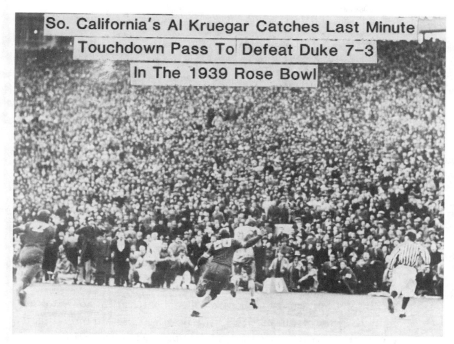

So. California's Al Kruegar Catches Last Minute Touchdown Pass To Defeat Duke 7-3 In The 1939 Rose Bowl

Krueger (misspelled on the photo) catches the winning pass.
Courtesy of Duke University Archives.

From there, Nave drifted back with seconds remaining, looked to the right for an open receiver, then looked left. He spotted Krueger alone in one corner of the end zone. Eric Tipton and Bill Bailey saw what was happening and ran toward Krueger, but it was too late. The ball sailed into Krueger's arms as he fell into the end zone. Gaspar converted for a 7-3 lead.

There was no quitting in Wallace Wade's team, but just a few ticks of the clock remained. On the game's last play, Tipton threw a pass to McAfee who carried it 17 yards to the Trojan 40. The game ended there. Duke had finally been scored upon, and worse, its undefeated season had come to an end.

During WWII, Doyle Nave was serving as a Navy officer on an aircraft carrier in the South Pacific. On an adjoining carrier was Dan Hill of Duke. They met again, and Nave asked Hill if he had had any idea that he (Nave) was going to start passing when he came into that 1939 Rose Bowl. Hill replied, "Hell no. We didn't even know who you were."

After the game, Coach Wade said of his team, "They made me proud of them. They played the greatest game any of my teams ever played in the Rose Bowl. I'm sick for their sake. I hate to see a bunch of boys lose who played and

A game during the 1939 season. In the upper left background
Duke Indoor Stadium can be seen, now called Cameron Indoor Stadium,
being built. Money from the 1939 Rose Bowl was used to build this
famous basketball arena. Courtesy of Duke University Archives.

fought like they did." Dan Hill was disappointed, but said, "We came within a few seconds of doing something nobody had ever done and probably never will. We were moving the ball back toward their goal when time gave out."

Even though it lost, Duke captured the nation's attention during the season of 1938 and the Rose Bowl game of 1939. On the return trip home, huge crowds turned out to welcome the team. The Iron Dukes were greeted by scores of people in Sanderson, Texas, and New Orleans. After arriving back home in North Carolina, 2,500 turned out in Charlotte and Salisbury, 3,000 in Lexington, 4,000 in Thomasville, 1,000 in High Point, and 2,000 in Greensboro, all just to get a glimpse of the boys and congratulate them on their season. The crowd that awaited the team train as it pulled into Union Station in Durham was estimated at 10,000 with thousands more lining the streets. A great roar went up from the crowd as it caught sight of the train, with some people even perched atop the roof of the railroad station. A local reporter guessed that it was the largest crowd in downtown Durham for an event since the Armistice was signed in 1918.

* * *

The money Duke earned in the 1939 Rose Bowl started the construction of Duke Indoor Stadium, now called Cameron Indoor Stadium, perhaps the most famous college basketball arena in the country. As coach of the football team Wade earned the money, and as athletic director he allocated the funds for the new basketball stadium, which opened in 1940.

* * *

In 1980, many of the members of the 1939 team attended the Rose Bowl at the invitation of none other than Doyle Nave, the USC quarterback who beat them with the touchdown pass. Wade, then 87, and his wife Peg, made the event out west. Still spry at his advanced age, Wade kept up with his former players, who were around 60 themselves. "These men have been crazy about each other ever since they played together. And I'm crazy enough to figure I better come along and keep my eye on them. This, after all, is what college football is all about."

For years the 1939 Rose Bowl team would hold a reunion. One member, Bill Sally, was killed in combat during World War II. Another year, Frank Ribar, a member of the Iron Dukes, was killed in a car wreck on his way to the gathering. After that, each time a member died the remaining players would send 39 red roses to the family.

The following are excerpts from a story on the Iron Dukes by Elizabeth Williams:

> Best of all was the football coach, fresh from triumph with Alabama's Crimson Tide. His name was Wallace Wade, and he looked the way a football coach ought to look, wiry, saturnine, with steely eyes shaded by the brim of his fedora.
>
> Wade drilled the Big Blue Team for the Rose Bowl through December. On the 20th, when the train—the Blue Devil Special—pulled out of Durham, thousands of fans lined the tracks as it chugged west, bound for Pasadena. They arrived in Los Angeles on Christmas Eve and were housed at Pasadena's Hotel Huntington, one of the most famous and beautiful hostelries in the state of California.
>
> January 2, 1939, was a cold gray day in North Carolina. Finally, as dusk fell in Durham, at 2 p.m. Pacific Time, Duke's gladiators in blue burst into the arena. Beside their Atwater Kents, North Carolinians listened tensely as the Iron Dukes withstood one onslaught after another from the Trojans. Finally, early in the fourth quarter, Tony Ruffa kicked a field goal. Three-nothing, Duke.
>
> Then it happened. A sophomore reserve named Doyle Nave threw USC's 32nd pass of the game. Al Krueger caught it in the end zone. USC made the extra point. Seven-three, USC.

In Durham, strong men wept.

At all the little railroad stations, the crowds were bigger than the ones that had cheered the team west. The trip home took five days. When the boys got to Durham, 10,000 people turned out to welcome them at the station. The heroes were loaded into open cars and escorted up Main Street by marching bands from every high school that had one. Somebody had written new lyrics to the tune of "She'll Be Comin' Round the Mountain":

> We will all go down to meet them when they come,
> We'll forget about that Krueger and that Nave,
> We'll think of Tipton, Hill and Ruffa,
> They don't make them any tougher....

The fame of the Duke team spread far and wide. The annual Duke Summer School for Coaches had more registrants in 1939 than ever, and the school became recognized as one of the finest of its kind in the nation. Wade spoke at the New Jersey State Interscholastic Athletic Association meeting and at the National Coaches Association meeting in Los Angeles. The Durham City Council passed a resolution commending Wade for his contribution to the city and state. The AP selected Duke as one of the outstanding sports teams of 1938, just behind the world champion New York Yankees baseball team.

Wade was chosen as the nation's outstanding coach for 1938 by the Detroit Yacht Club. By the end of the 1938 season, Wade had a record of 61 wins against 14 losses and three ties during his first eight years at Duke. This was almost an exact replica of his eight years at Alabama, where he was 61-13-3.

Eric Tipton signed with the Philadelphia Athletics major league team in 1939. In his first big league game, he was introduced at Detroit over the public address system as a former member of the "famed Iron Dukes team of 1938 that was unbeaten, untied, and unscored upon during the college football season." James Isaminger of the *Philadelphia Inquirer* was there:

> Eric Tipton, famed Duke athlete, had his christening as a major league player in the ninth with the bases loaded and one out. He received waves of applause as he was introduced with some detail, his university football reputation being mentioned by the announcer. A right-handed hitter, Tipton hammered a smoking liner to right, but Foxx turned tail and made a brilliant catch of the ball.

CHAPTER TWENTY-FIVE

1939 — 8 AND 1

It is doubtful that any coach other than Wallace Wade had experienced more success by the age of 47, when he began the 1939 season at Duke. He had a coaching record of 122-27-6 at Alabama and Duke, and if you were to take all the teams he was associated with as a player and coach up to that point: Brown, Fitzgerald and Clark, and Vanderbilt, the combined record would be 171 wins, 37 losses, and 8 ties. In addition, he had played on a Brown team that went to a Rose Bowl, and his was the first team to defeat both Harvard and Yale in the same year. He had won a state high school championship in Tennessee at Fitzgerald and Clark, then, while an assistant at Vanderbilt, the Commodores had gone undefeated in back-to-back seasons for the only time in their history. Then came his stints at Alabama and Duke, where he had won three national titles, participated in four Rose Bowls and won eight Southern Conference championships.

Wade believed strongly that playing football built character, but that only winning, not losing, really molded a person. He did not like to lose a game, and scoffed at the notion that sometimes a coach or player learned more through losing than winning. He once said, "What good did it ever do anybody to get kicked around?"

The Blue Devils downed Clemson in the spring practice game, as George McAfee, now healed from his foot injury, scored three touchdowns. Since Eric Tipton and Dan Hill had since left, McAfee was expected to be the star of the 1939 team. True to form, Gorgeous George would not disappoint anyone with his performance in the coming season.

Construction on Duke Indoor Stadium proceeded through 1939. In April the *Duke Chronicle* reported on the plans for the arena:

The indoor stadium, when completed, will be the finest of its kind in the South and perhaps the country. The structure, to be of materials and architecture corresponding to the other buildings on the university campus, will measure 175 feet by 262 feet, and will have a maximum seating capacity of approximately 10,500 persons. It will be situated 60 feet west of the gymnasium and be connected with it by an underground passage.

A gallery with 6,000 permanent seats will extend around the four sides of a hardwood floor to measure 96 by 200 feet. The court will be large enough for three regulation basketball courts, and when one court only is used, 3,000 roll-back seats may be placed on the floor. For such occasions as commencement and community gatherings, musicals, and addresses, nearly 2,000 additional seats can be placed. All of Duke's indoor sports contests will be held in the indoor stadium, leaving the present gymnasium (Card Gym) available for an expanded physical education program. The building will have many interesting appointments and facilities. There will be an entrance at each end, the North for students and the South end, which will be near the present freshman athletic field, will be used by the general public.

In the third game of the season, Duke lost to Pittsburgh 14 to 13. This would be Duke's only loss of the season, as the Blue Devils finished 8 and 1. The sole loss was more disappointing due to the fact that Pittsburgh was not nearly the team it had been in 1938 when Duke had beaten them. In his first year at Pitt after replacing the legendary Jock Sutherland, Charles Bowser led the Panthers to only a 5-4 record, so Duke's only loss that year came to a very beatable team.

George McAfee scored three touchdowns in a 33 to 6 win over Syracuse, with one of the scoring plays featuring a 46-yard reception from his brother, Wes. On November 4, Duke traveled to Atlanta to play Georgia Tech. Duke won 7 to 6 against a Tech team that ended up losing only two games all year, to Duke and Notre Dame, and which beat Missouri in the Orange Bowl. Jack Troy of the *Atlanta Constitution* reported on the Duke-Tech game,

> It was, as the lady said, 'the game is in the air and lawdy what I'd give to have a ticket.' The setting for the Tech-Duke game was as close to ideal as any setting at Grant Field ever will be. The game was an absolute sellout. All stadium seats and temporary bleachers were taken, and on adjoining roof tops. The stadium was a riot of color as is customary with crowds of 30,000. The old east stand press box was filled with visiting writers and scouts. A sun, playing hide and seek with gray-tinted clouds, occasionally broke through and lighted up the corsages of the ladies in a manner reminiscent of balls of fire. And it was quite a sight, indeed, when the Duke team, wearing bright blue uniforms, mingled on the field with the golden-jersied Engineers.

Built around the celebration of VMI's Centennial, the 1939 game with Duke was part of a twin bill, with Washington and Lee playing Virginia on Friday, and then Duke playing VMI Saturday. The Duke-VMI game marked a reunion for Coach Wade and Pooley Hubert, who was now head coach at VMI. Hubert pretty much used the same system of football as he had learned under Wade at Alabama back in the 1920s. Hubert and his old coach remained very close; Wade had recommended his former quarterback for the position at VMI. In the two times Duke faced VMI while Wade and Hubert were coaching at their respective schools, Wade won both games, 20-7 in 1939 and 23-0 in 1940.

The UNC game was preceded by the freshman Blue Imps of Duke playing the Tar Babies of North Carolina in Fayetteville. The Imps-Tar Babies game drew over 4,000 fans and ended in a scoreless tie. On the other hand, the Duke-UNC varsity game of 1939 drew a crowd in excess of 52,000 fans to Durham. Well before the game, Duke officials sent out this release: "Tickets: None available. Positively no standing room will be sold. Officials request nobody come to Durham with intention of seeing game who does not have ticket."

All the newsreel companies came: Paramount News, Hearst Metrotone, Pathe News, and Universal. The AP sent a reporter, as did such newspapers as the *Baltimore Sun* and the *Washington (DC) Times-Herald.*

UNC came into the game 7-0-1, their only tie coming against Tulane. The Heels were ranked number seven in the country, while Duke was 13th with a record of six and one.

Early in the game's third quarter, Duke's Bill Bailey blocked a UNC punt into the end zone, where he recovered the ball for a touchdown. Winston Siegfried scored on a short run in the final period, and Duke won 13 to 3. The win bumped the Blue Devils up to eighth in the AP poll, while the Tar Heels dropped to seventeenth. The win also pushed Coach Wade's record against Carolina to 6-2-1 in his first nine seasons at Duke.

Duke later beat NC State, for the seventh year in a row, by a score of 28 to 0 to end the season 8-1, earning Duke a ranking of eighth in the nation. As one of the top programs in the nation, and the dominant team of the Southern Conference, the Blue Devils got the best shot from teams on their schedule. Shakespeare once wrote "Uneasy lies the head that wears a crown," and Duke, as a team of national renown, had become a game their opponents aimed for with special focus.

George McAfee had a magnificent 1939 season. He rushed the ball for 596 yards, caught 10 passes for 229 yards, and completed nine passes for 138 yards. In addition, McAfee punted 40 times for a 38.2 yard average, returned punts

George McAfee. Courtesy of Duke Sports Information Department.

for 365 yards for an average punt return of 10 yards, and returned five kick-offs. He also scored seven touchdowns and intercepted three passes.

Drafted in the first round by the NFL, as the second player chosen, McAfee went on to a pro career that landed him in the NFL Hall of Fame. He also se-cured a spot in the College Football Hall of Fame for his great career at Duke. McAfee still holds the career record for punt-return average in the NFL, re-turning 112 punts for a 12.78 yard average. Amazingly, he also returned a kickoff 93 yards for a touchdown in his first pro game as a Chicago Bear. In 1941, McAfee was named to the All-NFL team, and would be named to the NFL's 1940s All-Decade Team. In 1940 he returned an interception for a touchdown in the Bears 73-0 win over the Washington Redskins in the NFL

Championship Game. Still ranking sixth on the Bears career interception list, McAfee pilfered 25, and leads the rankings with 4 career postseason interceptions.

George McAfee grew up in Ironton, Ohio, where he played quarterback on an undefeated high school team his senior year. Ohio State thought they had recruited him, but when he was invited to Duke to meet Coach Wade, he fell in love with both the coach and the picturesque Duke campus.

* * *

As Duke was celebrating victories on the football field, Adolf Hitler rode triumphantly into Czechoslovakia and invaded Poland. Reports of torture and death beyond imagination in Nazi concentration camps made their way to America. In other news, Lou Gehrig made his famous "I am the luckiest man alive" speech before 62,000 teary-eyed fans at Yankee Stadium. Two all-time classic movies debuted in 1939: "Gone With The Wind" and "The Wizard of Oz."

CHAPTER TWENTY-SIX

1940

Duke Indoor Stadium was formally opened on January 6, 1940, as Duke defeated Princeton in basketball. The stadium had been started with money earned from Duke's 1939 Rose Bowl game. Athletic Director Wallace Wade was on hand for the festivities. President Few gave credit to Coach Wade, saying "For the great success that has been achieved I heartily congratulate the athletic division of the university and Mr. Wade and those associated with him as coaches." Dean Wannamaker, in his speech, talked of the value, to the university, of sports:

> It has to be kept in mind that while many fine sports are encouraged and well provided for here, only football pays its way. It must and does, as is well known, provide the means for all other sports. With greater accommodations for basketball games, that sport will soon be able, we hope, to get along without aid. It has been for some time the hope and aim of Mr. Wade and those serving with him to put inter-collegiate sports in position to contribute materially to our physical layout and thus improve our program. A larger gymnasium, especially increased space for basketball, has been for some time greatly needed, and they have centered their efforts on such a project. The building in which we are tonight is the result of these hopes and efforts.

A local reporter who toured the new facility wrote about other features of the building:

> Despite its large volume, the building can be readily and comfortably heated by a combination of radiators and unit heating, with thermostat controls. Good ventilation in all weather has been assured. The electrical features of the new gym include superb lighting by the use of 42 1,000 watt lights. A special light fixture is provided at the center of the building to illuminate the boxing ring. Base for the maple playing floor are five-inch concrete slabs, cresoted wood sub-flooring, and waterproofing paper. The 6,000 theatre-type seats are

designed for comfort and are 19 inches wide. Other features of the gym include physical education department offices, a conference room, dressing rooms, large lobbies, and dirt floor rooms for practice use by outdoor teams in bad weather. There are trophy displaying cabinets in the south lobby.

Obviously not forseeing the huge impact that basketball now makes on the Duke campus, President Few also said, "With the new gymnasium, basketball might make a moderate yield if the people are willing to pay a reasonable admission fee."

Also around campus, former U.S. Senator Furnifold Simmons, an alumnus and trustee of Duke, died in April of 1939. Senator Simmons served from 1900 to 1930, and right up to his last years was a frequent attendant at commencement occasions and other functions for the university.

Dr. Paul Linebarger, a political scientist at Duke, was hosted in China by President Chiang Kai-shek, who invited him to deliver an address over the Voice of China radio. The address was broadcast throughout the world.

Total enrollment at Duke by June 1940 had reached 3,685 students, a number which represented a 75 percent increase over the 2,106 students in 1930. Having one of the best football teams in the nation certainly helped to increase Duke's exposure to prospective students.

Coach Wade was in demand, as usual. In late May 1940, Wade instructed at a coaching school at Mississippi State, then in early June he spoke at Utah State. In late June he was at Southwestern University in Memphis, and immediately after that he went to Centre College in Kentucky, returning to Durham on July 6 to finalize plans for his own coaching school scheduled to start at Duke later that month. Over 100 coaches attended his clinic in 1940, including coaches from Pennsylvania, Johns Hopkins, Kentucky and Cornell. Several of his former players who were now coaching attended, including Horace Hendrickson and Joe Brunansky of Elon, Carney Laslie, who played for Wade at Alabama and now of VMI, and Tom Rogers of Wake Forest. Coach Wade, as he had done since his days at Alabama, would lecture on a certain aspect of football in the morning and then demonstrate his points on the field in the afternoon. In 1940, one of his subjects was defending against the run. He emphasized to the coaches that one of the fundamentals of defending against running plays was to instruct the player to watch the ball carrier, and to stay stationary until he knew what the ball carrier was going to do. On backfield defense he said that one of the hardest things to get a man to do was to protect his own territory. Too many men left their positions to help out a teammate, only to find the play going over the spot they just left. This was a tenet of Wade's great defensive teams through the years: playing a type of zone defense in which players were taught to protect their own areas of the field.

Along with speaking about plays, formations, drills, and other technical aspects of football, Coach Wade spoke to groups about youth education, building character, and the value of hard work. Over 200 people attended a father-son banquet to hear Wade speak in Thomasville, North Carolina, and a similar number attended a Boy Scout gathering in Burlington. To the Boy Scouts he cited the attributes of scouting "as the finest possible basis for development. The first job of every boy is to be a boy and the second is to grow into a useful, honest man."

As 1940 moved into the start of fall classes, the threat of America becoming involved in war hung over the Duke campus. President William Preston Few, who had served Duke so ably since 1910 and was most responsible for leading Duke into a position of prominence as a national university, spoke to an assembly of students in October of 1940. He would die less than two weeks later. With the specter of war looming, Few told the young eyes that were riveted on him, "This generation is to be tested as by fire. I earnestly hope that everyone of you tested by fire may prove to be of true gold." As the 1200 or so young men filed out of the auditorium, silence reigned, as the future beckoned with both promise and with an ugliness that had rarely been seen in the history of man.

By 1940, there were campus efforts in support of British war relief. Mussolini and Hitler had announced an alliance between Italy and Germany, Norway and Denmark had fallen to the Nazis, Paris had been taken, and a devastating aerial attack on England had started. On September 16, the United States required men from 21 to 35 years of age to register for military training.

* * *

Football games started in late September of 1940, and helped to alleviate war concerns to a degree. Many key players were back from the 8 and 1 1939 team, including Tony Ruffa, Mike Karmazin, Tommy Prothro, and Steve Lach. Even though George McAfee was now starring for the Chicago Bears, his brother Wes was back at halfback.

In a preseason rating compiled by the widely used Williamson National Rating System, Duke was ranked number one in the country, Ohio State was ranked second and Washington was ranked third. But in the second game of the season, which was played on Shield-Watkins Field at the University of Tennessee in Knoxville, Robert Neyland's Volunteers beat Duke 13 to 0. Coach Wade, as was his custom, offered absolutely no excuses, saying "Tennessee just outplayed us in every department." The Volunteers would go 10 and 0 in the 1940 regular season, losing only to Boston College in the 1941 Sugar Bowl.

On this visit to Knoxville, Coach Wade and Coach Neyland displayed the tremendous respect each had for the other. A couple of days before the game, Tennessee was finishing its practice just as Duke was beginning its own. Coach Neyland and Coach Wade started talking, and Coach Neyland asked Coach Wade what was wrong with Tennessee's reverse play, knowing that Coach Wade was well known for his reverse-play timing. Generously, Wade then proceeded to take a stick and illustrate, in the dirt of the field, the problem. He drew two teams lined up, and showed Neyland what he had seen of the Tennessee reverse, recommending that the Volunteers should keep their ball carrier closer to the line of scrimmage, and a little more to one side of the field. This conversation, an example of how both men always learned from each other, went on and on. Finally, one of Duke's assistant coaches got up the nerve to ask Coach Wade if the team should go ahead and start practice without him.

Coach Wade enjoyed needling Coach Neyland. Once before a game with Tennessee, Wade had his sports publicist, Ted Mann, plant a story in the newspaper suggesting that Duke had used the T-formation in spring practice and had been running it in preparation for the Tennessee game. Wade had always relied, of course, on the single wing attack. The day before the game, Neyland asked Wade, "Wallace, are you going to use that damn T on me?" Coach Wade looked at his friend, gave a little smile, and just commented on the good points of the formation, but never directly answered Neyland. Wade didn't use it, and never had any plan to, but he knew that it would at least worry Neyland, and just might help Duke in the game.

On October 19, Duke went to Hamilton, New York, to play Colgate. Before the kickoff, the 14,000 fans in attendance stood for a moment of silence in honor of Dr. William Few, the long-time Duke president who had died on the sixteenth. Dr. Few had been president of the University during many changes in the athletic program: from when Duke had no football team because football itself had been banned, to when it was reinstated in 1920, to when the new football program had developed into a powerful force. Coach Wade always admired Dr. Few, calling him "a most honorable man, a principled man who was a good leader. He always supported me and my football program and athletics as a way to build young men."

After shutting out Colgate and Wake Forest, Coach Wade's defense looked imposing, as had been the case for most of his teams. In a column Wade wrote in 1940 before the season, some of his defensive philosophy can be seen:

> The big aim of varying the defense is to confuse offensive players in their assignments. This can really create havoc in the best attacks. The quarterback calls for a certain play and then, much to his dismay,

the defense, instead of playing the way he expected, will suddenly shift into a six or even a five man line. Defensive backfield alignments shift accordingly.

The most important requirement of a defensive player is the ability to recognize an attacking play as early as possible. As soon as he has the attack figured out, he should maneuver to meet the play according to some pre-arranged plan in cooperation with his teammates.

Instead of trying to guess what the next play is to be, the defense should try to anticipate the purpose of the offense, whether the offense is trying for a first down by a short gain, or whether a touchdown or long gain is to be undertaken.

There are many variations of defensive play, embracing the five, six, or seven man line. It can be the 7-1-2-1, the 7-2-2, a 6-2-2-1, 5-3-2-1, or just about any alignment a coach can devise.

North Carolina beat Duke 6 to 3 in Chapel Hill. This was Duke's first Southern Conference loss in three years, and it kept Duke from winning another conference crown. Duke's next opponent was NC State, and before that game sportswriter Chauncey Durden observed a Blue Devil practice:

A Duke football practice is all work and no play. The coaches and players are on the field for but one purpose—to perfect through practice. The practice sessions are not overly long, but there's no wasted time. It's dig, dig, dig the entire time. There is nothing to disconcert the players, practice takes place in comparative privacy. There isn't a water fountain anywhere on the field. It's a stern football school Wade conducts.

Wade is a great one for detail, and he takes an active part in practice. There's an old saying among observers of Duke practices that the weakest spots in the Duke machine can be spotted by following the coach during practice. Wednesday he was working with the tailbacks most of the time. After every maneuver the coach would come up and explain the tiny faults of the players. Then they'd try again.

The practice wound up with 20 minutes of blocking. My, how those Dukes do glory in hard blocking. Finally, after a play had been run letter-perfect, Wade called it an afternoon. Then, as the players began running off the field in the direction of the gymnasium, Coach Wade yelled, "seven-thirty tonight."

Football is a serious business at Duke.

Wins over NC State and Pittsburgh in the last two games finished Duke's season with seven wins and two losses. It was a disappointing season, considering that they had been ranked number one in the country in the pre-season, and that the two losses were to old rivals Tennessee and North Carolina.

CHAPTER TWENTY-SEVEN

1941—THE ROSE BOWL COMES TO DURHAM

In June 1941 Germany invaded Russia, and in October a U-boat sunk the destroyer, Reuben James, killing 100 Americans. It seemed inevitable that the United States would be drawn into World War II. Male Duke students began to be drafted into the service, and some faculty left campus to serve in the armed forces, or in the federal government in some other capacity. In May, the Department of the Navy selected Duke as the location of a Naval Reserve Officers Training site. Changes in the curriculum accommodated the specter of war, such as the implementation of an accelerated, three-year degree program, academic credit for some types of military training, and more emphasis on physical education courses.

The beauty of the Duke campus probably made it harder for students to accept that they were about to be drafted and taken away. Ovid Pierce captured some of the campus scenery in an essay:

> Beginning at a circular drive, there is a long beautiful approach to the tower. The road rides high above the slopes and gardens below, which in spring, drop down and down in terraces of color. The tower reaches up, then, suddenly, to the right and left, and the quadrangle has received you—a vast greensward enclosed by buildings of greenish-gray stone.
>
> It is strange to pass a tobacco barn, a crossroads store, a little white church, and to come suddenly to the center of this Gothic world. Here in the middle of North Carolina is a re-creation of the Middle Ages, as complete as a town. The chapel tower reaches above the lesser towers. Arches and cloisters are worked into a unifying design. Flagstone walks cross the green. Chimneys and spires rising from the deep slope of moss-gray slate reach into the sky with the tops of the pines. And there inside the chapel are the bodies of the founders of the Duke dynasty, each marble sarcophagus as cold, as permanent as that of any European saint.

Bob Gantt and a pretty coed on the Duke campus. Courtesy of Duke Sports Information Department.

Bill Woodruff, a student at Duke in 1936, also wrote about his Duke "home," after walking through campus one day:

These buildings and all that they represented in themselves and be-yond themselves—the whacking paddles of fraternity initiation and the learning and decorum of the classroom; the roar and color of the stadium and the painstaking accuracy of the lab; the clamorous bull-session with its cloud of tobacco smoke and the awe-inspiring hush of the Sunday chapel service, the cheerful clatter of knives and forks in the Union dining halls and the quiet of the library study rooms— these many things and more these buildings meant for me. These buildings, all the manifold ideas they incorporated and represented, all the activities, for which they furnished the background, all of this suddenly crystallized into one quality—home. This school, this university, this home had somehow or other got itself so tangled in my heart strings, had become so much a part of me that I know I should never cease to belong to it, and I caught myself fervently hoping that it would never forget me.

Durham itself was a growing town, with tobacco the driving force of the economy. Tobacco money, of course, had also built Duke University. Some of the highlights of Durham were advertised in a 1941 report:

> The population of Durham in the 1940 census was 60,195 persons, making the city the third largest in North Carolina. The large tobacco industries manufacture such well known brands as Duke's Mixture and Bull Durham smoking tobacco, and four brands of cigarettes including the famous Chesterfields and Lucky Strikes. Here was made 24 per cent of the nation's cigarettes.
>
> Amusements in Durham include seven moving picture theaters. The Armory Auditorium seats 2,500 persons. Daily newspapers include *The Durham Sun* and *The Durham Morning Herald*.
>
> 'The Friendly City' is in the greatest tobacco growing area in the world with over 42,000,000 pounds of the 'weed' being sold during 1940–41 in Durham auction markets.
>
> For transportation the city has five railroads. Nine hotels have a total of 800 rooms, the largest being the Washington Duke, constructed in 1925 at a cost of $1,800,000, with 300 rooms and baths. The Malbourne has 200 rooms. The City Athletic Park has a seating capacity of 4,000 and Durham is the national headquarters of all minor league baseball.
>
> Chief medical center south of Baltimore, Durham boasts four hospitals with a total of 944 beds: Watts Hospital, Duke Hospital, Lincoln Hospital and McPherson Hospital.

As the fall of 1941 approached, Wallace Wade, now in his eleventh year at Duke, gathered about him the players of his gridiron team. Returning to his center spot was Bob Barnett, captain of the team. Other key players for 1941 would be Tommy Prothro, Tom Davis, Steve Lach, Bob Gantt, and Winston Siegfried, among others. Good things were expected of this team, and they delivered. As Ted Mann put it, "This team simply beat the hell out of everyone."

After opening with a 43 to 14 win over Wake Forest, Duke hosted Tennessee. As many as 48,000 fans packed Duke Stadium. The Blue Devils scored three touchdowns in the first half to beat the Volunteers 19 to 0. Duke next played Maryland in Baltimore, where Duke scored 25 points in the first quarter to put the game away, winning 50 to 0.

1941 team. Courtesy of Duke University Archives.

Duke then played and beat Colgate 27 to 14, but it was a tough contest. Bill Geyer of Colgate returned a third-quarter kickoff for a touchdown to put the Red Raiders up, 14 to 13. But on Duke's next possession it drove 65 yards for a go-ahead touchdown from Winston Siegfried, and then scored again in the fourth quarter.

At Pittsburgh, Duke won 27 to 7 and climbed to number three in the nation in the AP poll. Georgia Tech next fell, 14 to 0. Davidson was no match for Duke, and fell 56 to 0. Duke remained number three behind Minnesota and Texas, having recorded a 7 and 0 record.

In a 20-to-0 win over North Carolina, Duke's Steve Lach had a sensational performance. He ran for 61 yards, scored a touchdown, played excellent defense and kept UNC backed up with his punting all afternoon. The game was the last one at UNC for head coach Ray Wolf, who had won two and lost four to Duke since taking over the Carolina program in 1936.

Duke beat NC State for the ninth year in a row to end the regular season 9 and 0. Duke had outscored its nine opponents 311 to 41, beating all nine by an average score of 35 to 5. In the AP's final poll of the regular season, Duke moved up to number two, behind only Minnesota. Notre Dame ranked third,

Homecoming 1941. Courtesy of Duke University Archives.

Texas ranked fourth and Michigan ranked five. That year, Duke won its sixth Southern Conference title under Wade.

Although Duke was again a great team defensively in 1941, as was typical of Wade-coached teams, it was more celebrated for its offense. Duke finished first in the nation in total offense per game, averaging 372 yards, compared to second-place Arizona, at 357 yards. 266 of Duke's yards-per-game came from rushing, with Tom Davis running for 461 yards for the season, Winston Siegfried running for 434 yards, Steve Lach running for 405 yards, and Leo Long running for 326 yards. Davis finished fourth in the nation in total offense, also passing for 517 yards. Lach showed his amazing all-around ability as he led the country in punting with an average of 45 yards per kick, caught 22 passes for 366 yards, along with his rushing yardage. He also intercepted three passes.

Duke accepted an invitation to play Oregon State in the 1942 Rose Bowl. The Beavers had gone 7 and 2 and were champions of the Pacific Coast Conference. Lon Stiner had been head coach in Corvallis since 1933, and through 1948 compiled a record of 74-49-7.

* * *

Duke students celebrate the news of the Rose Bowl invitation
at the Goody Shop. Courtesy of Duke University Archives.

Coach Wade made reduced-price, 50-cent tickets available to service men for all the 1941 home games. A total of 8,000 service men attended both the Wake Forest and Tennessee games. More than a hundred soldiers attended one Duke practice, and afterwards Coach Wade signed autographs for everyone and showed much interest in their welfare. Having been a captain in WWI, Wade respected the military men very much, and unbeknownst to the soldiers in 1941, Coach Wade would soon become Major Wade, and then Lieutenant Colonel Wade.

On a lighter note, that same year, two students became Duke's first female cheerleaders. Toni Salley and Vivian Driver were chosen to cheer by a vote of the entire Woman's College. A report of their debut in the Wake Forest game noted, "they added spirit and color to the game."

* * *

One day after President Roosevelt appealed to Emperor Hirohito to use his influence to avert war, the Japanese attacked Pearl Harbor, killing 2,403 Americans. The date was December 7, 1941. The next day, Roosevelt told Congress that, "no matter how long it may take us to overcome this premeditated invasion, the American people, in their righteous might, will win through to absolute victory."

On December 13, Lieutenant General John Dewitt, commander of the Fourth Army and in charge of military operations on the west coast, ordered that the Rose Bowl game between Duke and Oregon State be canceled. California Governor Culbert Olson announced that, "the unusually large gathering of people known to the enemy, exposing them to the dangers now threatening, requires that plans for the holding of this tournament and football game be abandoned."

On December 14, Wallace Wade telephoned Oregon State athletic director Percy Locey and Tournament of Roses chairman Robert McCurdy and offered to host the game in Durham. Oregon State accepted. North Carolina Governor J. Melville Broughton assured the War Department that the game would not interfere with the state's military preparedness, and the War Department agreed to let the game go on.

Coach Wade, in an article he wrote some years later, covered many details of the events leading up to the 1942 Rose Bowl:

> Plans for the trip to Pasadena were developing smoothly when news of the sneak attack on Pearl Harbor by the Japanese came. As a matter of fact, I heard the news on the radio in my car that Sunday afternoon as I was on my way to my office in the gymnasium to work on arrangements for the trip. Due to the declaration of war against Japan and the firing of some shells onto the California coast by a Japanese submarine, our government banned the gathering of large crowds in California and this meant that the game could not be played in Pasadena. In order to try to maintain the continuity of the games, I recommended at a meeting with President Flowers and Vice-President Wannamaker and Dwire that we invite Oregon State to play the game in the Duke Stadium. With their approval I telephoned Mr. Robert McCurdy, President of the Tournament of Roses and extended the invitation on behalf of Duke University and the city of Durham.

The respect McCurdy and Oregon State's Locey had for Coach Wade was shown by the fact that when Wade told them that he did not know what kind of crowd the game would attract, but that he would attempt to distribute gate receipts in a fair manner, McCurdy and Locey said that Coach Wade's word was good enough for them. That conversation was the extent of the contract for moving the game.

Such details as installing temporary seats, printing tickets, enlarging the press box, and coordinating game logistics all had to be done quickly, since the game was scheduled to be played in just over two weeks. Duke borrowed bleachers from the University of North Carolina, Wake Forest, and NC State. UNC offered Oregon State the Carolina Inn as its headquarters, and Oregon State accepted. Coach Wade later commented that, "Throughout the occasion the University of North Carolina cooperated most generously by providing quarters and practice facilities for the Oregon State team, by furnishing extra bleachers to supplement the seating capacity of the Duke Stadium, by assis-

Bob Barnett stands next to a scroll signed by UNC students congratulating Duke on its Rose Bowl invitation. Courtesy of Duke University Archives.

tance of its athletic administrative and maintenance staffs, as well as many other ways."

Tickets went on sale on December 16, and on the eighteenth sales were stopped. More than 50,000 tickets had been sold in just 48 hours. Lines jammed the ticket office, and orders piled up on the desk of the athletic business manager, Dayton Dean. There was a snafu. As Wade explained it,

> Several days before the game, the Western Union messengers left several boxes of telegraphic money orders in a vacant room in the old gym. Of course, these orders were not filled nor acknowledged and soon people started calling about their tickets for which we had no record. A few days after the game the telegrams were found. This solved the mystery of the missing tickets but it did not satisfy the people who failed to get to the game.

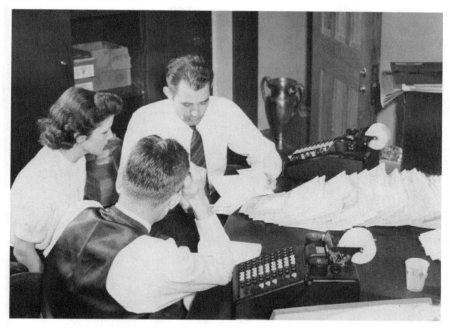

Rose Bowl 1942 ticket orders. Courtesy of Duke University Archives.

A band and thousands of local people met Oregon State at the train station in Durham. There was a breakfast held for both teams and the press at the Washington Duke Hotel, and the Durham Chamber of Commerce entertained the teams at the famous Turnage Barbecue Restaurant. The Durham Kiwanis Club continued the traditional "Kickoff Luncheon" regularly held by the Pasadena Kiwanis Club.

Coach Wade had two other problems: his players had been looking forward to the trip to California, and the war that many would soon be involved in made football seem a little less important. As the captain of that team, Bob Barnett, explained, "The seniors knew we were about to be drafted. Also, the luster of the trip to California was gone. Coach Wade had to be convinced to give us three days off for Christmas, as we knew we would be leaving our families soon for the war, so we wanted a little time at home."

Duke was favored to win the game. New Year's Day in Durham was cool and wet with a light rain falling. This did not affect the crowd, as over 56,000 fans attended. Barnett recalls that "the rain and the mud were terrible that day."

Oregon State scored first on a Don Durden touchdown run in the first quarter. Steve Lach scored in the second quarter to tie the game at seven all,

Promoting the 1942 Rose Bowl. Courtesy of Duke University Archives.

and that's the way the half ended. In the third quarter, Oregon Sate's Bob De-
thman threw a touchdown to George Zellick. Two minutes later, Steve Lach
ran for 37 yards on a reverse, setting up Winston Siegfried for a one-yard
plunge to tie the game at 14. Oregon State came right back, by scoring on a
long touchdown pass. It missed the extra point, making the score 20 to 14.

In the fourth quarter, Lach pinned the Beavers back on their three-yard-
line with a punt, and Duke scored a safety moments later, making the score
20-16, Oregon State. Duke penetrated into Oregon State territory three times
in the final period but could not put the ball in the end zone.

Turnovers cost Duke the game, as the team lost three fumbles and allowed
four pass interceptions. Turning the ball over was very uncharacteristic for a
Wade-coached team but as usual, he took the blame, saying he had made a
mistake in letting the players go home for Christmas, and that he had spent
too much time handling arrangements for the game when he should have
been more focused on his team. It is possible that while Coach Wade saved
the 1942 Rose Bowl, the action costs his team an unbeaten season and a Rose
Bowl win.

Lach was sensational, running for 124 yards on 12 carries. Tom Davis ran
for 80 yards, and Bob Gantt caught four passes for 93 yards. But Oregon State

Fans in Durham at the 1942 Rose Bowl. Courtesy
of Duke Sports Information Department.

Aerial view of the 1942 Rose Bowl. Courtesy of Duke University Archives.

just deserved to win on this rainy day in Durham, scoring the most points against a Wallace Wade-coached Duke team since 1931.

Oregon State officials and fans were very effusive in their praise of the friendliness they had been shown by Duke and Durham. A Corvallis newspaper maintained that "nowhere in this country are people more hospitable than in North Carolina." Led by the efforts of Coach Wade, Duke University and the city of Durham had done a great job of transplanting the Rose Bowl.

Oregon State did not play in another Rose Bowl until 1956, when it was led by Tommy Prothro, quarterback for Duke on the 1942 Rose Bowl team.

At a reunion of the Rose Bowl team in 1991, Bob Barnett, who went on to become President and CEO of ICI Americas, the second largest chemical company in the nation and now called Astra-Zeneca, recalled the significance of the game. "It meant a great deal to Durham and to Duke. It will never be repeated. It's the only one that has ever been played outside Pasadena, and unless they have an earthquake out there, it will be the only one that ever is."

Add Penfield, long-time "Voice of the Blue Devils," thought the loss to Oregon State was mainly due to the threat of war:

> Personally, I think Coach Wade's preparation wasn't up to standard, perhaps for one big reason. Very much on his mind was the threat to the country. He had been a captain in the cavalry in World War I. I think that by December he'd already made up his mind to go back into the Army as soon as possible. And he did just that. When he went into the Army shortly after the Oregon State game, he made one stop on his way to Fort Bragg. That was at my home in Durham. He had a request to make of Virginia, my wife ... would she please go to his home on the campus and sit with Mrs. Wade for awhile. He knew she needed comforting. Virginia caught the next bus to Campus Drive.

* * *

Steve Lach not only was an All-American in 1941, but he set the Southern Conference record for the shot-put. After graduating from Duke, he played for the Great Lakes Naval Station team, helping it to beat Notre Dame on a last-second touchdown pass. The 19 to 14 defeat in 1943, in the last game of the season for the Irish, cost it both an unbeaten season and a national championship. It finished 9 and 1. Lach, one of many of Wade's former players who are now in the College Football Hall of Fame, died in 1961 of a heart attack.

Bob Gantt was only a sophomore in 1941, but by 1942 he was an All-American in football, and also made the All-Southern Conference team in basketball. That year "Look" magazine placed Gantt on its cover, calling him "Dixie's finest athlete." Gantt had starred at Durham High School in football, basketball, and track. In basketball, Gantt played on one of the nation's best high school teams, in which Durham High won over 70 games in a row and featured Gordon Carver, who later played at Duke, and Horace "Bones" McKinney, who later coached basketball at Wake Forest. In football, Durham High won the state championship Gantt's senior year under coach Carey Brewbaker.

Tommy Prothro became a very successful college head coach, compiling a 63-37-2 record at Oregon Sate from 1955 to 1964 and two Rose Bowl appearances. At UCLA he went 41-18-3 from 1965 to 1970, winning the Rose Bowl in 1966 over Michigan State. He was also a head coach in the NFL.

CHAPTER TWENTY-EIGHT

WORLD WAR II

In early February of 1942, Duke University had its first air-raid drill. For ten minutes bells and whistles sounded as students and staff went to their assigned locations. A "patriotic dance" was held. The Dope Shops on both campuses ran out of syrup for Coca-Cola, as a sugar shortage spread.

Early in 1942, Ted Mann had jokingly remarked to Coach Wade, "You know, Coach, before this war is over they might call you up." Mann then noticed the look in Wade's eyes as he replied, "They may not have to call me, Ted." In March of 1942 Coach Wade, 49 years of age and respected as one of the truly great coaches in all of college football, voluntarily applied to the army.

His overall record as he left Duke for WWII was a sparkling 146 wins, 32 losses, and six ties, for a won-loss percentage of 81% through 19 seasons as a head coach at Alabama and Duke. By 1942, Coach Wade stood at the pinnacle of his profession, and at his age, certainly could have chosen to finish his career out at Duke, But this intense man of duty, this man who loved his country, who had attended a military prep school, who had organized his own company and served as a captain in WWI, and who was a life-time reader of military history, didn't hesitate. He felt it was his duty to serve his country.

Another big reason Wade went into the army was because, as he said later in life, "My boys were going in and I felt like we should stay together as a team; we were just participating in a different battle".

In a diary Coach Wade kept during 1942, he wrote on March 27: "Turned keys over to Eddie. Felt very queer to be no longer connected with Duke University after 11⅓ years." Eddie Cameron replaced Wade as head football coach and athletic director. Later that day, as word spread the Duke campus that its coach was about to leave for service, hundreds gathered on the steps of the Duke Chapel. They then walked to Wade's home across campus and asked him to come out, which he did. For 15 minutes the students sang songs and wished Coach Wade well. They then presented him with a 25-foot scroll signed by more than 2,000 members of the student body and the university community. At the top of the scroll was the official United States coat of arms, followed by this message: "Best of luck, Coach Wade. We, the students of Duke Univer-

Wallace Wade and Eddie Cameron. Courtesy of Duke University Archives.

sity, wish to take this opportunity to express our sincere admiration to a fine gentleman, a great coach, and a true soldier."

On March 29, Wade left Duke for his first assignment. He wrote in his diary:

> Left home with Wallace [Wallace Wade, Jr., his son, who was also in the army], Mother [Frances, his wife] at home alone, was awfully hard to leave her. She seemed to be very brave about it. Hope she does not mind too much and does not get too lonely. Arrived at Bragg at 10 p.m.

March 30: "Had my first day, got an idea as to how much I have to learn. On Ft. Bragg radio program with Wallace." For some time while stationed at Fort Bragg, Wade was under the command of Colonel John Butner, who had been his teammate at Brown some 25 years before.

Wade, now a major, made this entry for April 2: "Went out to firing range. Ate lunch with D Battery in field." On April 14: "Wallace and I went to dinner with Captain Victor Robinson, formerly of Tullahoma, Tennessee." (Wade had coached in high school in Tullahoma in 1919 and 1920.)

Duke celebrated a War Day rally on May 15. Brigadier General Edwin Parker, commanding officer of the Field Artillery Replacement Center at Fort

Bragg, was invited to speak. Wade introduced Parker. "Spent day at Duke in observation of War Day. General Parker made speech. Mrs. Parker and Gen. Parker were offered use of Few home by Dr. Flowers. Returned to post at night." A mass student rally was held in Duke Stadium to heighten campus enthusiasm for the war effort, and the Duke band participated with the Fort Bragg Drum and Bugle Corps in a parade.

On May 27, Wade wrote just a two-word entry into his diary, which many Duke students would no doubt have been tickled to have read, written by the most famous man on their campus, simply. "Exams end." He was referring to the instruction he was receiving in field artillery.

On June 8, Wade received news he did not welcome. His diary entry for that day read, "Had letter from Major General Surles, offering me assignment to coach All-Army football team this fall. Asked to be relieved of assignment in order to have better chance of getting combat duty." His June 9 entry was: "Sis [his daughter] graduated with honors, unable to attend." On June 13, Wade finished the Field Artillery Replacement Center course. His June 15 entry read: "My fiftieth birthday. Took charge of 5th Battalion of FARC."

Along with his command of the 5th Battalion, Wade assisted in the physical fitness training of Fort Bragg soldiers. Brigadier General Parker had recruited Wade for this task, saying that "Major Wade's knowledge of physical training and body building will prove valuable to us in developing a finer physical training and conditioning program for trainees." Wade had helped the Durham recreation department in 1941 to start a program of exercise to condition potential draftees so that the number of men being rejected for "physical defects" into the armed services would be lowered. Also assisting in this program was W.F. Burkhardt, the football coach of North Carolina Central University in Durham.

Wade had also assisted in another, more subtle, way before leaving Duke for Fort Bragg. An AP story covered it:

> A travel-by-bicycle movement hit the Duke campus today with the latest recruit being Coach Wallace Wade. Wade has ordered his bike and expects it to arrive shortly. The Blue Devil coach will put his automobile, for which he is unable to obtain new tires because of restrictions, into the garage and use the bicycle to travel about the campus and Durham.

Wade's diary on June 25 read: "Battalion reviewed by Gen. Cubbison. He was very complimentary." His entries starting on July 12 were about his disappointment at being selected to coach the army football team and preparations for the games.

**Wallace Wade as WWII Officer. Courtesy of Duke
Sports Information Department.**

July 12: 1:00 p.m. Had telephone call from Col. Dalfores saying orders were at Ft. Bragg for me to report to Washington at 11 a.m. to
Director of Public Relations War Department. Took train from Fayetteville to Washington.

July 13: Arrived Washington 7:00 a.m. Reported to Major Gen.
Surles at 10:00 a.m. Said he was going to talk to Gen. Marshall about
Neyland [Robert Neyland of Tennessee] and me coaching All-Army
teams. I told him that I wanted to stay in Field Artillery. At 3:00 p.m.
Gen. Surles told Neyland and me that Gen. Marshall had picked us
to coach the Army team. I was terribly disappointed, about as low as
any time in my life. Arrived Fayetteville at midnight.

July 14: 10:00 p.m. Notified that Army plane was at Pope Field
ready to take me to Washington for news conference in regard to football games.

July 15: Left Fort Bragg at 6:00 a.m. in Army plane. Went to Norfolk and picked up Col. Neyland. Flew up Atlanta coast to NY. Arrived NY about 11 a.m. Left NY at 6:00 p.m., arrived Norfolk 8:00 p.m. Left Norfolk 9:00 p.m., reached Ft. Bragg about 10:30 p.m. A most interesting trip.

Around the middle of 1942, reports started coming back to Duke that alumni had been killed in the war. Gayle Louis Hermann, who had graduated in 1937, was killed in action while fighting a Japanese plane in the Pacific. William Anderson, a 1941 graduate, was killed in a plane crash in Mississippi during training. Preston King was killed in a similar plane crash in Florida. David Pinkerton was killed in the Battle of Midway Island.

Starting on July 20, Wade covered some of his coaching duties with the All-Army Western team. Coach Neyland was coaching the All-Army Eastern team. Both teams would be playing NFL teams to raise money for the war.

July 20: Arrived Washington 10:00 a.m. Reported to Gen. Surles and started work on arrangements for football game. Found very little had been done and whole thing was a mess.

July 23: Sat in on Secretary of War Stimson's press conference, Sec. Stimson was impressive.

July 28: Turned names of 40 football players over to Adjutant Generals Office to be ordered to Camp Cook, Santa Monica, Cal. to train for team.

August 2: Arrived Los Angeles noon. Drove to Camp Cook. Arrived Camp Cook about 9 p.m., is a desolate place.

August 5: Went to Los Angeles for press conference.

August 7: Back to Camp Cook and first practice.

August 22: Last practice. Drove to Pasadena. Arrived at Vista Del Arroyo Hotel about 8:00 p.m. [Wade had stayed here with some of his Rose Bowl teams.]

August 23: Went to San Diego to see Washington [Redskins] play.

August 24: Practiced in Rose Bowl. [It was during this visit that the Rose Bowl presented Coach Wade with a plaque thanking him for hosting the 1942 Rose Bowl in Durham.]

August 30: Played Redskins, we lost to a great team. Sammy Baugh was superb. Took train at 8:00 p.m. for Denver.

While scouting Washington in San Diego, Wade complimented not only Sammy Baugh, the great Redskins quarterback, but also one of the Redskins pass receiving ends. "Their ends were exceedingly fine in catching the passes.

One of them, Krueger, looked great." A reporter then asked Wade if he remembered Krueger. Wade chuckled, "I'll say I do." Al Krueger had caught the touchdown pass from Doyle Nave in the 1939 Rose Bowl to spoil Duke's unbeaten season.

As many as 60,000 fans saw the Redskins beat the Army team 26 to 7 in the Los Angeles Memorial Coliseum. Baugh threw two touchdown passes. "Thank goodness we won't meet any more Sammy Baughs on this tour," Wade said after the game. Receipts totaled $80,000, of which $45,000 went to the Army Relief Fund.

On September 6, Wade's Army team defeated the Chicago Cardinals 16 to 10 in Denver. John Kimbrough of Texas A&M scored twice for Army, and Marshall Goldberg, the former Pittsburgh All-American who lost to Duke in the 1938 season, played for the Cardinals. Over 20,000 attended the game, and $27,000 was raised for Army relief. Wade's diary for that day read: "Played Chicago Cardinals, we won a sloppy game. Left 7:15 p.m. for Detroit."

On September 9, Wade's team beat the Detroit Lions, and then lost to the Green Bay Packers on September 13. On the 19th, Army lost to the New York Giants 10 to 7. The Army team finished 2 and 3 against NFL teams that had been together much longer than the few weeks Wade's team had had to practice. On September 22 Wade recorded, "Banquet in NYC with Grantland Rice and others. Left NYC 9:30 p.m."

> September 23: Arrived Hendersonville 9:30 a.m. Dumpy [Dumpy Hagler, his longtime assistant coach at Duke] met me. Arrived Durham. Watched Duke practice in afternoon.
> September 24: Arrived Fort Bragg 4:00 p.m. Terribly let down and feeling very much out of place. [Wade records that he feels out of place because he never wanted to leave Fort Bragg to coach in the first place, and felt that he had fallen behind in his wish to see combat.]
> September 25: Spent balance of day in field with 6th Battalion. Helped to get me to thinking of soldiering again.

The month of October was an eventful one for Wade, involving a wedding and promotion, along with his command now of the 6th Battalion.

> October 1: Left Ft. Bragg for home. Frances was waiting to see me. Awfully glad to get home. Watched Duke practice in afternoon.
> October 2: Had rehearsal at Duke Chapel for Sis's wedding.
> October 3: Sis married at 4:30 p.m. Everybody said it was a pretty wedding. Reception at home afterward, many of our friends came.

Wallace Wade and Wallace Wade Jr. Courtesy of Nancy Wade.

Sis and Bobby left about 6:30 p.m. on honeymoon. They certainly looked like two kids. Sis looked very sweet and happy.

October 5: Left for Bragg. I got the same sad feeling, leaving Frances at home all alone. She is so little and needs somebody with her.

October 6: Wallace left in afternoon to report to 9th Div. They expect to go overseas very soon. Hated to see him start off alone, but it should be a fine experience for him. Our family is certainly split up now.

October 9: Was promoted today from Major to Lieutenant Colonel by special order #275 War Department.

October 14: Went out to see Wallace and tell him good-bye. They expect to leave tonight. I think that his outfit is to form part of a task force to land somewhere in Africa.

Although Wade loved the military life, he couldn't completely forget coaching football. The fact that Duke was a relatively short distance from Fort Bragg made it possible for him to attend a couple of games during 1942, such as the Georgia Tech game on October 31. In November he sat on the bench with the team as Duke beat NC State 47 to 0.

Lieutenant Colonel Wade spent Christmas at home in Durham. "Had a great Christmas Day. Bobby and Sis came over last night and spent the day with us. We all enjoyed the day very much except that we were saddened by the thought that Wallace was in Africa not able to be home and enjoy Christmas."

After being sent to Fort Sill, Oklahoma, for a short while in 1943, Wade assumed command of the 272nd Field Artillery Battalion at Camp Butner, very near Durham. In September of that year, Wade received word that his mother, Sallie Wade, had passed away at the age of 84. In November, Wade suffered a broken leg when a jeep he was riding in during blackout maneuvers overturned on the Camp Butner range. Major Lorance Dennis was driving the jeep when he became blinded by the lights of an approaching vehicle. The accident occurred around 10 p.m. The injury, said by doctors to be "long and tedious in healing," was another setback in Wade's wish to get into combat.

Just before the accident had taken place, Wade's field artillery unit had won first place honors in competition with other units in field maneuvers. Colonel W.E. Evans at that time called Wade "one of the finest officers I've ever seen and his ability to handle young men is remarkable."

Wade recovered at the Oliver General Hospital in Augusta, Georgia. In February of 1944, he returned to Fort Bragg to assume command of the 272nd unit again.

In early 1944, two Duke alumni were awarded the Distinguished Flying Cross. First Lieutenant Maxwell Holder was given the award

> for extraordinary achievement while participating in flight missions in the Pacific. Flights involved flying at low altitudes over mountainous terrain under adverse weather conditions in an unarmed transport plane and often necessitated landing within a few miles of enemy bases.

Lieutenant Edwin Wilson was awarded for piloting a dive-bomber in the Solomons. Military officials cited him for "participating in an attack against enemy shipping in strongly defended waters of Kahili, which resulted in the sinking of four destroyers. During the attack he scored a direct hit on one of the destroyers." Duke's Navy students treated him like a celebrity when Wilson visited campus for a couple of days.

As of March 1944, 43 Duke alumni had been killed in WWII, with 20 being held as prisoners and 12 missing in action. The Duke Alumni Office worked hard to keep in touch with its graduates and former students, answering every letter it received. Former athletes got news of football under Eddie Cameron and baseball news under Jack Coombs, former music students received notices of current campus productions, and so on.

In May of 1944, news reached the Duke campus that First Lieutenant Robert McCormick, Jr. had been shot down over Sardinia and was being held as a prisoner by the Germans. In June, two large liberty ships were christened in Georgia bearing the names of James B. Duke, whose money made Duke University possible, and William P. Few, long-time president of Duke.

In April 1944, Lieutenant Colonel Wade took his 272nd Field Artillery Battalion overseas. His unit was composed of 240-millimeter howitzers, the heaviest field artillery in the US arsenal. The 272nd served at various times with the Third, First, and Ninth Armies. Under Wade, it participated in the Battle of Normandy, the Siegfried Line Battle, the Battle of the Bulge, the crossing of the Rhine, and the Ninth Army drive through Germany. At the end of the war it was one of the units closest to Berlin. Wade went through the entire European campaign without a day's leave despite being 52 years old. He was in range of enemy fire constantly for nine months, dodging enemy mine fields and spending time in foxholes.

While overseas, Wade heard about a soldier about to be court martialed for violating procedure, even though the soldier had performed a heroic act in saving another man's life. Wade thought such a court martial in this special circumstance was very unjustified, and used his national prominence by letting it be known that he would let some friends of his in the press back home in America know how the military was treating this heroic soldier. The charges were then dropped, and the young soldier's career was saved.

Back home, Duke had been invited to play in the Sugar Bowl against Alabama on January 1, 1945. Eddie Cameron had led Duke to a fine record since Wade had departed. Duke was 5-4-1 in 1942, 8-1 in 1943, 6-4 in 1944, and would go 6-2 in 1945. In 1943 Duke beat its most keen rival, North Carolina, 14 to 7 on October 16, then turned around and beat UNC again 27 to 6 on November 20. Cameron's overall record against UNC in his four seasons as football coach was 4-0-1.

The 1945 Sugar Bowl matched Wallace Wade's old team, Alabama, against his former team, Duke. Frank Thomas, who had succeeded Wade at Alabama and done a wonderful job, was still the Crimson Tide coach. Fans numbering 72,000 watched the game in Tulane Stadium in New Orleans. The lead changed hands four times, and the score was not settled until the final gun.

Sugar Bowl pre-game festivities, 1945. Courtesy of Duke University Archives.

Alabama, behind the brilliant passing of Harry Gilmer, jumped to a 19-7 lead. Duke scored before half-time to make it 19-13.

In the third period, Tom Davis of Duke carried the ball 11 times on a 12-play 64-yard touchdown drive, then scored to put Duke up 20-19. Hugh Morrow of the Crimson Tide then intercepted a pass and ran it back for a touchdown to make it 26-20 Alabama. Duke got the ball back and drove to Alabama's one-yard line, but the Tide defense somehow kept Duke out of the end zone. Only three minutes remained in the game.

Thomas called for a safety to get a free kick from the 20, making it 26-22. But Duke took possession as George Clark caught Alabama's punt on the Duke 40 and returned it to the Tide 39. Jim Larue then carried the ball for 19 yards on a reverse. Then Clark went over right tackle for the remaining 20 yards,

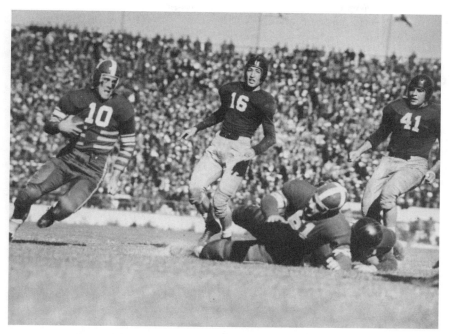

1945 Sugar Bowl action. Courtesy of Duke University Archives.

and Duke led 29-26. But Alabama was not through. Gilmer passed to Ralph Jones to the Duke 24 before the game ended.

Lieutenant Colonel Wade had sent word through a letter to Cameron and the Duke team that he would stop fighting to hear the game from France, where he was still involved in combat. In the letter, he sent an "order for victory." He added that he was "setting up a special cheering section over here to help the boys along. Tell the boys they've got to win this one." Wade had asked the War Department to approve the Duke-Alabama game for reception to overseas troops, and the famous coach-turned soldier got his wish.

* * *

The war continued, of course, not stopping for football or anything else. On March 7, 1945, American forces crossed the Rhine River, and by the end of the month, all German forces had been pushed back into Germany. On April 12, President Franklin Roosevelt died. Duke canceled all social activities as a tribute, a memorial service was held at the Duke Chapel in honor of FDR, and classes were called off so that university students and staff could attend.

In early 1945 John Lanahan, a former Duke student, wrote a letter from New Guinea back to friends at Duke:

> At a time when the entire world is seething, restless, and troubled, Duke represents what we are fighting for—peace, rational thinking, and an equal change for one to develop his potentialities free of suppression and "governmental guidance."
>
> Duke, and all it stands for, means something different to all of us, I imagine. It's a composite of Chapel steps between classes, the Dope Shop, last minute term papers, fraternity rivalries, football games, the Goody Shop, a request to "drop in and see H.J. Herring," a constant suspicion that the "cut book" is an animate object incapable of human understanding, and the 10:30 p.m. rush on East Campus.
>
> I've run into quite a few Duke lads out here. Three of us that left college before we finished look forward to the day when we can trade a uniform for a sport coat and the deck of a ship for the Duke campus.

The year 1945 also saw the death of Lewis Frederick and his dog Jerry. Frederick was a member of the Duke class of 1944 and gained fame as a pilot on the Air Transport Command, winning a presidential citation among other awards. Frederick always flew with his Dalmation dog, Jerry. "Major" Jerry was reputed to be able to sight enemy planes before members of the crew could. This pair had been featured in *Life* magazine and many newspapers. Frederick and Jerry both died when their plane went down over England.

The Navy V-12 school at Duke closed in July of 1945. In all, 353 Navy trainees received diplomas from Duke.

In May of 1945, Wade was named athletic director of the 12th Army Group, a post in which he had charge of athletics for some 1.5 million soldiers in Europe. Headquartered in Wiesbaden, Germany, Wade coordinated recreation activities for occupational troops. Traveling throughout Europe, Wade held conferences with athletic leaders and gave lectures on the value of physical fitness.

Wade came home in late 1945. He discussed some of his experiences and thoughts of war in several interviews:

> The Germans are a contradictory constituency. Civilians caused practically no trouble at all for us as we advanced, but their soldiers fought furiously. The civilians violated few regulations and were often valuable assets for information and direction. The German people believed the vicious stories related to them concerning the Jews, and

when convinced of the awful treatment administered to the Jews and
others they immediately lay it to the government by saying, "we did
not select the government."

It will take a long time to teach and develop the idea of democracy
in the minds of these people. They are impressed with the militaris-
tic ideals and display as seen in the German army. Germany cannot
wage war again in 10 years. However, we must look out for them in
the next 15 and 25 years from now.

They will doubtless respond to a program of guidance and teaching over a period of years. If we undertake to knock their ears down
it will be altogether different.

At another talk to the Durham Civitan Club, Wade said, "The thing that
whipped Germany and her army was our great mass production of war
equipment for our allies and ourselves. The German Army was a great fighting machine."

The French government awarded Wade the Croix de Guerre with Palm, and
he received a Bronze Star and four battle stars on the European Theater Campaign Ribbon.

With WWII over, Lieutenant Colonel Wade now had to decide if he wanted
to resume being Coach Wade.

CHAPTER TWENTY-NINE

1946–1950

Wade decided to coach again, starting with the 1946 season. Eddie Cameron had done a good job coaching the football team while Wade served in World War II. It was decided that Wade would continue his athletic director duties in 1945, as he had held that position from 1931 to 1942. But Wade, who had been involved with football for over 30 years of his life, wanted to get back into coaching. In 1946, Wade gave up the athletic director job to just coach.

Eddie Cameron was himself a legend on the Duke campus. After a brilliant football playing career at Washington and Lee, playing for James DeHart, who became Duke's head coach and was succeeded by Wallace Wade, Cameron came to Duke in 1926 with DeHart and coached freshman football and freshman basketball. He became head varsity basketball coach in 1929 and held that position until 1942, winning 229 games against 99 losses. He also served as an assistant coach in football from 1930 to 1942, then as head coach of football from 1942 to 1945, compiling a 25-11-1 record with the Sugar Bowl victory over Alabama. He then became an assistant football coach again from 1946 to 1951 while also serving as director of both physical education and athletics. He held the latter two positions until 1972.

As athletic director at Duke, Cameron raised the money for the Duke University Golf Course, and held many national appointments to organizations such as on the Board of Directors of the US Olympic Association.

Perhaps the most famous college basketball arena in the country, Cameron Indoor Stadium, now bears his name.

Wade would not have as much success in his last five years of coaching at Duke, from 1946 to 1950, compiling a 25-17-4 record, with his only losing record for a season in his 24 years as a head coach coming in 1946 at 4 and 5. The players had changed to a degree, many of them had experienced a war, they were older, some were married, many were on the GI Bill, and they were not as much dependent on athletic scholarships. Wade, too, did not have the same drive and single-minded focus he was known for, as he had seen so much death and destruction from his service in WWII that football suddenly just didn't seem as important, this from a man whose life had been football.

A comment he made in later years best sums up his feelings during these post-war years, and at least partially explains why Duke slipped just a bit. He said, "When you try just to stay alive for two years, football doesn't amount to much."

Most of his players in 1946 were veterans. Bob Barnett, a player for Wade before the war, came back to Duke to attend law school and also as a graduate assistant coach to Wade. While serving in the Marines, Barnett once left on a patrol on Iwo Jima with four officers and 27 men, only one officer and four men returned. John Muse had participated in the destruction of Berchtesgarden in Germany, flying eight bombing missions on B-24s. Bill Milner participated in the occupation of Japan. C.P. Youmans fought in the European Theater with the Third Army, earning three battle stars. Roger Neighborgall was a member of a 500-man Ranger battalion that spent 14 days behind German lines. Only 135 returned safely. Fred Folger served with a bombing squadron and was awarded several ribbons and medals, Jack Eslick was a high speed radio operator in China and India. Bob Gantt served on a destroyer that was credited with downing 17 enemy craft and took part in invasions of Iwo Jima and Okinawa.

These players that walked on Duke's practice field in 1946 were now men, not typical freshmen or returning players whose minds were on football, classes, and pretty coeds. No, these young men still loved football, but their experiences had given them a more mature, perhaps sedate, and emotional way of thinking.

Bob Cox and Carmen Falcone were two new additions to the coaching staff. Falcone had been a star football player and wrestler at Kent State, then served in WWII, some of that time in the Navy V-12 program at Duke. After the war Falcone received his master's degree in physical education from Ohio State. Falcone coached football as an assistant at Duke from 1946 to 1972, and the Carmen Falcone Award is given annually to Duke's most valuable player. Coach Falcone's son, Sonny Falcone, has served as the Head Strength and Conditioning Coach at Duke since 1980. Cox had been an All-Southern player at Duke for Wade in 1932 and 1933.

Before the season started, there was a little controversy over the recruitment of a player by the name of Charlie "Choo Choo" Justice. Justice would lead the University of North Carolina to some of its greatest success. UNC would play in its first-ever bowl game, the Sugar, in 1947, and also in the Sugar Bowl again in 1949 and the Cotton Bowl on January 1, 1950. Justice was runner-up for the Heisman Trophy in both 1948 and 1949.

The *Duke Chronicle*, Duke's student newspaper, ran the following story in 1946 concerning Justice.

It appears that when Carolina bought (pardon, brought) Charlie Justice into their fold, they not only got another football player but a very efficient scout and high pressure salesman. Gridiron fans will remember Choo Choo Justice as the All-American service player who served a short hitch in the navy, playing ball for the powerful Bainbridge aggregation.

After getting out of the service, it was rumored that he was on his way to Duke University to attend college. It was about this time that more than a dozen colleges allegedly started bidding for the amateur player.

Last week while attending a spring workout here at Duke as an uninvited guest, he noticed the playing of one Tony Yovicsin, a freshman out for the squad. It so happened that after the practice Choo Choo began to tell Tony of a more "profitable" education at Carolina. It was not long after Justice had pointed out these "advantages" that Mr. Tony's school spirit suddenly changed to Carolina. But not only was he contented with taking himself over to Carolina, he also wanted to take a few memories with him. These memories were in the form of a complete set of Blue Devil plays worked out during spring practice.

In the last publication of the *Carolina* magazine, the advertising department, or the dirty dig department, published a fictitious ad containing the words: "Athletes, learn as you earn at Dook University." Has it ever occurred to the members of said magazine that maybe one or two of their star basketball players are not attending the school because of the good old college spirit of Carolina? Justice turned up at Carolina after it was rumored that South Carolina had offered him the fat sum of $8,000. Yes, it was school spirit that brought Choo Choo, his wife, and his football ability to Carolina. Justice just might bring glory to the Tar Heel football team, but to take the words from that famous play: "What Price Glory?"

Duke lost to North Carolina State in Wade's first game back. Another big game in 1946 that Duke lost was to Army 19 to 0 at the Polo Grounds in New York City. Army would finish 9-0-1, the tie against Notre Dame, and was led by Glenn Davis and Doc Blanchard, the Heisman Trophy winners of 1945 and 1946. Army, under Coach Red Blaik, was the most powerful team in the nation from 1944 to 1946, going 27-0-1. The glory days of Army football can be summed up by a telegram wired to West Point following its undefeated 1944 season: "We have stopped the war to celebrate your magnificent success. MacArthur."

Wade had wanted to beat Army in the worst way, but not from any antagonism toward it. He had great respect for Coach Blaik and his program, and he admired the Army players for their spirit and service to the country. It is more than probable that coaching football at Army would have been a position Coach Wade would have relished. Of course, one of his favorite players at Duke, Eric Tipton, ended up coaching at Army for some 20 years, and very successfully. An example of Wade looking to the Army game is shown from this article by Frank Spencer:

> There's an old saying around Dixie that when Wallace Wade "points" for a game there will be fur a-flying. Seldom in his long, colorful, and successful career has Wade witnessed an opposing team in action. He leaves the scouting job to his capable aides. But when Oklahoma met Army, Wade was in the stands watching the Cadets in action.

Duke and Wallace Wade still held much national appeal in 1946, as a sell-out crowd of over 59,000 attended the Army game. Coach Blaik said after the game that "we could go on packing the Polo Grounds with Duke." Of course, Army was a drawing card unto itself. But for the game, Army was just too good, even though the 19 points scored was the lowest total for Army in its last 24 games.

Duke finished 4 and 5, not only Wade's first losing season as a head coach, but the only losing season he was ever connected with as a player or assistant coach, ever, starting as a high school player.

In November of 1946 Wallace Wade Jr. married Evelyn Weygandt in Ohio, and Wade served as best man.

1947 brought a 4-3-2 record, highlighted by a win over Tennessee in Knoxville. After starting the season 4-0-1, tying Navy, the Blue Devils were ranked number nine in the nation. But they then lost to Georgia Tech and Missouri and tied South Carolina. Their last game was in front of 57,000, a Duke Stadium record, against Choo Choo Justice and UNC. UNC dominated the game, and won 21 to 0, the score being kept down by virtue of UNC's six turnovers and 150 yards in penalties.

Wade still was able to recruit good players, and as at Alabama he had a network of former players coaching high school football, which aided the talent pool coming to Durham. An example of this was Emory Adkins, who coached at Greensboro High, Wilmington New Hanover, and Rocky Mount. Buddy Luper and Pete Goddard were two players that Adkins sent to Duke to play for Wade. Winston Siegfried, after a stellar playing career at Duke, developed some of the top teams in the state at Sanford High School.

Although Duke had good players, an 8-8-2 record over 1946 and 1947 was definitely not up to par with Wade's splendid teams of the 1930s, which boasted the best overall record in the country. 1947 was not only not a good

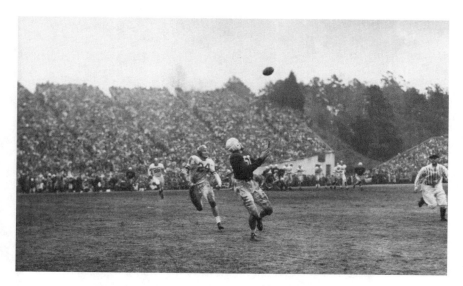

Duke-UNC, 1947. Courtesy of Duke University Archives.

season on the football field, but a terrible one for Wade off the field. His dear wife of 30 years, Frances Bell Wade, died on June 2 at her home in Durham after having been in declining health for several months. The love Wade had for his wife is shown in the diary he kept in 1942; he constantly referred to her, worrying about her feelings and health while he was in the army, mentioning several times how glad he was to see her and how sad it was to leave her. Anita Caldwell recalls how although Coach Wade seemed to always be in charge and the center of attention away from home, that Mrs. Wade ran things around the Wade house. According to Mrs. Caldwell, if Mrs. Wade had announced dinner to be at 6 p.m., Coach Wade would leave for home in plenty of time to be there by 6, no matter if he was having a staff meeting or what, the meeting would just have to wait. Just as Coach Wade did not tolerate players being late to practices, he knew Mrs. Wade did not tolerate her husband showing up late to the dinner table. As noted earlier, she also made Coach Wade store the many apples that his brother Mark sent him out in a shed, as she did not particularly like their smell.

Mrs. Wade enjoyed being wife to a football coach, as is somewhat expressed in a letter to her sister Claire, written in late December of 1938 from the Rose Bowl in Pasadena.

> We had a lot of excitement getting away from Durham—mobs of people at the train. I really felt like Mrs. Roosevelt as I sat in my train

Larry Karl, 1948. Courtesy of Duke University Archives.

window waving and smiling at the crowd outside! Every place we stopped, more mobs of people met us at stations. Once in Pasadena, we drove out here to the hotel with Johnny Mack in his car. We had a fine time yesterday. We drove through Beverly Hills, where our driver pointed out homes of movie stars. The boys were thrilled at this. Then we went to Santa Monica, where we had dinner at a beach club right on the beach. After dinner we drove to Westwood to the Ice Carnival—this was swell! Wally was crazy about it, wants to try it. Tonight we go to a play, a comedy called "El Capitan."

As the 1948 season neared, there was a little unrest among Duke fans. One reason whey Duke was perhaps not doing as well was suggested by Harry Beaudouin of the *Charlotte News*:

In 1946, Wallace Wade's first season of football coaching since serving on European battlefields as an artillery colonel, his Duke team won four games and lost five. This record, shabby compared with those established by the Old Man's pre-war juggernauts, elicited considerable Yaketty-yak among Durham partisans.

More than a few Duke students said, yeah, that single-wing stuff is out-dated, what Wade needs is a new technique—spelled with a capital T.

In 1947, it was practically the same story—four victories, three defeats, and two ties. Pretty mediocre for Duke. Again the Blue Devils were disembowled by their Chapel Hill neighbors (21-0), marking the first time since 1929 that the Dukes had dropped two in a row to Carolina.

By this time it wasn't just the student body that asked, "What goes?" It was alumni, Duke followers, and the collegiate sporting world in general. Outsiders were prone to theorize that Wade had lost his touch, that he no longer ranked with America's greatest coaches.

Despite their chagrin over losing, the University's authorities steadfastly refused to take the road which would obviously remedy the situation, i.e. recruiting high school stars with fat offers and inducements. Wallace Wade is of like mind.

Because of his reluctance to keep athletes happy with engravings of Abe Lincoln, Wade has suffered. In 1946, the most promising center to enroll at Duke in years, Frank Sinkovitz, quit school. Reason: he was married and fed up with living on the government's GI allowances of $90 a month.

Most of Duke's football men, like those elsewhere, are service veterans. Uncle Sam foots the bill for their expenses, except meals and room rent. A football "scholarship" at Duke these days consists of weekly meal books and involves having the Athletic Association pay the University for the athlete's dormitory room. Thus, the boy is free to use his GI subsistence of $85 for other purposes: laundry, social life, etc.

In short, the deal at Duke is room and board—and tuition for the non-veterans. It differs in no way from the set-up at certain institutions in the oh-so-unspeakably-pure Ivy League.

Since the war, proselytizing has reached ludicrous proportions to be sure. Illinois, for example, pays football players for "working" as "highway inspectors" (between classes, no doubt). Ohio State's heroes were on the State of Ohio's payroll for the month of October to the tune of $3,436—a pay scale at the rate of $30,000 a year for part-time jobs.

A Notre Dame man told me that some of the more valued Fighting Irish receive a cut of the stadium parking lot receipts.

A freshman basketball player at Georgia said that he was permitted to draw up to $100 in cash per semester—this, of course, in addition to his monthly GI stipend.

Athletes have been getting smaller deals in colleges the country over ... Duke is one place where they are not.... Duke wants to win— but not with high-priced beef imported from the hinterlands.

While on the subject, let us briefly consider some interesting statistics—the percentage of "foreign" players on the 1947 football squad of Southern Conference rivals in Duke's immediate territory. Official rosters were used.

Wake Forest's quad is 47% Yankee. North Carolina is second with 45%, while 41% of NC State's legions migrated from north of the Mason-Dixon Line.

Duke's squad, on the other hand is 25% Union-bred—a modest percentage indeed, considering that 50% of the entire student body hails from up yonder.

Duke people ... point out that it is no accident that five of the seven men in Carolina's first-string line last season were dyed-in-the-wool, hot-blooded Southerners from Newark, NJ, Powell, Pa., Buffalo, NY, Frankfort, Ind., and Shippenburg, Pa. Tar Heel coaches, if they so desired, could set apart their 30 Yankees and stage an annual North-South game of their own.

Witness the case of a young man from Dan Hill's hometown of Asheville, NC, Charlie "Choo-Choo" Justice. It is known that Duke had A-1 priority while Charlie was romping to high school touchdowns. The Navy engulfed him, however, and when he emerged he was perhaps the most sought-after service athlete in the country. Married and discharged, Justice went to see Dan Hill first. He told Dan what he wanted. Dan told Duke, and Duke told Charlie, "You-funny-boy-you."

Justice next visited South Carolina ... then North Carolina—and stayed, presumably because he felt that Chapel Hill's atmosphere was conducive to the study of Tibetan semantics. Needless to report, he has been prominent in the severe whackings which Carolina has dealt Duke the past two seasons.

The Duke opinion is that any boy willing to sacrifice the time and lumps that collegiate football entails is certainly deserving of financial assistance in obtaining his education. Assistance, that is, within the bounds of common sense.

Practice, 1948. Courtesy of Duke University Archives.

Just as significant—and consequential—as its abiding reluctance to part with bullion is the fact that Duke's academic requirements have been stiffened in recent years. Veterans who returned found that whereas they have been able to get by in "the old days" merely by hitting the books with bulldog courage on the eve of final exams, they now had to stay eager from one week to the next. Class cuts were reduced to three per semester.

And those athletes who arrived expecting a four-year fiesta discovered that ... the chauvinism of the faculty is not such that professors will overlook the fact that a term paper is three weeks late, even though its author may be a simply devastating halfback.

The muscle men are in the same boat with the rest of the undergraduate history majors, engineers, or business administration students. They sink or swim.

Because of a curious regard for something known as "academic standards," Duke shut the door in the face of a potentially great college player. But, as Dan Hill philosophically observes, "Hell—that's been happening every day here."

Practice, 1948. Courtesy of Duke University Archives.

Duke finished 4-3-2 for the second straight year in 1948, including losses to North Carolina and Wake Forest. Just as in 1947, it got off to a good start, as they were 3-0-2 after the first five games and ranked fifteenth in the nation, but lost three of the final four games. UNC won 20 to 0 behind Justice's 120 yards rushing. UNC had been ranked number one in the country at one point in the season and finished 9-1-1, losing only to Oklahoma in the Sugar Bowl.

Al DeRogatis played his last game for Duke in 1948, and is considered one of the greatest defensive linemen ever to play for the Blue Devils. DeRogatis was six-feet-two inches tall and weighed 220 pounds, and combined that size with bone-crushing wrath on the field. Coach Wade had to ask DeRogatis to take it a bit easy on his teammates in practice. Tom Chambers, a teammate, said,

> I almost bust a gut myself trying to get out of Al's way when I see him coming, because he is going after the ball-carrier no matter who gets in his way, friend or foe. You can imagine how the other fellow feels when DeRogatis charges across the line.

When Duke played Army in 1946, Doc Blanchard was known to barrel over quite a few defenders. One of the Army offensive lineman, early in the game, told his Duke counterpart across the line, "Mister, Doc Blanchard is coming right through here this time. I don't know what you are going to do, but I'm getting the hell out of the way." That counterpart happened to be DeRogatis, and he replied, "Let's just see who backs up first." According to reports of the game, neither great player backed up the whole game, as the collisions between these two All-Americans could be heard throughout the Polo Grounds that afternoon.

Carlton Byrd of the *Winston-Salem Twin City Sentinel* described DeRogatis as having "a physique like that fellow who goes around carrying the world on his shoulders—Atlas, they call him—and when DeRogatis twitches one of his biceps it resembles the Rock of Gibraltar doing a rhumba dance." Once during a practice to get ready for Duke, Peahead Walker, the Wake Forest coach, stopped a drill and screamed to his defense, "Hold everything. That mess isn't going to work on DeRogatis. He'll kill a couple of you boys if you try to work that on him."

After Duke, DeRogatis had a distinguished career with the New York Giants in the NFL before a knee injury forced him to retire. He is well known also for his 17 years as a pro-football analyst for NBC television.

* * *

By 1949 the spread of communism had the Truman administration making containment its top priority in foreign policy. Winston Churchill had warned of communism being spread by the Soviet Union, declaring, "From Stettin in the Baltic to Trieste in the Adriatic, an iron curtain has descended across the Continent." For entertainment, Americans watched "The Lone Ranger", played with a toy that every kid wanted, the Slinky, jumped on pogo sticks, and twisted inside hula-hoops. The Broadway musical "South Pacific" debuted in 1949, and the first Volkswagen went on sale in the US.

Duke football rebounded to go 6 and 3 in 1949, getting big wins over Virginia Tech, NC State, and Tennessee. The losses were to Navy, Wake Forest, and North Carolina.

The Tennessee game in Knoxville marked a relatively new method of travel for the Blue Devils, as they flew on a Capital Airlines 60-passenger plane. They had flown once before. The meal served on the way home consisted of chicken on toast, green beans, cream potatoes, Bartlett pear salad, butter and French rolls, ice cream and cake, and coffee or milk to drink. Leaving Knoxville at 6:30 p.m. and arriving in Durham at 8:00 p.m. also convinced the players that the airplane was the way to go over the train.

Coach Wade was adapting to the times by the late 1940s, even trying some T formation plays in practices and using more of a separate offensive team and a defensive team, as opposed to the single-wing formation and one-pla-toon football he had used throughout his career. Ed Danforth of the *Atlanta Journal* noticed these changes:

> After watching all that ultra-modern stuff going on, one turns to look at the tall figure of Wallace Wade in his baseball cap [his tradi-tional attire for practices] and it seems strange again ... and hearten-ing. The "Bear" is cutting away old conceptions of football. He is swimming strong with the tide.
>
> I asked him, "You used to play 'em all the way at Alabama and be-fore the war you just made spot substitutions here at Duke. Are the boys getting soft?"
>
> Wade replied, "No, but we coaches have learned something about keeping football players fit. We used to play them until they were ex-hausted before substituting. They got along all right because they were playing against men who were just as tired. Late in those games both sides were out on their feet as often as not. We have learned now that frequent rest periods are better for them. It keeps them sharp for the whole game. We are going through with it although we do not yet have the personnel to make it really effective." Coach Wade also likes many ideas in the T offense and he is working on them with an idea of going further next year.

Wade, in fact, hired Billy Hickman, a T specialist from the University of Virginia, to coach at Duke in 1950.

Wade was also using the pass more, as evidenced by Billy Cox throwing 18 times in the 21 to 7 win over Tennessee for 172 yards.

57,500 spectators were in the stands of Duke Stadium as UNC, fresh off a 42 to 6 loss to Notre Dame before 67,000 in Yankee Stadium, beat Duke 21 to 20. The Tar Heels led 7 to 6 at half-time, then recorded a safety to go up 9 to 6 early in the third quarter. Choo Choo Justice scored on a short run to make it 15 to 6 mid-way through the third quarter. Late in the third, Justice con-nected on a touchdown pass to Art Weiner to put the Heels up 21-6. Tom Powers of Duke then returned UNC's kickoff 93 yards for a touchdown, and with the conversion it was 21-13. Billy Cox of Duke ran into the end zone with four minutes to go, and Mike Souchak, the future professional golfer, kicked the extra point, and it was 21-20.

With 20 seconds remaining Duke had the ball on the Carolina 19. Billy Cox threw two incomplete passes, and now four seconds remained. As Duke lined up for a field goal, referee J.D. Rogers signaled that the game was over. UNC fans came onto the field, but after realizing his mistake, Rogers cleared the field after several minutes. Mike Souchak came back in to attempt a field goal, but Art Weiner blocked the kick.

After the game, Coach Wade said,

> Of course we wanted to win this game more than any other one on our schedule. All of our boys played their hearts out, but it just wasn't in the books for us to win. I found out a long time ago that a football takes a lot of crazy bounces, but it is a good game.

As he had throughout his career, Wade made no excuses, blamed no one, said nothing negative about the mistake the referee made, even though it obviously upset the rhythm of the game. Rogers admitted his blunder, and apologized, saying, "I blew it." Rogers came over to Wade after the game, and the two shook hands.

While Duke had beaten UNC seven times against three defeats and a tie during Wade's first eleven years, UNC had now won four straight from 1946 to 1949, and it was the play of Charlie Justice who had led the way. Talmadge Little, a UNC supporter, rubbed it in a little with this poem written shortly after the Duke-UNC game of 1949:

> On November 19, 1949, at Duke Stadium I arrived, just in time.
> As I took my seat in the big horseshoe,
> Up pulled "Choo Choo" at the South gate
> A little later, about quarter to two I looked down on the field,
> And there went number 22.
> He took a seat on the bench with the rest of the bunch
> Coach Wade said to Ace Parker,
> "I got a hunch, we're going to get beat the fourth time."
>
> Justice said to Coach Snavely,
> "I never felt finer ... and I'll complete my first pass for a touchdown to Weiner."
> UNC moved down field to the Duke 32.
> Coach Snavely waved his hand and in went "The Great Choo Choo."
>
> He faked a run to his right, he didn't have a care
> For down in his heart he knew big Art would be there.
> He cocked that right arm and gave the pigskin a flip,
> Big Art leaped high in the air, and gave
> That football a grip.
> He fell across the goal line and rolled

All around,
He yelled to Justice, "We've got a touchdown!"

Carolina relaxed, they never felt finer;
They had just got a touchdown from Justice to Weiner.
With the game about over, the score 21-20.
Cox said to Powers: "Let's have some fun."
They got up steam and began to roll,
Then all of a sudden they ran out of coal.
They were all excited, each poor soul,
When Coach Wade shouted, "Try a field goal!"
They all lined up,
Souchak gave the ball a sock,
And all of a sudden they knew the kick
Had been blocked.
Coach Wade said to Parker,
"I told you about that hunch, we are beaten again by that same old
bunch."

Louis Allen made third team All-American for Duke for the 1949 season from
his tackle position. He also made All-Southern Conference for the third straight
year, joining Ace Parker and Tom Davis as the only Duke players to do so. Billy
Cox, the Blue Devil quarterback, set a new Duke record for total offense in one
season with 1,268 yards, eclipsing Parker's record of 1,190, which had stood for
13 years. Wade was named Southern Conference Coach of the Year, as he won
six out of nine against a tough schedule with the fewest returning lettermen in
his career.

* * *

President Hollis Edens of Duke received a letter from a Duke supporter of
lower admission standards for athletes in 1949. Duke today stands for academic excellence and is one of the best overall athletic programs in the nation,
which sets an example for true student-athletes.

> Now it is very evident that boys cannot excel in athletics and studies
> at the same time. They sacrifice the one to the other. I think that the
> boys of our country, through their athletic activities, are doing more
> for secondary education than any other one influence. Is it fair to
> allow them to continue to do this at the expense of their preparation
> for college and then penalize them by making them compete with the
> horn-rimmed spectacled group whose chief athletic activity was suck-
> ing soda through a straw?

**Wallace Wade with Sam Snead. Courtesy of Duke
Sports Information Department.**

* * *

Wade and Coach Carl Snavely of UNC always had much respect for each other. During the summer of 1950 they appeared together as guest actors in the drama "The Lost Colony" in Manteo, North Carolina. Dressed up as colonists, they did a peace pipe smoking scene. As they smoked, a little boy colonist, about seven years old, came on stage. Wade said, "He looks like a pretty good prospect. Son! Have you thought about what college you'd like to attend?" "Wait a minute, Wallace. Look son, we can offer you the best of everything at Chapel Hill. Remember Choo Choo? This boy wouldn't be happy at Duke, Wallace," Snavely retorted. To which Wade replied, "That's what you think. If you think you can get this one away from me...." Snavely then reminded Wade of the peace pipe. "Peace pipe nothing. From now on this is war," Wade said, as the little boy ran off the stage. "That's okay by me, I'll see you in Chapel Hill in November," said Snavely.

In the second game of the 1950 season, Duke hosted Pittsburgh. Coming on the heels of an impressive win over South Carolina in Columbia, the Duke team had high hopes for the upcoming season. Duke beat Pitt handily 28 to 14, but the game was more significant for those who played in the game. Flint Greene was a black player for Pittsburgh, and still in 1950, it was customary

**Homecoming 1950 window display in Belk-Leggett store in Durham.
Courtesy of Duke University Archives.**

for a visiting team to not play any black players it had when going against a team in North Carolina or the rest of the south. Wade, who had been friends with Fritz Pollard at Brown and had allowed a black player for Syracuse to play in 1938 in a game at Syracuse, took another stand for the integration of college athletics in the Pitt game. With Wade's approval, Duke issued the following statement before the game:

> Yes, we have heard that the Pittsburgh team has a Negro on the squad. When we schedule a team we of course expect to play on fair and even terms. The coaches of each team have the unquestioned right to play any eligible man they choose to play. We have neither the right nor the desire to ask a coach to restrict or limit his team's participation because of creed or color. Duke fans and students have a fine record of treating visiting teams courteously. We have every reason to believe that this record will be continued.

Greene played and became the first black player to play an integrated college football game in North Carolina.

Herman Riddick, a very successful football coach at North Carolina Central University in Durham, very graciously wrote a letter to Greene, telling him that "I will be very happy to have you stay at my home as my guest during your stay in Durham." Eddie Cameron, as athletic director at Duke in 1950, supplied Riddick five tickets to the game as guests of Duke.

Bill Stern, one of the most famous sports announcers in the United States, had this to say on his national NBC radio show from New York City in the RCA Building. The broadcast occurred two days after the Duke-Pitt game.

> Yes ... history was made at Durham last Saturday when Flint Greene, a Negro tackle of the University of Pittsburgh, played against Duke at Durham in the heart of the South. Not only was he allowed to play, but he was a welcome member of the Pitt squad. To the Duke student body, to its coaches, to its President, and to the team itself, my sincere congratulations.

* * *

Along with Herschel Caldwell and Eddie Cameron, no one was more help to Wade during his Duke years than Ellis "Dumpy" Hagler. Hagler had been born in Blue Springs, Alabama, became a top lineman for Wade in Tuscaloosa, and had been at Duke since 1930. Hagler coached football at Duke from 1930 to 1956. He also served as the golf coach, winning thirteen Southern Conference championships and five ACC titles. Hagler was inducted into the National Collegiate Golf Coaches Hall of Fame.

Mike Souchak, a member of the 1950 team, who played both golf and football under Hagler before having an excellent career on the PGA tour, once said that, "He was gruff on the outside but once you proved yourself, once you won his confidence, he was a friend for life. When he put his arm around your shoulder and gave you encouragement, you knew he meant it."

* * *

In a game at Richmond, Tom Powers scored six touchdowns, tying the national record, in a 41 to 0 win. On November 25 Duke went to Chapel Hill with a 6 and 3 record. Duke won 7 to 0 in biting cold, as the temperature was around 15 degrees and a northerly wind swept through Kenan Stadium. In the third period, Wade gambled on fourth down. With the ball on the Carolina 34 and needing seven yards for a first down, Billy Cox threw a touchdown pass to Tom Powers. The game ended 7 to 0. At the final gun, Wade's players came up to him ready to hoist him on their shoulders, but in characteristic fashion, he did not want to show too much exuberance, out of respect

Homecoming display, 1950. Courtesy of Duke University Archives.

for his opponent. As he walked calmly across the field to shake Coach Snavely's hand, he told his players, "No, no, boys, there'll be none of that. Let's go shake their hands."

At the time, no one knew it was to be Wade's last game. Four days after the game, another happy day came for Wade, when he married Virginia Jones. Shortly after returning from a honeymoon in New York, Wade announced he was resigning his position at Duke to become the commissioner of the Southern Conference.

Duke finished 7 and 3 in Wade's last year, giving him a 110-36-7 record at Duke for his 16 years.

Billy Cox was a first team All-American in 1950, breaking his own record for offense in a season at Duke with 567 yards rushing and 1,428 yards passing. Cox had graced the cover of the 1950 *Illustrated Football Annual*. Another first team All-American in 1950 was Blaine Earon for Duke.

Wade was simply ready for another challenge as he left Duke. His teams had gone 13 and 6 over his last two years, and prospects looked good for 1951. Over the three years after Wade left, 14 players who Wade signed to Duke were drafted into the NFL. Wade had opened up the offense, with Billy Cox attempting 206 passes during 1950. His job was never in jeopardy, even though Duke was not the national power it had been prior to WWII. He was 58 years old, and the Southern Conference wanted him as its leader. Wade had been a coach in the conference for 26 years, and decided to accept this new challenge.

* * *

Even though Wade coached Ed Meadows as a freshman, he was not at Duke for the years when Meadows developed into one of the all-time best players at Duke. Meadows, from Oxford, very near Durham, became Duke's second two-time first team All-American in 1952 and 1953. He then went on to an outstanding career in the NFL.

During a practice in 1950, Wade noticed that Meadows, as a freshman, was simply dominating the offense during a practice. Wade walked into the huddle, called a play for the offense, and watched as a double team on Meadows literally lifted him off his feet and threw him back several yards. With a sly smile, Wade lifted his familiar baseball cap off his head, and said, "Meadows, where were you on that play?" The "old man" still had it.

* * *

There were many applicants to replace Wade at Duke. E.C. Brooks, Jr. wrote, "Major Stem [Thad Stem, member of the athletic council] and Mr. Josh Horne advised me this morning that they felt that Eddie Cameron should be asked to take the football coaching position on a temporary basis." Cameron was offered the position but turned it down to concentrate on his athletic director duties. Another writer suggested Art Guepe, the Virginia head coach.

Duke selected Bill Murray, a Duke graduate in 1931, who had been an outstanding player for Duke. From 1931 to 1940 Murray won 69 games against nine losses at The Children's Home in Winston-Salem, North Carolina, playing against some of the best high school and prep teams in the state. At Delaware he won 51, lost 17, and tied three. He spent 15 years at Duke and went 93-51-9. In addition, his teams won eight conference titles and beat Nebraska in the 1955 Orange Bowl, lost to Oklahoma in the 1958 Orange Bowl, and beat Arkansas in the 1961 Cotton Bowl.

There is no question the best era of Duke football was from 1931, with the arrival of Wade, to 1965, Bill Murray's last season. During those 35 seasons, Duke won 228 games with 98 losses, and appeared in the Rose Bowl, Orange

Bowl, Cotton Bowl, and Sugar Bowl. This era includes the 25-11 record of Eddie Cameron during WWII. There were only three losing records in those 35 years, and these were records of 4-5 in 1946, 4-6 in 1959 and 4-5-1 in 1964.

But since 1965, when Tom Harp succeeded Murray, only Steve Spurrier has had a winning career record at Duke, as he went 20-13-1 from 1987 to 1989 before going to Florida.

It could have been different. Duke officials asked Wade to help in the search for Murray's successor in 1965. Wade met with an old friend of his, and reports circulated, which Wade confirmed, that this friend was almost ready to take the job. This old friend and coaching buddy of Wade's was none other than Bud Wilkinson. Wilkinson had just lost in his bid for a United States Senate position, and felt an itch to get back into coaching. Wilkinson had won 145 games with only 29 losses and three national titles at Oklahoma from 1947 to 1963, including a 47-game winning streak, the longest ever in college football history. Coach Wilkinson's son, Jay, had been an All-American and ACC Player of the year at Duke in 1963 as a halfback.

Jay Wilkinson confirmed to me in an interview that his father almost accepted the Duke job.

> Coach Wade was a coaching icon to my dad. Dad was greatly influenced by Coach Wade's brand of football, especially defense and kicking, and his philosophy on life in general. I often talked about the 1938 Iron Duke team with him. Dad also liked the values off the field that Coach Wade stressed.

Who knows, but the arrival of Bud Wilkinson on the Duke campus probably would have continued the golden era of Duke football. Dr. Robert Rankin, chairman of the Duke athletic council in 1968, made this rather accurate prediction of the future,

> Sure, when the administration raised entrance requirements here a couple of years ago, Eddie Cameron and I said we could live with them. Which we can, but I think from now on, Duke may consider itself as having a relatively successful football season when it ends up with a 5-5 record. And I don't think we'll be getting many bowl invitations on that basis.

Duke has played in two bowl games in the last 40 years, with only eight winning records in that span.

CHAPTER THIRTY

RETIREMENT

Wade began his job as the first commissioner of the Southern Conference in December of 1950. The league had never had a full-time commissioner. Upon Wade's appointment, the Southern Conference headquarters were set up in the Carolina Theatre Complex in Durham.

Wade was a man who got things done, so he was a good choice to lead the conference. An example of his take-charge personality was exhibited at a meeting of Durham civic leaders once. A discussion went on and on about how to accomplish a particular task. Wade got tired of the chit-chat, as he would call it, stood up, and said, "It seems to me you ought to quit talking in circles, vote on a couple of things, and start doing some work." Within minutes the meeting had some direction.

At the time of his appointment as commissioner, there were 17 members of the conference. On May 8, 1953, seven institutions announced their intentions to leave the conference to form a new league. These schools were Duke, Wake Forest, Clemson, Maryland, North Carolina, NC State, and South Carolina. From this meeting the Atlanta Coast Conference was born, leaving ten schools in the Southern Conference. Commissioner Wade was instrumental in lending guidance to the ACC in its first couple of years, as he was, of course, very familiar with the schools.

Among the famous athletes in the Southern Conference during Wade's time as commissioner were basketball players Jerry West of West Virginia, Frank Selvy of Furman, "Hot Rod" Hundley of West Virginia, and Dick Groat of Duke, who was a two-time All-Southern Conference performer in both basketball and baseball and was the MVP of the National League in 1960 as the Pittsburgh Pirates won the World Series.

Wade announced his retirement in 1960 after ten years. He thought it was time to retire to his farm on the outskirts of Durham. He was succeeded as commissioner by Lloyd Jordan, former head football coach at Harvard.

* * *

Bill Murray, Eddie Cameron, Wallace Wade, and Tom Harp. Courtesy of Duke University Archives.

In 1953 Frank Thomas, former Alabama coach, wrote a letter recommending Wade for the College Football Hall of Fame. Thomas and Wade had remained friends through the years, and had much respect for each other.

> I would like to submit to the Football Hall of Fame a man whom I have known eminently for the past thirty years. I would like to submit the name of Wallace Wade, the present Commissioner of the Southern Conference.
>
> While Wade was here at Alabama, I was at the University of Georgia and competed against his teams, so I have known him from that angle. Wade was not only a great coach, he was a fine sportsman and a man of high integrity and character. It is true that he was a hard taskmaster on the field. I never heard of Wallace using any underhanded methods in any of his coaching. I am fully convinced that Wallace was one of the great coaches of his day and most certainly belongs in the Hall of Fame.

Wade was inducted into the College Football Hall of Fame in 1955.

* * *

Wade devoted his energy to many things after retiring in 1960 as commissioner. Among these were raising prize beef cattle, being a good husband, father, and grandfather, reading military history, walking around his farm, watching football, keeping up with former players and coaches, serving on the national football rules committee, and being honored. He was inducted into many Halls of Fame, such as Alabama's, North Carolina's, Duke's, Brown's, and the Rose Bowl's.

Wade was asked to speak to numerous groups, clubs, organizations, and athletic teams. He spoke to the Durham Rotary Club, the Northern Durham High School athletic banquet, the Durham High student body, the Durham Elks, and the Dunn High School athletic teams, just to name a few. Newspapers, television, and radio reporters requested interviews. He stayed busy, the only way of life this aging but very robust man had ever known.

In 1967 Duke University gave Wade what he considered his highest honor, the naming of Duke Stadium to Wallace Wade Stadium. Art Vann, a former player for Wade, spearheaded the effort to honor Wade with the stadium naming. "I just didn't want to see Coach Wade die out there on his farm without somebody doing something to honor him while he's living," said Vann. Little did Vann know that Wade, who was 75 at the time, would live another 19 years.

Words of praise poured in as old players, coaching acquaintances, and friends spoke about how appropriate the naming of the stadium was. His former player at Alabama, Frank Howard, said that it

> was a great honor to a man who dedicated his entire life to football. When he was coaching me at Alabama, I used to think at times he was the meanest man on earth but after becoming a head coach myself, he wasn't near as tough as I thought he was. There is no telling how many lives of boys he has touched. I know that he is a successful cattle rancher now so tell him I'll pick up my free side of beef this fall when we come up to play the Blue Devils.

Howard was coaching Clemson at the time.

Furman Bisher of the *Atlanta Journal* wrote that "there is no doubt in my mind of one thing: Wallace Wade did to Southern Conference football several years in advance what Everett Case did for it in basketball. He made it necessary that the other colleges play the game or get out."

Bill Currie, a sports director of WSOC Television in Charlotte, perhaps summed up Coach Wade's career better than anyone.

**Mr. and Mrs. Wade on the day Duke Stadium became Wallace Wade
Stadium. Courtesy of Duke University Archives.**

The true measure of Wallace Wade's greatness as a man is not fully
reflected in his overwhelming won-lost record on the field, nor in his
patriotic devotion to our country in combat during two world wars;
rather, it is reflected in the dignity and bearing of the man, which
makes him a giant among his peers and successors.

Hugo Germino of the Durham Sun wrote, "What better monument to me-
morialize the man who brought big-time football to the South in general and
to Duke and North Carolina in particular?" Bill Cox wrote that "Wade established Duke as a permanent bastion for good in college athletics." Ed Seaman
of the *Fayetteville Observer*, wrote "Many feared him because of his strictness
and devotion to a set goal, but they respected him. And under his guidance
they became real men."

Coach Wade talks to the Duke team in the 1970s.
Courtesy of Duke Sports Information Department.

A special dinner and presentation of a portrait of Wade was held in the Great Hall on the Duke campus. Many former players and coaching friends came, such as Jess Neely, Eric Tipton, Dan Hill, and Bob Barnett. The dinner menu that night chronicled Wade's career.

Menu
Crimson Tide Punch
Served with
Single-Wing Wafer
Hall of Fame Salad
Roast Prime Ribs of Bahama Beef Au Jus
Southern Conference Baked Potatoes with Rose Bowl Garni
Iron Dukes Rolls and Butter
Blue Devil Parfait & Brown Bear Petits Fours
The Colonel's Coffee

After dinner there were speeches from Dillard Teer, representing the Durham Chamber of Commerce, Dick Herbert of the *Raleigh News & Observer*, his long-time friend and coaching companion Herschel Caldwell, Eddie Cameron, and others. Coach Wade, in his remarks said,

I have had a lot of pleasant experiences, and some unpleasant experiences, but never have I been overcome as I have on this occasion. It's something to think that a former barefooted farm boy from Tennessee is being honored in this fashion tonight. What success we had can be attributed to the coaching staff and players. I'm thankful for the players and coaches and fans who are here tonight. I'm thankful for what they have said about me. I'm thankful for the messages received from those unable to attend. In fact, I'm thankful for everything tonight.

Dr. Hersey Spence of Duke wrote this poem to honor Coach Wade:

> What means the sound of revelry and joy,
> Where tens of thousands all their powers employ?
> Where mingled shouts of Rah! Rah! Wade are raised,
> And "Dear Old Duke" whose name is proudly praised?
> What means the blaring of the marching bands?
> The deafening sound of yells and clapping hands?
> In the vast stadium joy and sadness blend;
> Gloom that a great career has reached an end;
> Gladness at memories of the long ago;
> Praise given one we love and honor so.
>
> Why are they here with all their pomp and splendor;
> Due honor to an "all-time Great" to render;
> Whose prowess countless football fans has thrilled;
> Whose sportsmanship with pride our hearts filled;
> He feared no foe, now did he lightly yield
> To foe, however strong, no football field,
> With trivial easy tasks was discontent;
> Built football empires wheresoever he went,
> But more than empires men to man them trained;
> Whose high ideals with them have e'er remained,
> He taught them taste of victory without vaunting;
> To lose, without despair their memory haunting.
> Who is this man by noble, impulse swayed?
> The greatest of the great, Coach Wallace Wade.
>
> Old Glory floats high o'er the stadium walls;
> The bands once more play "Stars and Stripes Forever"
> In memory he again that day recalls
> When he awhile his ties with sports must sever.
> A soldier now, and for his country's sake

Must run great risks and fearsome chances take:
War's whirlwind, bursting bomb and screaming shell;
Foul and fierce furies, horrible as hell;
Answering the call of duty unafraid—
The calm, courageous, Colonel Wallace Wade.

Back from the battlefields, the war now o'er,
The gridiron battles he returns once more.
But larger task was proffered, there was need
For one who through the conference maze could lead:
Vexatious difficulties to be solved;
Cool judgments needed for the task involved;
Tedious the task; decisions must be made,
Fair and yet firm, Commissioner Wallace Wade.

In quietude the great man wends his ways,
No longer dreading coming Saturdays;
Not troubled now with "talks between the halves'"
His interests, mooing cows and bleating calves.
Still he at times must feel the football urge,
And long to see his warriors, stopless surge
A down the filed, and hear above the low
Of bulls, the cry: "Go, Blue Devils, go."
However many cattle he possessed
He'll doubtless always love his football best.
Long may he live, triumphant, undismayed:
Coach, soldier, statesman, William Wallace Wade.

* * *

Wade received another award later in 1967 that meant very much to him also, because of the man the award was named for. The Knoxville Quarterback Club named Wade the recipient of the Robert R. Neyland Memorial Award, which was presented to Wade at the Tennessee football banquet. Wade and Neyland had met many times on the football field. Lenox Baker, who became one of the nation's most renowned orthopedic surgeons, had worked as an athletic trainer for both Neyland at Tennessee and Wade at Duke. At the award ceremony, Baker said, "No two coaches ever had a fiercer rivalry on the football field and yet two men never admired each other as much."

In 1970 Wade was inducted into the Alabama Sports Hall of Fame. He spent a couple of days meeting old friends before the ceremony in Birmingham. Hank Crisp, long-time coach and athletic administrator at Alabama, was

Wallace and Mrs. Wade with Mike and Ginger McGee. Mike McGee
won the Outland Trophy at Duke in 1959 and was the head coach at
Duke from 1971 to 1978. Courtesy of Duke University Archives.

inducted along with his old friend Wade. Also inducted in 1970 were Jesse
Owens, the great track athlete, and William Van de Graaf, the first All-Amer-
ican football player for Alabama and a former coach for Wade at the Capstone.
Bear Bryant attended the banquet along with Johnny Mack Brown. Alf Van
Hoose of the *Birmingham News*, after seeing Bryant and Wade talking, wrote
this: "Wade, 'The Bear' long before Paul Bryant ever left Moro Bottom,
Arkansas, because he coached and dealt with most people as if he'd been a
grizzly who'd missed meals for weeks, had left Alabama for Duke in 1931."

A tragic event happened at a reception before the official ceremony. Hank
Crisp collapsed and was dead on arrival at a hospital only blocks away. Coach
Wade said it was "a real tragedy to lose such a man as Hank." Coach Bryant,
who thought as highly of Crisp as anyone he knew, said that "Coach Crisp was
one of the sweetest men who ever lived. To every man who ever wore the red
jersey he was the greatest. It is a great loss to all of us."

Despite his comings and goings, Wade spent most of his retirement on his
farm near Durham, which he named Wadehill Farm. Registered Hereford cattle roamed the pastures of his 120-acre farm. His house set well back off the
public road, with a winding path leading to his house running alongside trees
and a wooden fence. A huge white feed and storage barn stood near the pas-

tures, and a small shed was near the house. Mrs. Wade made Coach Wade keep the boxes of apples he was sent by his brother Mark out in the small shed, as she didn't so much like them cluttering space up in the house. Mark owned one of the largest apple orchards in the country, so one type of food the Wades of Durham were never low on was apples.

As with everything else Wade had tried in his life, he didn't "mess around with it," but did his best. He didn't just raise cattle, he raised prize beef cattle, winning ribbons at the nearby NC State Fair in Raleigh. Wade enjoyed walking along the pastures to check on his "pets." He also enjoyed asking guests to his farm, "Tell me, what do you see out there?" as they gazed at his cattle. The guest would invariable reply to the effect of "You sure do have some nice looking cows, Coach Wade." Wade would always reply, "No! That's money you see, money!" Coach Wade never forgot the value of a dollar.

Planting his garden, sewing oats, feeding his cows, cutting grass, and mending fences made life enjoyable. He also enjoyed driving his truck around the dirt paths through the woods and pasture land. Wade's granddaughter, Nancy, fondly remembers riding around the farm with her grandfather.

Mrs. Wade (Peggy) also worked alongside Coach Wade. Once, when one of their cows died giving birth to her calf, Mrs. Wade saved the baby calf's life by wrapping him in blankets and rubbing his body to get the circulation going, while Coach Wade went off to get the special milk the calf needed. Mrs. Wade once said that

> cattle do have distinct personalities. They're just as different from one another as humans. Sometimes they're quite cantankerous and sometimes very docile. They're very sensitive creatures. My husband always wanted some activity and some hobby when he retired. Now we both enjoy it. We're never satisfied. We're always striving for some goal in our herd—confirmation or better and larger portions of beef.

Ted Mann, the sports information director at Duke during the Wade years at Duke, visited Wadehill Farm with two friends in 1970. He tells this story:

> After fording a creek with the "Old Man" at the wheel, we found the cattle, lolling in the shade of some trees. Sparks, the photographer, and Coach Wade went into the trees to take a picture, at the end of which the cattle were "supposed" to have gone into an open field for another shot. Coach Wade started his round-up but some of the cattle had another idea and went a different way from which he intended. Lord knows what would have happened if one of his football players had ever done that.

Wallace Wade in 1970. Courtesy of Duke University Archives.

Anyway, Coach Wade came out of the woods giving all three of us hell for not turning the cattle back where he wanted them to go. But, believe me, they all had long horns and none of us wanted to be impaled on a cow's horn. So Coach Wade cranked up his truck and we followed the herd and finally we were in shape to get the desired pictures. After shooting the pictures, Coach Wade let down a piece of fence to make a short-cut back to the farmhouse. As he started back to the truck, he told Sparks not to let any of the cattle through the fence. He had a little trouble starting the truck and one of those long-horned rascals started toward Sparks and the opening. Sparks made, and I agree with him, little or no effort to head off that big rascal.

And then the climax came. The 78-year-old Wade jumped out of the truck and ran, repeat ran, around the cow to get her back where she belonged, in the meanwhile letting out some right strong expressions about Sparks' ability as a cattleman. Some of his comments would have done General Patton proud.

A special trip for Wade took place in 1981, as he visited President Reagan in the Oval Office. The visit was arranged by Senator Jesse Helms. Accompa-

**Wallace Wade with President Ronald Reagan in the Oval Office.
Courtesy of Duke University Archives.**

nying Wade and his wife Peggy were Wade's daughter Frances and son-in-law Robert Clark. Reagan had seen a couple of the Rose Bowl games of Wade's teams and had also met Wade when Wade had appeared on the "This Is Your Life" television program back in the 1950s. Wade enjoyed the meeting, saying that "President Reagan was so cordial and nice. My wife Peg was completely smitten with him. She thought he looked younger than his age." Afterward, the Wades had lunch in the Senate Dining Room with the Helms.

Wade donated his 1942 Rose Bowl trophy to Duke in 1982 so that it could be auctioned off to raise money for children's cancer research. "It's an attractive trophy and has meant a lot to me over the years," Wade said. "But it's going for a good cause."

Turning 90 on June 15 of 1982, Wade was asked how he felt. He replied, "It's the first time I've ever been 90, so I haven't been there long enough to know what it's like yet." Upon turning 92, the US Senate sent him birthday greetings, saying, "You are a remarkable American, and we are very proud of you and grateful for the high standards you established during your illustrious career."

In a wide-ranging interview very late in his life, Wade looked back over his career. He said he was proud of what he had accomplished at Alabama and Duke. "They didn't do too well before I came," he said. "Now understand, I'm not trying to blow myself up. But it's a fact." When asked to comment on his toughest loss, he said it was probably the 1939 Rose Bowl defeat to USC.

> I never saw that last pass that beat us. The players were all standing in front of me. I asked George McAfee if they caught it and he said they did. That loss hurt more than any other. Here we were, on the verge of achieving something no one else had ever done. But coaching was like that. The wins were nice, but the losses took so much out of me. They linger so long.

When asked about his time at Duke when he came back to coach after WWII, Wade said,

> I was whipped down. I got back into coaching before I should have, and I didn't do very well. But I had been in a bigger game over in Europe. Coaches always talk about plays like they're life and death situations, but I had been in a position where my moves really did involve life and death. Football just didn't seem as important anymore.

Of Eddie Cameron, Wade said that he knew for sure Cameron would take over for him in 1942 and do an excellent job. "Eddie was a great leader of boys, and they respected him so much. He was just a good man, that's about all you can say." Other long-time assistants, Dumpy Hagler and Herschel Caldwell, were remembered fondly also. Of Hagler, Wade said, "You've got to have a coach who's inspired to coach the line. We had one when I was at Duke. Dumpy would go through hell teaching the discipline of blocking and tackling." Wade said Caldwell, who won 46 games with only nine losses and five ties as a freshman football coach,

> was such an outstanding individual from the standpoint of character, which made him a good teacher. He was a good influence on the incoming players. He had been an expert football player—a great pass catcher, blocker, and defensive player.

Herschel Caldwell's wife, Anita, must have some kind of record going herself. A very attractive, elegant lady now of 98, she has not missed a Duke home football game since 1933. She met Herschel at Alabama when they were both students in Tuscaloosa in the 1920s, and they were married in 1933 after Herschel had come to Duke as an assistant to Wade. Mrs. Caldwell still remembers her student days at Alabama, serving as a sponsor of the football team at

Wallace Wade in retirement. Courtesy of Duke University Archives.

Denny Field, Herschel coaching at Sidney Lanier High School in Montgomery, Dr. Denny, the Alabama president, the early days of Wade and Duke and the great years of the 1932 to 1941 teams, Duke having the best record in the nation. She remembers the Rose Bowl and of dining at Johnny Mack Brown's mansion in California. She remembers the many unbeaten seasons her husband coached for the Blue Imps, the freshman team.

In another interview after he retired, Wade was asked who the best coach was he had gone up against.

> General Neyland was the best I knew anything about. His teams seemed better drilled and more complete. He was the toughest person for me to beat. Bobby Dodd was another good one. But Neyland was excellent in every phase of coaching, but I most admired the way he'd come back at you when you stopped the things he did best.

Wade underwent surgery at Duke Hospital late in life, and Tom Rogers, a former player who became head coach at Wake Forest, visited him. Wade, who always liked for his teams to finish strong, was still quite ill. "Coach, you always told us that the fourth quarter was ours," Rogers reminded his

Wallace Wade and his wife Virginia (Peg) at home.
Courtesy of Nell Breeden.

old coach. Two days later, Wade left the hospital in a remarkable turn-around.

* * *

On October 6, 1986, Wallace Wade passed away from complications of pneumonia at Duke Hospital. He was 94 years old. There would be no more big football games to win, no more world wars to fight, and no more turning boys into men. It was time for Coach Wade to rest after such a life well lived.

His wife, Virginia, whom he called Peg, would die three years later, in 1989.

A bright autumn day, perfect football weather, greeted guests at Wade's funeral at the Duke Chapel. A huge crowd filled the ornate cathedral, from family to friends to former players and coaches. The service included a eulogy

**Wallace Wade bust outside Wallace Wade Stadium.
Courtesy of Duke Sports Information Department.**

from Terry Sanford, the former Duke president and North Carolina governor. "When Wallace Wade talked, I listened," said Sanford.

> He had complete composure in all circumstances. He demanded of himself nothing short of perfection and demanded that of all around him. Thank God for sending Wallace Wade into the lives of each of us, and give us the guidance and dedication to live up to the life he expected of us.

The Reverend William H. Willimon of Duke and the Reverend Robert T. Young also spoke. Young paid tribute to Wade by reading from scripture, "I have fought the fight, finished the race, and kept the faith."

Pallbearers were Carl Schock, George McAfee, Dan Hill, Elmore Hackney, Eric Tipton, Ace Parker, Billy Cox, Earl Wentz, Al DeRogatis, Tom Davis, and Kidd Brewer. Among the honorary pallbearers were Terry Sanford, Herschel Caldwell, Eddie Cameron, Dumpy Hagler, Lenox Baker, Bobby Dodd, and Senator Jesse Helms.

A bronze bust of Wade that stands outside Wallace Wade Stadium was dedicated shortly after his death. The bust was done by Frank Creech, a former Duke football player.

Also shortly after Wade's death, an announcement was made of a gift of $100,000 to Duke from Wade for a scholarship fund to help student-athletes. The Wallace Wade Endowment Fund is based on character, leadership, academic achievement, and financial need.

In 1998, the city of Tuscaloosa, Alabama, named a street for Coach Wade. Wallace Wade Avenue now runs alongside Bryant-Denny Stadium between Bryant Drive and University Boulevard.

CHAPTER THIRTY-ONE

COACH WADE IN WORDS

Many former players responded to a questionnaire sent to them for this book about Wade or talked to me over the phone. I have included some of their comments in previous chapters. This chapter is devoted for the most part to those players, but also included are comments from others who knew Wade, and there are some quotations straight from the man himself.

* * *

"Jelly beans who are not connected with either school are usually the source of trouble between two keen rivals." — Wade

"Athletics are part of a man-building program." — Wade

"My favorite moment with Coach Wade was my last year as trainer, in the spring of 1933, when I was down in the gym getting ready to start spring practice, and Coach Wade came in, wanted to know what I was doing there. When I told him I was getting ready for practice, he said, 'Well come out to the hall, I want to talk to you.' He told me, 'You've got one job to do this year, for me and for the department of athletics, and that is to get that MD degree in June. Now, I don't want you to come down here unless I call you. You stay up there at that School of Medicine, because that degree is the most important thing to me. Do what you have to.'" — Dr. Lenox Baker

"One word describes him better than any other — indomitable. He was a great football coach, an honorable man of great integrity, and to use a word you don't hear that often today, he was a patriot all his life. He demanded better than the best from you and he had a way of getting it." — Dan Hill

"I don't know where I'd be today if I hadn't played for Coach Wade. I went to Alabama because I wanted to play for him. I wanted to play in the Rose Bowl and I knew he'd get us there." — Frank Howard

"He was never satisfied with less than 100 percent and most of the time expected 150 percent." — Art Vann

"He wouldn't take any foolishness from any of his players. He'd just bench 'em or suspend 'em or kick 'em clean off the team. Even sports writers were scared of him. I mean, you were just sort of in awe." — Hugo Germino of the *Durham Sun*

"When he talked, everybody — I don't care who was there, everybody just shut up and listened." — Hugo Germino

"I would just as soon have called the Queen of England 'Lizzie' as to have called Coach Wade by his first name." — Dr. Hersey Spence

"I didn't believe in a college boy surrendering, and a fair catch is a surrender, like raising a white flag." — Wade

"Sick! Sick! Boy, get sick on Christmas Day, get sick on the 4th of July, get sick any time, but don't get sick in the middle of a football game!" — Wade, after a player told him he felt sick during half-time.

One day Tom Rogers failed to emerge from a pileup. He lay groaning on the ground. Wade asked, "What's the matter, Rogers?" "I believe my right leg is broken, Coach," Rogers said. "Well, you've got another one, haven't you?" said Wade.

"Once in spring practice I was running the ball downfield when I was blind-sided by Bolo Perdue, all 230 pounds of him (I was 160). He knocked me all the way to the bench practically in front of Coach Wade. I was barely conscious when I heard in that strong southern drawl, 'Dammit Brown, get up! You can't play football on your back!'" — Werner Brown

"If Coach Wade wanted something to happen, he arranged the events to make it happen. He was a powerful presence on the Duke campus." — Ted Mann

"Giving your best is not good enough if it doesn't get the job done." — Wade

"The road to failure is paved with players who did their best. The best player is the one who does what is necessary." — Wade

"What good did it ever do anybody to get kicked around?" — Wade on his dislike of losing.

"Nobody ever got backslapped into winning anything." — Wade, on not celebrating too much.

"The world is not interested in how hard you tried, but did you get the job done." — Wade

"Wallace Wade held presence, commanded attention, and demanded excellence." — Terry Sanford

"You build up character just like muscles. You use the same plan. Use a muscle and it develops. Use character and it develops." — Wade

"When everything is done for you, you don't have a chance to develop. Man becomes strong by doing things — by doing things that he doesn't want to do." — Wade

"I have more respect for him than any other man I ever knew. I spent a career as an Air Force officer and never met a Colonel or General that commanded the respect that Coach Wade did." — William Mozingo

"Coach Wade remains one of the most impressive people I have ever met. He was fair, he was thorough in his preparations, he was very well-versed in knowledge of the game." — Walter Smith

"In 1950 we went to Atlanta to play Tech. At our hotel, Sam Eberdt, a sophomore running back, entered the lobby with his father, who was a US Navy Commander and had played for Coach Wade at Alabama. Commander Eberdt entered the lobby with a cigarette in his mouth. Upon entrance he came face to face with Coach Wade. Commander Eberdt swallowed his cigarette — he knew that Coach Wade smoked but did not condone such from players." — Walter Smith

"The number one aspect of his relationship to players was the respect, even fear, all had for him. Most were too afraid to even let Coach Wade hear them joke about getting rained out of practice. Not only the players, but our assistant coaches respected him totally. He was strict about team departures from the hotel on out-of-town game days. On one trip to South Carolina, a new player was talking on the telephone, and Coach Wade told the driver to pull out. In 1949, two married players didn't return to Durham with the team, and he dismissed them from the team. One was the starting blocking back, and UNC was the next game." — Robert Deyton, Jr.

"Practices were extremely intense, no standing around. Coach Wade felt that you would play in a game like you performed in practices, thus you were pushed hard. Every practice was a learning experience. Good physical conditioning was a must and was expected. He always stressed that you were attending Duke with the expectation of graduation. He did not tolerate incompetency in your studies as well your football endeavors." — Leonard Smith

"Duke was fortunate to have him. Whatever success I may have accomplished was due to Coach Wade, Herschel Caldwell, and, of course, the team.

Coach Wade, even though he was definitely tough, was a gentle man, quiet and compassionate, unassuming, who offered effective encouragement, and never asked for attention who always diverted praise to others. He was that rare individual who could have willed himself to the top of virtually any profession he chose.

"My two most memorable games were the 1949 Tennessee and 1950 Georgia Tech games. We beat Tennessee 21 to 7, earning Coach Wade the honor of being the only coach to defeat Neyland's team in Knoxville twice. In a 30 to 21 win over Tech we gave up 21 points in 8 minutes to fall behind 21-0, but came back to win.

"Practices were tough compared to today's standards. We had more contact and less water. You were fighting for your position in every practice. We ends had the best position coach, Herschel Caldwell. Coach Caldwell taught me moves that helped when I went to the NFL." — Blaine Earon

"In practice, he was a hands-on coach. At his age, 54, he still showed backs and ends how to block and take first steps in a play. Though his expertise was in defense, he really had a mind for offense. He had a reason for every play, even punting on third down if there was too much risk. Our practices were hard and well organized, and early in the season, hot as hell. We scrimmaged and ran a lot; the games were much easier than our practices.

"I was the first lineman since Dan Hill to call offensive plays, which I did for several games in 1950, so I was around Coach Wade more during that time in QB meetings, game plan sessions, etc. I found him very patient. I gained a lot of respect for his football mind." — James Gibson, Jr.

"One day, the football team had a long hard scrimmage and the temperature was in the 90s. As we approached the closing minutes of the scrimmage, we were totally exhausted and felt we couldn't continue. Coach Wade, sensing our feelings, pointed out that in the games to come there would be times late in the fourth quarter that we would feel the same exhausted way. However, he pointed out that our opponent across the line of scrimmage would also feel exhausted and think he couldn't go on. Coach Wade told us the one who forced himself to take the extra step would prevail.

"During my life, I have been a combat soldier in World War II, a US Attorney, a business executive, a father of three girls, and a husband. I have always remembered Coach Wade's words, and I have always forced myself to take that extra step, and it proved invaluable to me." — Walter Lenox

"Coach Wade was a 'myth' by the time I arrived at Duke. Many would have characterized him as aloof, but to me he was a very human person who cared about the players and the staff. Integrity, intensity, and involvement are words that come to mind about Coach Wade." — Robert Price

"I was a freshman during his last year of coaching, and we always ran the plays of the opposing team in practice each week before a game. One day I remember so vividly while running the single wing offense after a certain play, he chewed each player out because they didn't do exactly what the play called for. I was amazed how he could see so many details in a given play. When he spoke no one moved and no one ever questioned him or talked back." — Dr. Bernard Jack

"I had played under Coach Cameron from 1943 to 1945 while Coach Wade was in the service. The adjustment to Coach Wade was considerable! He told me in some later years that the adjustment for him to civilian life after the war was very difficult.

"In the UNC game of 1946, I was on the bench seated next to Coach Wade. Charlie Justice made an end run in front of our bench. Louis Allen, our tackle, dived at Charlie and missed him as he started to reverse his field. Coach Wade said "Get up, get up Lou, he'll [Charlie] be back this way in a minute." Justice was known for reversing the field. — George Clark

"Who else was strong enough to take Duke to the Rose Bowl and bring the Rose Bowl to Duke?" — Howard Ris

"He was a great man, a great coach, and a patriotic American. If he mentioned your name at practice, you had 'arrived.' In the late 1940s we had great camaraderie and esprit de corps among the players, many of whom were returning vets. I was a 17-year-old kid, and they were all like my big brothers. Coach Wade valued academics and put an emphasis on the quality and character of the individual he recruited. There were no bums at Duke." — Charles Adams

"What Coach Wade said was the law. There was never a question in my mind that he was not the greatest coach that a growing boy could have. Once during practice, my brother Tom was running a particular drill. After trying to tackle him three times, Coach Wade told me there 'was no place for brotherly love on a football field.' I tackled Tom good the next time but dislocated my right little finger. Doc Chambers taped it back straight. I still live today with a stiff right little finger, thanks to my brother." — Jasper "Jap" Davis

"Coach Wade had the candid ability to see the actions of all 22 players on any play. He was truly a mentor of student athletes. What I learned under Coach Wade prepared me for the Marine Corps."—Judge James Wolfe, Jr.

"Coach Wade was a great coach and leader. I have tried to follow his example all my life and what success I have had I attribute much to him."—Paul Stephanz

"During practice one day I was bumping up against my good friend Fred Sink, a 220-pound tackle. I was 160 pounds. All linemen will remember this drill—one-on-one, 1, 2, 3, hit. I hit fast, dropped to the ground quick (before Fred O. creamed me). We both rolled over, came up with both legs churning to hit, hit, and hit again. Coach Wade, I'm told, jumped a foot in the air, came running over, and grabbed us both, yelling, 'Great, great, this is what we need more of, never stop moving and hitting until the whistle blows.' I remember that compliment and lesson on a day 63 years ago like it was yesterday."—Dick Lenox

"Coach Wade emphasized to us that we were there to get an education foremost, and to play football secondarily. I learned that character and preparation were the keys to success."—W.D. McRoy

"Coach Cameron was our coach in 1945, but when we were in the Polo Grounds to pay the Blanchard and Davis powerhouse Army team, Coach Wade in full uniform of an Army Colonel appeared in our locker room. While he didn't interfere or take over, we sensed the presence of a strong leader as he quietly talked with our coaches offering, I'm sure, some sound advice as we faced tough odds.

"After playing with a sore throat against Georgia Tech when I boarded the train (yes, we still made a train trip to some away games back then), that night Coach Wade asked how I felt and had me sit at his table for dinner, which I could not eat, so he had the trainers get me some soup which my throat would tolerate.

"While there were times when his age and demeanor might send misleading signals, he had a kind inner side that the soup incident portrayed. It also was evident later when on a Sunday morning visit to the training room after a Saturday home game in 1949. I had gone in for some treatment and took my toddler son with me. Coach Wade came in while I was there and was like a kindly grandfather playfully entertaining little Larry for several minutes as he checked with the trainers on injuries from the day before.

"In an earlier situation, when my grades weren't something to brag about, he pulled me aside at the end of a practice inside the gym and commented on my borderline status in a couple of classrooms and asked if I was spending too much time on the East Campus. He got both messages across, i.e., improve my grades and spend less time on the ladies. He then told me to see Dan [Hill] to arrange for some tutoring help.

"There are a lot of memories, but one that stands out was a game in Washington, DC, against Maryland that bears out Coach Wade's attempt to confuse or defuse the idea that he was old fashioned. We were going to kick-off to open the game and in those early days of two platooning, you could only substitute during a timeout or change of possession. Maryland had their offensive team on the field to receive the kickoff and we pulled a successful onside kickoff. Since we were still basically a two-way team, our kick-off team was an offensive unit and as we recovered the kickoff, Maryland could not get their defensive unit into the game. After a big brouhaha with then Terp Coach Jim Tatum storming the officials, the original call stood and we proceeded to go on to score what eventually was the difference. You can check into this—as I said earlier it's been a long time.

"I'm not sure if that was in '48 or '49. But, it does show Wade's inventiveness. Another different yet similar "prank" was early in one of those seasons when we were still a single-wing team. On our first possession of the game we came out with a T formation with Jimmy Brown, who ran the T against us in practice, at QB. We ran from the T for that one possession and you never saw it again. But, it gave future opponents something to think about and spend time in practice in case we were switching. Prior to our showing that one bit of T, teams had to work the week prior to a game with Duke against the single-wing. Now they had to worry about a T also and thus spend time preparing to face the single-wing and the T.

"In a game in 1949, long before the term or use of a "blitz" was employed, he sent me into a game with instructions to NOT lineup in a down-lineman position as part of our normal 6-2-2-1 defense, but rather to standup in the middle as a linebacker and on or just before the snap to jump in and crash straight through. We had not practiced this, so even our own linemen were yelling at me to get down in the line in my normal guard position.... What I am trying to get across here, is that while he was being badgered about staying with the single wing and not changing as it seemed everyone else was doing, he was doing some things differently."—Larry Karl

"Coach Wade spoke with a finality that always punctuated his conversations."—Add Penfield

"To me, character is the capacity to do something you ought to do that you don't want to."—Wade

"Sure, academics eliminates some players, but football requires character and background. A chap with good grades has better potential to be a football player, as he has proven he is willing to work." — Wade

"At Brown, I had to get out and hump to keep up with those damn Yankees. I worked my way through. I had a laundry service, fired furnaces, and shoveled snow. I was proud when they made me president of a fraternity." — Wade

"I learned early you had to be boss, and I expected my instructions to be carried out." — Wade

"Coach Wade was a superb human being in everything he did, was as good as his word. He was a splendid teacher of young men, a person of impeccable integrity." — Jesse Helms

"Men, I'd like you to meet Coach Wallace Wade, the man who is most responsible for the University of Alabama football tradition. In many ways, he is the reason I'm here and the reason you're here." — Bear Bryant, introducing Wade to his team in 1980.

"Coach Wade was like a blood-thirsty army officer. We all wanted to hate him, but when it got down to it, we loved him. He was a helluva coach who developed us into an outstanding team in 1930." — John Suther

"There is a young backfield coach at Georgia who should become one of the greatest coaches in the country. He played football under Rockne at Notre Dame. Rock called him one of the smartest players he ever coached. He is Frank Thomas, and I don't believe you could pick a better man." — Wade to Dr. George Denny, recommending a successor to him at Alabama.

"Coach Wade just had a real bearing, and carried himself with authority. Even Coach Bryant was a little intimidated around Coach Wade, who he had great respect for." — Clem Gryska

"There was good football played in Arkansas in those days, at Henderson-Brown and Arkansas Tech as well as the university. But we read and heard more about Alabama, and that's where I wanted to go. If you were any kind of football fan, you knew about the Crimson Tide and Wallace Wade, who had been head coach there since 1923 and took them to three Rose Bowl games.

"I remember going down to a college all-star game in Dallas with Fred Thomsen, the Arkansas coach. He wanted me to come there. And at the half I slipped off and rode a streetcar back to town to listen to Alabama beat Washington State 24-0 in the 1931 Rose Bowl, Wade's last Alabama team. So when they came over to ask the Jordan twins, our best players, about coming to Alabama, they didn't have to recruit me. I was ready." — Bear Bryant in *Bear*, his autobiography.

"You can look at the 1926 Rose Bowl as the most significant event in southern football history." — Andrew Doyle, Winthrop University

"They told me boys from the south would fight." — Wade, to his Alabama team at half-time in the 1926 Rose Bowl.

"What I try to do is get the very best out of every boy who becomes a member of the Crimson Tide team. I never ask a boy to try to win a game for my sake, but on the other hand, put him on his mettle to do his level best and failing, he feels the discomfort of not having done his duty, measuring up to the best that is in him." — Wade

"I am going to Alabama and the University of Kentucky will never win a football game from a team of mine." — Wade, after getting tired of waiting after interviewing for the Kentucky job. Wade would go 11 and 0 against Kentucky at Alabama and Duke.

"A 'Bear' led Alabama football through its first great era and established the rich tradition of the Crimson Tide. No, not that Bear. This Bear was Wallace Wade. Some people call him the Godfather of Alabama football, but his players called him The Bear." — Wayne Hester, *Birmingham News*

"All the boys were scared of him. They called him Bear because they feared him." — Hoyt "Wu" Winslett

"I had great respect for Coach Wade. He even came and talked to a couple of my teams when I was at Duke. All of us at Duke knew that Coach Wade was responsible for the tradition of football we had at Duke." — Mike McGee

"Wade put Alabama football on the map. The enrollment at Alabama dramatically increased during his time in Tuscaloosa, the 1920s and 1930s." — Andrew Doyle, Winthrop University

"Coach Bryant said that before Wade there was no tradition at Alabama, that Wade had developed the foundation for the teams that followed." — Fred Sington, Jr.

"It was the money from that football game [1939 Rose Bowl] that enabled Duke to build the basketball arena that today carries Cameron's name."— Bill Brill

"It was the Wallace Wade powerhouse at Duke in the 1930s and 1940s that brought national attention to North Carolina and gave football firm claim to center stage. The participation of two Wade teams in the Rose Bowl, the marvel of his unscored-on 1938 team, and the renown of stars such as Ace Parker and George McAfee made Duke a catalyst for rival schools in the state.—Joe Mobley

"I had always wanted to attend Duke, but my football abilities and finances would not permit this opportunity. I was lucky enough to get a scholarship to Georgia Military Academy at College Park, Georgia. This gave me an opportunity to improve my football and academic abilities. We had a great team at GMA and many of our players got scholarship offers from various schools. I was lucky enough to receive a letter from Dan Hill, who was the Duke football recruiter at the time. He didn't offer me a scholarship but said Duke was interested in me and they would like for me to come for a visit and to talk to Coach Wade. Needless to say, I was delighted for this opportunity. It was arranged for me to come for this visit during the Thanksgiving holiday of 1940. After being shown around the campus, Dan said we would now go to Coach Wade's office. I was scared to death as well as being so excited to finally have the chance to meet the greatest coach in college football, Coach Wallace Wade. In his office was Coach Wade, Coach Eddie Cameron, Coach Dumpy Hagler, Dan Hill, and me.

"After shaking hands with everyone, Coach Wade told me to sit down in the chair across from his desk. After exchanging a few pleasantries, he looked me straight in the eyes and said in his slow southern drawl, 'Bethune, do you want to come to Duke?' I could hardly answer I was so excited and pleased that he asked me. I managed to blurt out, 'Yes, yes sir.' He then said, and I'll never forget this, 'I'm in the position to offer you the opportunity to get a four year education at Duke University, the best college in the USA. But to make this happen there are three things you have to do. First, you must pass your schoolwork. We will provide tutors and night study classes that you must attend. If you don't pass your schoolwork, you're gone! Second, you must conduct yourself as a gentleman. If you do anything to embarrass this football team, this university or your teammates and coaches, you're gone. The third thing is you must work in the student dining hall at meal-time your freshman year. This is required by all freshman football players and basketball players on athletic scholarships. Now if you agree to these three things, I'll offer you a four-year scholarship to Duke

University.' (He never mentioned that I had to be a great football player or any-thing like that. I only had to remain on the squad as long as I was physically able). This was one of the happiest days of my life.

"I agreed and was about to leave his office when I remembered a recent news-paper article condemning some colleges for offering scholarships to football players, but after the 1st semester, if they didn't make one of the 1st three teams they would kick them out. I turned and asked Coach Wade if we needed to sign a contract or an agreement. He stood up and looked me square in the eyes as he stretched his hand out across the desk and said as he looked at his hand 'Bethune, this is our contract and it is good as gold.' I shook his hand and left the office. Never in all the years I knew him did I ever hear of anyone who doubted Coach Wade's word. He was one of the most honest and straightfor-ward persons I have ever known and I owe him so much.

"... In June 1942, I joined the Air Corp Reserve, with several other football players. Coach Wade announced he was going to leave Duke to serve in the Army. During this period of time the US was at war and everyone at Duke was upset as to what the future would bring in our lives. I was concerned about what would happen to my scholarship, if I left Duke to serve my country. Well, the concern I had did not last long. Coach Wade called Johnny Muse, Jake Poole, and myself to his office. The three of us were from Charlotte, NC and had played football together. Dayton Dean, athletic business manager, and Dr. Charles Jordan, Duke vice president, were also present in Coach Wade's office. He said to us, 'Boys, the country is at war and we have no idea how long it will last. I know you are in the Air Corp Reserve and could be called at any time. I want you to know that if you have to leave school that when you re-turn your scholarships will still be here, just as I promised, whether I am here or not.' He said our records were in a box in the office safe, which Dayton Dean later showed us. 'I promised you four years of college and that is what you are going to get.' I can't tell you how much this relieved our minds.

"I was called into the service in Feb. 1943. I returned to Duke after three years in the Air Force in 1945. I played on the football team of 1946 with Coach Wade. I owe Coach Wade so much. I graduated from Duke in 1948. I was on the Dean's List and was president of my class, 1948. I obtained a job with Brown & Williamson Tobacco Corp. through the Duke Placement Center where I worked for 34 years. At retirement I was Director of Leaf Processing for all Brown & Williamson factories in the U.S. While at Duke I met my wife. We were married for 41 years and had two wonderful children. None of this would have happened to me if it wasn't for Coach Wallace Wade. He was one of the most outstanding men I have ever known and Duke is so lucky to have had him." —E.P. Bethune

REFERENCES

Agee, J. Evans, W. (1939). *Let Us Now Praise Famous Men.* Boston, MA and New York: Houghton Mifflin Company.

Barnes, B. (1989). *Coon Creek: A Tennessee Geological Treasure Chest.* The Tennessean Magazine.

Barra, A. (2005). *The Last Coach.* New York: W.W. Norton and Company.

Beadles, Z. (1963). *The Wades.* Jackson, TN: McCowat-Mercer Press.

Brister, R. (1994). *Bruce Wade: Tennessee's Forgotten Geologist.* Earth Sciences History.

Britt, A. (1976). *A Chronological Study Of Undergraduate Curriculum Revision At Duke University.*

Bryant, P. and Underwood, J. (1974). *Bear.* Boston, MA and Toronto, Canada: Little Brown and Company.

Carroll, J. (1992). *Fritz Pollard: Pioneer In Racial Advancement.* Urbana and Chicago, IL: University of Illinois Press.

Carroll, J. (1999). *Red Grange and the Rise of Modern Football.* Urbana and Chicago, IL: University of Illinois Press.

(2005). *The Chicago Bears Media Guide.* Broadview, IL: Rapid Impressions.

(2005). *Clemson University Football Media Guide.*

Cromartie, B. (1992). *Battle of the Blues.* Atlanta, Georgia: Gridiron Publishers.

Culp, F. and Ross, Mrs. R. (1961). *Gibson County: Past and Present.* Trenton, TN: Gibson County Historical Society.

Davis, K. (2003). *Don't Know Much About History.* New York: Harper Collins Publishers.

Doyle, A. (1997). *Foolish and Useless Sport: The Southern Evangelical Crusade Against Intercollegiate Football.*

(2005). *Duke University Football Media Guide.*

Dunnavant, K., (1996). *Coach.* New York: Simon and Schuster.

Durden, R. (1993). *The Launching of Duke University.* Durham, NC: Duke University Press.

Fitzgerald, W. and Butts, W. (1957). *Private Preparatory Schools for Boys in Tennessee.*

Gold, E. (2005). *Crimson Nation*. Nashville, TN: Rutledge Hill Press.

Grundy, P. (2001*). Learning To Win: Sports, Education, and Social Change in Twentieth-Century North Carolina*. Chapel Hill, NC: The University of North Carolina Press.

Hanlon, J., and Philips, D. (2003). *Ever True: The History of Brown Football*. Brown Sports Foundation.

Harvey Jr., E. (1994). *Our Glorious Century*. Pleasantville, NY: Readers Digest Association.

Hester, W. (1991). *Century of Champions*. Birmingham, AL: Seacoast Publishing.

Hoover, B. (2006). *Journey of Reconciliation*. Ivy League Sports.com.

Howard, F., (1990). *Howard: The Clemson Legend*.

Huie, W., (1942). *Mud on the Stars*. New York: L.B. Fischer Publishing.

Humm, Christopher. (2005). *Brown University Football Media Guide*. Providence, RI: Brown University Sports Information Department.

Kritzberg, B. *From Cadet to the College Football Hall of Fame*.

Langford, G. (1974). *The Crimson Tide: Alabama Football*. Chicago, IL: Henry Reynery Company.

Lester, R. (1995). *Stagg's University*. Urbana and Chicago, IL: University of Illinois Press.

Lougee, Jr. G. (1990). *Durham, My Hometown*. Durham, NC: Carolina Academic Press.

MacCambridge, M. (2005). *ESPN College Football Encyclopedia*; New York: Hyperion.

Mann, Ted. *A Story Of Glory: Duke University Football*.

Miller, P. (1999). *Slouching Toward a New Expediency: College Football and the Color Line During the Depression Decade*. American Studies.

Oriard, M. (1993). *Reading Football*. Chapel Hill, NC: The University of North Carolina Press.

Oriard, M. (2001). *King Football*. Chapel Hill, NC: The University of North Carolina Press.

Powell, W. (1989). *North Carolina Through Four Centuries*. Chapel Hill, NC: The University of North Carolina Press.

Rieland, T. (1997). *Roses of Crimson*. The University of Alabama Center For Public Television and Radio.

Rogers, W., Ward, R., Atkins, L. and Flynt, W. (1994). *Alabama: The History of a Deep South State*. Tuscaloosa, AL: The University of Alabama Press.

Scott, R. (2004). *Legends of Alabama Football*. Champaign, IL: Sports Publishing.

Sperling, D. and Chester, W. (2001). *Rites of Autumn* DVD Set. Lions Gate Home Entertainment.

St. John, W. (2004). *Rammer Jammer Yellow Hammer*. New York: Three Rivers Press.

Stone, R. (1987). *The Graham Plan of 1935: An Aborted Crusade to De-emphasize College Athletics*. The North Carolina Historical Review.

Sumner, J. (1990). *John Franklin Crowell, Methodism, and the Football Controversy at Trinity College, 1887–1894*. Journal of Sport History..

Sumner, J. (1991). *The Rose Bowl Comes to North Carolina*. Carolina Comments.

Watterson, J. (2000). *College Football*. Baltimore, MA: The Johns Hopkins University Press.

Whittingham, R. (2001). *Rites of Autumn*. New York: The Free Press.

Walker, E. (1994). *University Training School*, Trenton, TN.

Wise, J. (2002). *Durham: A Bull City Story*. Charleston, SC: Arcadia Publishing.

Other references used were the *Durham Morning Herald*, Add Penfield manuscript, *Knoxville News-Sentinel*, *The Duke Chronicle*, Duke University Archives, Duke University Sports Information Department, Paul W. Bryant Museum Archives in Tuscaloosa, AL, W.S. Hoole Special Collections Library in Tuscaloosa, AL., *Duke University Chanticleer*, *Nashville Tennessean*, *Nashville Banner*, *The Richmond Times-Dispatch*, *The Durham Sun*, *The Durham Herald-Sun*, *The Sporting News*, *Time Magazine*, *The Charlotte Observer*, *Greensboro News and Record*, *The Raleigh News and Observer*, *The Birmingham News*, *The Asheville Citizen*, *The Atlanta Journal*, *Trenton Herald Democrat*, *The Vanderbilt Alumnus Magazine*, Morgan Park Academy Alumni Files, *Vanderbilt Commodore Yearbook*, Vanderbilt Special Collections and University Archives, Duke University Alumni Register, Duke University News Service, *Collier's Magazine*, *Blue Devil Weekly*, *New York Herald Tribune*, Papers of William Wannamaker, Papers of William Few, Papers of George Denny, and University of Alabama Athletic Department Records.

INDEX

Longfellow, Henry Wadsworth, 157
Los Angeles Times, 107, 147
Louisiana State, 76
Loyola, 5
Lubbock, 240
Luper, Buddy, 292

M

MacIntyre, George, 42
Mann, Ted, 204, 207, 209, 217,
    230, 237–238, 258, 263, 275,
    317, 326
Marshall, Furber, 33
Mason, Lowell, 181, 184, 186
Mayfield, James, 106
McAfee, George, 199, 221, 225,
    227, 238, 244, 249–253, 257,
    320, 323, 334
McAfee, Wes, 227, 257
McCook, E.M., 51
McCormick, Jr., Robert, 283
McCurdy, Robert, 267
McEver, Gene, 180
McGugin, Dan, 29, 38–39, 41–43,
    46, 60, 100, 103, 112, 120, 133,
    143
McKinney, Horace, 273
McNairy County, 12
McNamee, Graham, 98
McRoy, W.D., 330
Meadows, Ed, 307
Meagher, Jack, 200
Mehre, Harry, 135
Memphis, 9, 179, 239, 256
Meridian, 72, 80, 87, 144
Michigan, 28–29, 43–45, 64, 76,
    197, 265, 273
Miller, Hugh, 130–131
Miller, Patrick, 230

Million Dollar Band, 56–57, 73,
    83, 108, 153
Milner, Bill, 290
Mobile, 9, 138, 140, 240
Mobley, Joe, 334
Monroe, 25, 239
Montgomery, 37, 44, 54–55, 59,
    61, 72, 78–80, 99, 102–103, 115,
    134, 139, 321
Moore, Jimmy, 134, 146
Morgan Park Academy, 20, 24
Moro Bottom, 151, 316
Morrison, Roy, 5
Morrow, Hugh, 284
Mozingo, William, 327
Mud on the Stars, 110
Murfee, James, 52
Murphy High School, 140
Murphy, Bob, 191
Murphy, Jimmy, 33
Murray, Bill, 180, 307, 310
Muse, John, 290

N

Napoleon, 16
Nashville Banner, 38
Nave, Doyle, 244–245, 247, 280
NCAA, 18, 41
Neely, Jess, 44, 114, 140, 220, 313
Neighborgall, Roger, 290
Nevers, Ernie, 104
New Mexico, 31
New York Herald Tribune, 65, 210
New York Times, 16
New York Tribune, 26–27
Newark Evening News, 16
Newman, Zipp, 56, 70, 73, 77, 85,
    97, 107, 130, 139, 144, 199
Newton, Doc, 189

R

Raleigh News and Observer, 313
Randolph County, 160
Rankin, Robert, 308
Raymond, Walter, 32
Reagan, Ronald, 319
Ribar, Frank, 228, 232, 247
Rice, Grantland, 41, 64, 97, 137, 197, 201, 211, 232, 280
Riddick, Herman, 305
Ris, Howard, 329
Roanoke Times, 207
Roberts, Jr., J.B., 135
Roberts, Scoop, 226, 228
Robinson, Edward, 23–24, 26, 60, 76
Robinson, Roger, 244
Rockefeller, Jr., John D., 24
Rockne, Knute, 22, 137, 149, 176, 178
Rocky Mount High School, 292
Rogers, J.D., 300
Rogers, Tom, 184, 200, 256, 321, 326
Roosevelt, Eleanor, 197
Roosevelt, Franklin, 160, 183, 285
Roosevelt, Theodore, 17, 160
Rose, Frank, 7, 86, 138, 149–150, 200, 325
Ruffa, Tony, 228, 231, 244, 247, 257
Runyon, Damon, 97
Russell, Fred, 39, 41

S

Salisbury, 246
Salley, Toni, 266
Sally, Bill, 247
Sanford High School, 292

Sanford, Terry, 322–323, 327
Schock, Carl, 192, 323
Scott, Xen, 44, 56, 60
Seaman, Ed, 312
Sewanee, 37, 46, 55–56, 64, 71, 101–102, 132
Shaughnessy, Clark, 5
Shelby, Isaac, 9
Shelley, Jim, 55
Sherman, William T., 183
Sidat-Singh, Wilmeth, 228–229
Siegfried, Winston, 231, 251, 263–265, 270, 292
Simmons, Furnifold, 256
single wing, 71, 104, 258, 329, 331
Sington, Fred, 7, 118, 129, 132, 136, 138, 140, 144, 146, 148, 154, 175, 333
Sink, Fred, 330
Small, Walter, 206
Smith, Andy, 25
Smith, Ben, 147
Smith, Earle, 112
Smith, Eugene, 50, 111
Smith, Harry, 240
Smith, Leonard, 327
Smith, Walter, 327
Snavely, Carl, 205, 303
Souchak, Mike, 300–301, 305
Southeastern Conference, 43, 134, 138
Southern Conference, 3, 5–7, 9, 41, 43–46, 61, 65–66, 72–73, 96, 98, 100, 103, 112, 135, 159, 178, 180, 186–187, 194, 200, 203, 205, 207, 213, 220, 230, 249, 251, 259, 265, 272, 296, 302, 305–307, 309–311, 313
Southern Methodist, 5